Finance: Plain and Simple

Finance: Plain and Simple

What you need to know to make better financial decisions

Sebastian Nokes

**Financial Times
Prentice Hall
is an imprint of**

Harlow, England • London • New York • Boston • San Francisco • Toronto • Sydney • Singapore • Hong Kong
Tokyo • Seoul • Taipei • New Delhi • Cape Town • Madrid • Mexico City • Amsterdam • Munich • Paris • Milan

PEARSON EDUCATION LIMITED

Edinburgh Gate
Harlow CM20 2JE
Tel: +44 (0)1279 623623
Fax: +44 (0)1279 431059
Website: www.pearsoned.co.uk

First published in Great Britain in 2011
© Pearson Education Limited 2011

The right of Sebastian Nokes to be identified as author of this work has been
asserted by him in accordance with the Copyright, Designs and Patents Act 1988.

Pearson Education is not responsible for the content of third party internet sites.

ISBN: 978-0-273-73129-0

British Library Cataloguing-in-Publication Data
A catalogue record for this book is available from the British Library

Library of Congress Cataloging-in-Publication Data
Nokes, Sebastian.
    Finance : plain and simple : what you need to know to make better
financial decisions / Sebastian Nokes.
        p. cm.
    Includes bibliographical references and index.
    ISBN 978-0-273-73129-0 (pbk.)
    1. Finance, Personal. 2. Financial literacy. 3. Consumer education.
I. Title.
    HG179 .N56 2011
    332. 024--dc22

                                                            2010040002

10 9 8 7 6 5 4 3 2 1
15 14 13 12 11

Typeset in 9.5pt/13.5pt Melior by 30
Printed by Ashford Colour Press, Gosport

Contents

Contents

Author's acknowledgements

This book crystallized as an idea over a number of years in the author's mind, and a great many people have played a part in this crystallization, many no doubt unwittingly. The seed of the crystal was planted by a, let us be charitable, somnolent independent financial adviser, at a cost of almost everything I had managed to save in the course of my (at that time) seven-year career. It is beyond my generosity to be grateful to that individual, but I am grateful to have lost everything at an early age when I had yet time, youth, health and energy to recover, for I have since seen many who having reached or even passed normal retirement age then suffered in the Equitable Life fiasco and in other financial scandals a fate far worse than mine. I am grateful for the many retail savers and investors, including many Equitable Life victims, who have spent time and effort in letting me know what kind of a book would be useful to them.

In the course of researching for this book a large number of organizations and individuals have been helpful. In particular I would like to thank the following:

Daniel Ward, Guy Treweek, Chris Booton, Nick McLeod-Clark, Simon Irish, Louis Plowden-Wardlaw, Aziz Musakhanov, Edmond Jackson, Peter Robin, Dawn Metcalfe, Omar Roberts, David Barker, Stuart Pugh, Tolga Uzuner, Mike Bevan, James Prichard, Daniel Davies, Andrew Capon, Alan Kerr, Charles Marment, Christine Brentani, George Shehadeh, Ian Cooper, Ronnie Barnes, Tanvi Davda, Dave Hastings, Graham Throp, Mark Stratford, Stephen Digby, David Brimacombe, Peter Burditt, Gordon Hogarth, Peter Wynter Bee, James Wilcox, George Palmer and Susan Lee Miller – who all provided detailed assistance and ideas on specific areas of content of this book, making it far more useful than it could ever otherwise have been. I would also like to thank all my classmates from London Business School Finance MSc MiF PT98 not already mentioned.

Author's acknowledgements

Nicola Nokes, my wife, who has a natural thrift and money sense and many other fine qualities, many of which I lack, and whose patience, encouragement and tolerance during the conception and creation of this book will be forever under-rewarded.

Julian Nokes, my father, who has worked in finance all his life but who was rarely been bedazzled by the spin that the industry sometimes emits to temporarily dazzle its workers and their clients. He has made excellent suggestions and corrections, especially in the field of pensions.

Humphrey Nokes, my brother, who introduced me to the delights and dis-delights of private equity investment, I hope in a favourable proportion.

Professor Chris Higson, whose view of the financial world at the time of Enron and the whole dot.com denouement was as sceptical as it was accurate, and who has seen through more acts of accounting leger de main than any junk bond trader has had hot bonuses.

Jeremy Johnson, who taught me much about the practical enforcement of contracts and the management of legal risk.

Dr Jade Prince has been an invaluable and indefatigable researcher, tackling assignments such as 'Find a catchy item that costs £2 billion or so in today's money' with unwavering efficiency and rigour.

Ian Major, who as my boss many years ago at IBM signed off approval for the corporation to pay my fees at the London Business School, thereby enabling me to study finance to a degree that would have done justice to minds far more powerful than mine.

Dr Diana Burton, whose knowledge of how to invest in the New Zealand property market is surpassed only by her knowledge of death in ancient Greece and of Roman numerals, and who was most generous with her time in reading proofs. And also to the Burton family, whose generous hospitality in the Marlborough Sounds in New Zealand enabled this book to be completed.

Colleagues at the UK Ministry of Defence (including 'Commonwealth Alley') and in 600 (City of London) Squadron RAuxAF, too numerous and too professionally discreet to mention, whose practical questioning on a range of financial matters, especially the Freeserve IPO, helped to make this book rather more practical than it might have been.

Steve Whiting and Sarah Ellis of the Debt Management Office, whose assistance was professional, generous and supremely efficient.

Special thanks must also go to Patrick Walsh of Conville & Walsh for having conceived the original idea which became this book, and for his patient, professional and generous handling of the idea and the rights.

Like many people, support from my bankers has been essential to my personal and business lives, and I would like to thank Matt Warren, Paul Williams, Lisa McNeice, Jodi Bruce, Chris Wiltshire, Jonathan Smith, Terry McCarthy, Ann Lumb and Joan Madsen.

It is only those who have written a book who probably really understand why authors feel the need to say in print that despite so much help from others all remaining errors and inadequacies are entirely their own. This is certainly the case here, and I ask forgiveness from all those who have helped me where it is the case that I have misformulated or failed to formulate at all the input that they so generously gave, there is no doubt the errors are mine.

This book is dedicated to the memory of Alastair John Stuart Shaw.

Publisher's acknowledgements

We are grateful to the following for permission to reproduce copyright material:

Text

Box on page 10 from Oxford English Dictionary, 2nd ed., Clarendon Press (1989).

Photographs

Page 21 from Shutterstock: Chris Curtis; page 66 from Shutterstock: Twisted Shots; page 89 from Shutterstock: stocker1970; page 95 from Shutterstock: Brian A Jackson; page 106 from Shutterstock: Andrejs Pidjass; page 149 from Shutterstock: Paul B. Moore.

In some instances we have been unable to trace the owners of copyright material, and we would appreciate any information that would enable us to do so.

Introduction

A man need not be a hen to judge the merits of an omelette.

Rudyard Kipling.

Very high IQ people can be completely useless. And many of them are;

Charley Munger (referring to academics behind the conventional measures of risk in investment banking)

No man in the country is under the smallest obligation, moral or other, so to arrange his legal relations to his business or property as to enable the Inland Revenue to put the largest possible shovel in his stores. The Inland Revenue is not slow, and quite rightly, to take every advantage which is open to it under the Taxing Statutes for the purposes of depleting the taxpayer's pocket. And the taxpayer is in like manner entitled to be astute to prevent, so far as he honestly can, the depletion of his means by the Inland Revenue.

James Avon Clyde, Lord Clyde (1863–1944)

Introduction

Can you afford to be financially illiterate? It has become increasingly dangerous to go through life without basic financial literacy. This book is intended to be your garlic to any financial vampires or vampire squids around you.

This book is about basic financial literacy. What do we mean by basic financial literacy? We mean understanding finance sufficiently to master the three parts of your financial existence. These are: first, making money through your work; secondly, deciding how to save, including deciding how much to save; and thirdly managing your finances so that you get the best financial returns given your circumstances and preferences. These three parts of your financial existence are related. If you are not financially literate then you'll be forced to rely completely on others for advice when you make decisions about your financial affairs. If you wish to run your finances yourself without relying on financial advisers, this book will help you do that; if on the other hand you do want to use financial advisers, this book will help you get better value from them and reduce your risks in using them.

The book is in two parts. Part 1 is a toolkit, and from it you can learn about the basic principles of finance and how to apply them to make better financial decisions in both your personal and business life – decisions that will make you richer or less prone to financial disaster, and that will make the organization in which you work more successful. Part 2 is a guided tour of the main types of financial product available to the retail investor. You may read Parts 1 and 2 in either order, alternatively you may read just one or the other.

1
part

Fundamentals
of finance

1 Assets and liabilities

An asset is the present right to the services (or uses) of an existing economic resource.

> Richard Gore and Richard Samuelson
> (in an undated Powerpoint presentation 'Redefining Assets:
> A Proposal for the Conceptual Framework')

The 'five Cs' of credit: character, capacity, capital, collateral, conditions.

> Traditional banking maxim

Every mania in financial history has been liquidity driven. You can go back to the South Sea Bubble or tulips in Holland. As long as the money is coming in, everything is fine.

> Raymond Devoe, 11 December 1995 – quoted on
> www.prudentbear.com

The aim of this chapter is to show clearly what a financial asset is and what a financial liability is. There are many definitions of assets (and liabilities) and even experts disagree. Often this is because different definitions suit different purposes and different industries. This chapter explains these terms from the point of view of a private individual who wants to be able to understand finance better as it affects them. If you don't have a clear understanding of what assets and liabilities are then you may be at the mercy of others who are in a position to take advantage of your possible confusion on this.

Assets

Let us take the nature of financial assets and liabilities as the
starting point for financial literacy. The basis of ordinary literacy
is the alphabet, and the first step in becoming literate is to learn
to recognize the letters of the alphabet. In financial literacy there
are, on this analogy, only two letters, *asset* and *liability*. The
two 'letters' of financial literacy are opposites of each other. If
this sounds too much of an oversimplification bear with me: the
difference between an asset and a liability is very important and
it is worth some effort to make sure that we are clear about the
difference. Even governments sometimes manage to confuse the
two letters of the financial alphabet, and when they do this it
tends to make people who cannot spot the mistake poorer than
those who can see the mistake. Those who find a way to bet on
the government's error can make a great profit. Pensions is an area
where the difference between assets and liabilities matters.

Liabilities disguised as assets

A financial asset is something that holds its value, a liability is
something that has costs attached. There are people who make it
their business to confuse you about what is an asset and what is a
liability. 'Think of it as an investment' is the cry of the salesman
who tries to get you to spend money by implying that you are
investing, because investment means you are building up an asset.
Sometimes we need no help from others in such deceits, and we
rationalize our mistakes even as we make them by confusing an
asset with a liability.

The young boy racer who spends all his money and more on a sports car instead of spending prudently is right, if unwise, to say that it is his money and he can do what he likes, but he is wrong to say that the sports car is an asset in financial terms. Unless you are a dealer in sports cars, your sports car is probably a financial liability. If you are lucky or skilled in buying and selling sports cars there is a chance it will be a financial asset, but in the main sports cars tend to be liabilities for the typical buyer – and similarly in the case of yachts, helicopters, private jets, football teams and horses. We assume that the typical reader of this book is not a habitual buyer of such things. There is nothing wrong with buying a yacht or a sports car if you want one and can afford it, just don't mislead yourself that it's an asset.

Financial assets as a special case of assets in general

The case of the boy racer and his sports car leads to the distinction between financial assets and assets generally. We can say in general terms that an asset is something worth having or is good to have. A good husband may be said to be an asset to his wife, and vice versa. The relevant criteria, for worth having or for good, depend on individual preferences, social norms or circumstance, and they need not be examined further for the purposes of this book. The point to note here is that not all assets are financial assets. A financial asset is something worth having because it is good financially. When you are thinking financially, the first rule where assets are concerned is to be clear in your own mind between assets that are financial assets and other kinds of asset. You need both in life.

In financial terms assets are good and liabilities are bad. However, there are many things that are good despite being financial liabilities, and there are some things which, notwithstanding that they are financial assets, are bad or even diabolical. For example, a profitable brothel is a financial asset, but is not a good thing. Healthcare for your dying mother may be a financial liability, but is a good thing. Being financially literate requires us to understand that the question of whether something is a financial asset or a liability is independent of and separate from the question of whether that thing is good or bad. One of the obstacles we face in thinking clearly about financial matters is that our emotions can get in the way.

Making money by understanding better than your government what assets are and why

George Soros is someone who made money betting that the UK government was wrong about assets. Soros is estimated to have made over a billion dollars when he sold short (see below) over £10 billion in the lead-up to Black Wednesday (16 September 1992). This was the day on which the UK government had to pull the UK currency out of the European Exchange Rate mechanism (a precursor to the Euro) and to devalue the currency, the pound sterling. What was the UK government wrong about? In a nutshell, the UK government had claimed that the UK currency would be as strong as the German Deutschmark, and, by implication, that the UK's economy was similar to Germany's. Soros and many others simply did not believe this claim, and found a way to bet that the UK government was wrong. The UK government spent £27 billion trying to prop up the pound before conceding defeat: it was treating sterling as an asset and one worth investing £27 billion into. In fact sterling was not an asset. Soros understood this and the British government did not.

Selling short

Suppose you have one fish. If then you sell one fish, you surrender (give up) the fish and, in return, you get money, i.e. payment for the fish. If you sell short one fish it's exactly the same, except that instead of starting with one fish, you start with no fish, and you end up with minus one fish. If you expect the price of fish to double in the next hour you would delay selling your fish in the expectation of making twice as much money. If on the other hand you expect the price of fish to halve you would want to sell as soon as possible. Of course, you cannot actually have minus one fish, physical objects don't work like that, and in fact nor do shares in companies. But you can still short fish, or shares, or anything else, by borrowing them and then selling. Why might you wish to short sell? Just as you buy or keep something if you expect it will rise in value, in the hope of making a profit, so you short-sell (or short) things in the hope of making a profit. Why would anyone buy from you if you stand to make a profit? It is not certain that you will make a profit, it is your opinion. Someone of a contrary opinion is likely to wish to trade with you. Markets are means of reconciling opinions.

An illegal brothel*	A legitimate business*
A people trafficking business*	A house with no mortgage
Proceeds of crime	A good reputation
ASSETS	*If profitable

LIABILITIES	
A large income tax bill	A large income tax bill
A congenitally unprofitable business	A daughter's wedding
Damage to your car which is not covered by insurance	A child's tuition fees at a top university
BAD THINGS	**GOOD THINGS**

Whether something is a financial asset or a liability has nothing to do with whether it is a good thing or not. Some assets are good things, others are bad things. And sometimes it depends on your own personal view of things, as with the case of an income tax bill. This is certainly a liability, it must be paid. But some people feel that a large income tax bill is a good thing, because then one must have had a large income. Others feel that income tax, or income tax above a certain rate, is a bad thing by its nature. As we will see later in this book, there are some cases where the same thing can be an asset to one person but a liability to another. What matters for financial literacy is that you are able to work out given who you are, what you want in life and how you feel about things, what assets and liabilities are to you. Note also that assets and liabilities may be intangible, as in the case of reputation.

FIGURE 1·1 Some examples of good and bad assets and liabilities

How to think about assets and financial assets

The point of life is not to accumulate as many financial assets as possible, and whatever point life has, if any, will entail a balance of financial assets and liabilities as part of an overall mix of wider, non-financial assets and liabilities. The benefit of being financially literate is that it helps us to judge, given our circumstances, what it is feasible to aim for in terms of assets and liabilities. That my aim in life is to have a sports car or that I think giving my daughter a pony is the right thing to do is not a matter of finance – these are personal decisions, and the most important ones, towards the daughter's pony end of the scale rather than the end with one's own sports car, are often moral in nature. The role of financial literacy is to help one make decisions and act in a way that achieves one's aims to the extent possible: will the pony live in a fenced off part of the garden or in its own 100-acre paddock? Will your sports car be a brand new Lamborghini Reventón or an MG Midget with a dozen previous owners?

Assets and liabilities in financial decision making

Our aim in life is to acquire financial assets up to some point and to manage our liabilities so that we take on only those liabilities which we must. Ideally, our liabilities will be smaller than our assets and will continue to become ever smaller in proportion to our assets. The vicissitudes of life are such that we may not always be in this happy situation. This aim holds even if our aim is not to get richer, but simply to be comfortable or to avoid getting poorer.

Throughout the rest of this book we will take *assets* and *liabilities* to mean financial assets and financial liabilities.

What are assets and liabilities? A more detailed look

An asset is something that:

■ can be realized for cash or

■ can be exchanged for other assets, or

■ generates cash beyond its cost or

■ is likely to generate cash beyond its cost.

A liability is the opposite, something that consumes more cash than it generates or is likely to do so. What kind of thing? Most things in the world can be categorized as either a financial asset or a financial liability, although it may not be wise or useful to do so. A gold mine is an asset if the value of the gold produced exceeds the cost of running the mine. If not, it is a liability. This shows that assets and liabilities can swap their natures. Other examples are:

- If you buy a rental property and it doubles in value, then it is an asset.

- If you buy a property, do not insure it and it burns down and the local council forces you to rebuild, it becomes a liability.

- If it burns down and you do not have to repair it, then it has become neither an asset nor a liability, it has simply vanished.

The example of the house shows that we may not know whether something is going to be an asset or a liability.

Dictionary definition of the word 'Asset'

Assets. [a. late Anglo-Fr. assets (Littleton §714). early AF. asetz (Briton I. XVI §5), OF assez enough, cogn. w. Pr. assatz, OSp asaz, Pg. assaz, assas, It. assais:– late pop. L ad satis 'to sufficiency', substituted for simple satis 'enough'. The origin of the English use is to be found in the Anglo-French law phrase aver assetz 'to have sufficient', viz. to meet certain claims; whence assets passed as a technical term into the vernacular. It was originally singular but was soon (from its final –s, and collective sense) treated as plural, and in modern use has a singular asset.]

Oxford English Dictionary, 2nd ed. Clarendon Press (1989)

By understanding the nature of assets and liabilities, their characteristics and the features that render the same thing an asset under some circumstances and a liability under others, we can manage assets. We buy insurance against fire and other risks, and we find out about, or pay someone else to find out on our behalf, what the local authority and other government bodies may require us to do, so that we can maintain the asset as such and avoid it becoming a liability.

Samuelson's view of assets

Richard Samuelson, a distinguished economist, says

> As an alternative, we suggest that assets be defined as rights to
> the services of an economic resource and that the definition of
> an economic resource focuses on the utility of the resource as
> opposed to the value of the resource.[1]

Assets can remain assets but create a loss for you

Instead of a house, suppose you buy a painting. Suppose the
paintings costs you £100 but you run short of cash and sell it for
£50. It is still an asset and in trading it you have lost £50, and the
new owner may have got a bargain. If you had to spend money
repairing the picture in order to sell it (as well as selling it at no
profit) then it will have been a liability because it consumed more
cash than it earned. Note that merely selling the asset for less than
you paid for it does not make it a liability. The test is whether it
generates more cash than it costs. If so, then it is an asset. If not,
then it is a liability.

Assets can become losses

Suppose now you decided to display your picture to the public and
charged £1 a time for people to look at it. If you can get 101 people
to pay their £1, then the picture is an asset. Suppose, however,
that the hundred-and-first person, after paying you their £1, grabs
the painting and leaps into a getaway car. You are not insured,
you hail a passing taxi and tell the cabbie 'Follow that car!' but,
tragically, your taxi driver loses the thief's car and you never see
your painting again. You have to pay the taxi driver £2, which
means that the painting has cost you £100 to buy, brought in £101,
and then cost you another £2. The painting was a liability. It cost
you £1 cash overall, in addition to your time and effort in finding
the picture, buying it, setting it up for display and talking to people
who wanted to look at it.

Cash flow diagrams help us to distinguish assets from liabilities

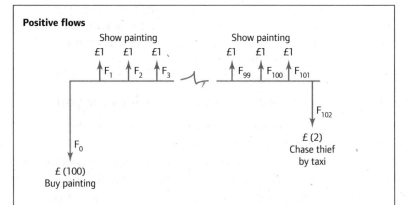

Positive flows

Negative flows

A cash flow diagram represents all cash flows associated with an asset, which in our example is a project to buy and show the painting. Each vertical line represents a cash flow, and the arrow on the line shows the direction in which the cash is flowing: lines pointing upwards represent cash flowing in; lines pointing downwards represent cash flowing out – positive and negative flows.

The length of each line indicates the size of the flow, so a longer line means a bigger flow than a shorter line. (In this particular diagram the line lengths are not proportional.) Each line is numbered, F_0, F_1, F_2... F_{102}, to indicate the first, second, third etc. units of cash flow. (Starting at F_0 rather than F_1 is merely a convention – you may use whatever convention you wish. This convention is especially helpful when F_0 is the acquisitions or start-up cost because it marks this cash flow out as being of a different kind, that is a capital cost rather than a revenue flow or operating cost.)

The point of a cash flow diagram is that it helps you to see how much cash goes out and comes in, and in what sequence.

FIGURE 1·2 Example of a cash flow diagram

It can be helpful to draw the cash flows associated with a financial situation or decision. Figure 1·2 is a cash flow diagram that shows the flows for this example of the picture. A cash flow diagram can help to illustrate many key areas in financial literacy, and we will make use of this format elsewhere in this book. In the context of assets, the key thing that this diagram illustrates is that an asset has revenue, that is, positive cash flows, associated with it. Anything that has cash flowing into it or that causes cash to flow into your life is an asset.

Figure 1·2 has more detail than we need, which makes it unwieldy. It would not be useful to see every single one of the 101 payments as separate lines. We can simplify this cash flow diagram while retaining its key features, as shown in Figure 1·3. The main test of whether something is an asset is whether the total cash flows associated with it are positive or not. It will be an asset if and only if there are cash flows associated with it and they are positive. Two questions then arise. What if we are not certain of what the cash flows will be? And whose cash flows are they? We must modify our definition of an asset slightly so that the cash flows which can *reasonably and probably be expected* to be associated with the thing in question are in total positive. The question of ownership clarifies that there is a necessary element of perspective in identifying assets (and liabilities). A loan is an asset to the bank, because the bank expects positive net cash flow (that is, interest payments and repayment of the principal) from it, but the same object, the loan, is a liability to the borrower.

The same information as is presented in Figures 1·2 and 1·3 can be shown in tabular form, as illustrated in Table 1·1. Some people prefer visual representation, some prefer tables of data and others text. Throughout this book all three methods of explaining ideas will be used. Pick whichever you prefer, and if you want to test your understanding, use one or two of the other methods of representation to check that you see the same idea irrespective of how it is explained.

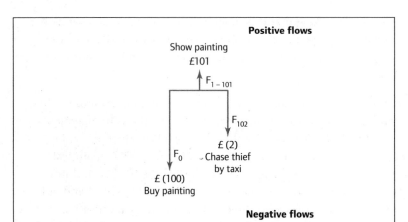

FIGURE 1·3 A cash flow diagram with the details hidden

TABLE 1·1 Cash flows and total of cash flows represented as a table of data.

Activity		Cash flow
Cost of acquiring the painting	£	(100)
Sale of 101 tickets at £1 each	£	101
Taxi fare for pursuing the thief	£	(2)
TOTAL CASH FLOW	£	(1)

Note the use of round brackets in this table. Brackets are used by convention in finance to indicate a negative number, where in other walks of life a minus sign might instead be used. We follow this convention in this book. What convention you use matters little, the key thing is to be clear about when cash is going out and when it is coming in.

Note that while these cash flow diagrams and the table show all cash flows associated with the asset, they show nothing about whether the asset continues to exist, and in our example it does not. This is a critical omission from the cash flow diagram. In return for the outflow of £100 in F_0, you get an asset worth, let us say, £100. But when the thief takes the asset you lose that asset, which means you have lost something worth £100. This loss is not shown in this diagram, at least not directly: if you had managed to catch the thief and regain possession of the picture, then there would be further positive cash flows, F_{103}, F_{104}, etc. continuing on to the right. So cash flow diagrams show cash flow, not assets. They are relevant to assets because we define financial assets by reference to the probable cash flows attached to them. In later chapters we will look at the notions of cash flow, cash, profit, options and risk. All of these can be different views of the same thing, and part of financial literacy is to understand how these different views relate to each other. This simple example has begun to show how assets and cash flow are related to each other, and how the idea of risk also fits in.

Using the concept of an asset to make better financial decisions

In your dealings with the wider world and its financial matters, including banks, financial advisers, pension providers and government, you may be presented with information in only one format and it may not be the one you prefer, so part of being financially literate is to be able to understand financial information even when it is not presented in your preferred format. Indeed, it is not unknown for some financial players to deliberately select a format that makes it difficult to understand what is really going on. Being able to identify an asset and its key features, especially cash flow and the risks associated with that cash flow, is your first defence against being misled by financial advisers, governments and financial institutions. Often there is no intention to mislead, simply the everyday difficulty of someone else not understanding exactly your circumstance and view of what you want.

The cash flow diagrams and the table of data given above to illustrate the example of buying the picture and then displaying it show the most obvious financial features of the chain of events, and sometimes the obvious features are the only ones that matter. Often, and especially in business decisions and more complicated personal transactions, some of the less obvious financial features matter, and may turn what seemed like an asset into a liability. In the case of this example, your time is worth something, so the whole episode has in fact cost you more than the £1 net cash cost shown in Table 1·1. There will also have been heating, lighting, property taxes and other costs associated with buying, showing and trying to protect the picture. However, the illustration serves to show the key features of an asset, and the concept of cash flow, whether we represent it as a diagram or as a table of numbers, can easily be extended to take account of any other costs as one so chooses.

We have identified the defining characteristic of an asset, which is that positive net cash flow attaches to it. (This definition satisfies the purposes of this book, which is basic financial literacy for personal purposes. In fact there are fundamental problems with defining an asset, and these are outlined below.) Some industries and professions have their own refinement of this fundamental definition of an asset. Financial accounting is accounting for the purposes of reporting information to shareholders in a company, and financial accounting sometimes uses this definition:

$$\text{Assets} = \text{Liabilities} + \text{Shareholder's equity}$$

Anyone who invests in shares (company stock) will find it useful to understand this definition. However, while this financial accounting one is a true definition, it merely puts the onus of understanding onto the terms 'Liability' and 'Capital'. *Capital* in this sense means the extent to which the company is an asset to its owners, that is, to the shareholders, and *Liability* is, as we shall see in a moment, the opposite of *Asset*. So while this financial accounting formula is useful in explaining how to calculate the value of a company, which can be seen to be intuitive by rearranging the formula thus:

$$\text{Shareholder's equity} = \text{Assets} - \text{Liabilities}$$

it is not useful in defining the nature of an asset or in showing how to recognize an asset, however it is useful in helping you understand what it is that you own as a shareholder in a company.

Key terms: total, net, gross

If there are three numbers, x, y and z, then the total of these numbers is x + y + z. If, say, z is tax, then the net amount is x + y, and the gross amount is x + y + z.

The term *gross profit* means profit before deducting tax and any other indirect cash flows such as overheads and interest. (Don't worry if some of these terms mean nothing, they are covered later in the book.) Net profit is profit after all such deductions. The net amount is what you end up with, the gross amount includes sums that go to other people, such as the tax authorities. The difference between net and gross matters, and a business that shows a gross profit can have a net loss.

The English word 'net' in this sense derives from the French word 'net' meaning neat or clear, which is related to 'nettoyer', 'to clean'.

So if a number is given net of tax, then there is a tax liability in addition to that figure. Tax is not the only everyday case where it is important to understand whether you are dealing with a net or a gross amount. If in our example of the painting you had bought the painting at auction, the prices being called out by the auctioneer as the painting was being sold were net of the buyer's commission, for which you would have been liable in addition to the so-called hammer price, the price at which the auctioneer announced the actual sale of the painting. If you have worked out the absolute maximum you can afford to pay for a painting that is coming up for sale at auction, remember that is the maximum *gross* price you can afford, and the net price, which is what you offer in the bidding, may be rather less.

Another definition often used in economics of the term 'asset' is 'economic resource'. For the purposes of this book, there is no difference between these two terms. However, this and the previous alternative definition of 'asset' does illustrate a key point about financial literacy, which is that often one will need to be able to recognize different terms being used to mean the same thing. The point of being financially literate is to be able to understand the financial world to the extent that one needs to for running one's own life, pursuing one's own interests and helping one's family, friends and allies in their endeavours, and, therefore, to make financial decisions. To do this one needs to understand certain key terms, the first of which is an asset. If someone you are dealing with calls the same thing that you call an asset by some other name, for example a resource, the point is not to argue with them about what it should be called nor to spend time trying to learn about the finer points of how it may have come to pass that two people can use different terms for the same thing. The point is to have the confidence to recognize the asset as such and to make a decision accordingly.

Now that we have laid out the fundamental characteristic of an asset by using the example of a painting, let us develop our understanding with some other examples of assets. Examples of the kinds of things that typically are assets include:

- gold and precious metals
- land and property
- shares in companies and certain other financial instruments
- oil and other mainstream commodities
- cash either in notes or on deposit in a bank
- a decent job or a set of clients
- major works of art
- certain kinds of intellectual property (for example, copyrights over popular songs or plays).

Examples of possibly less obvious assets include:

- certain kinds of knowledge or opinions
- attractive physical appearance (good looks)
- certain kinds of contracts
- good friends and personal relationships
- reputation, energy or drive

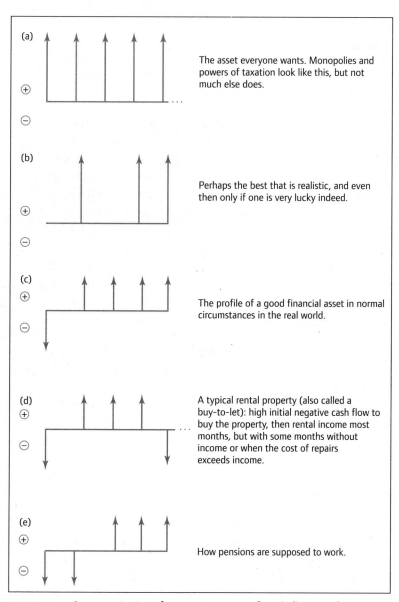

The asset everyone wants. Monopolies and powers of taxation look like this, but not much else does.

Perhaps the best that is realistic, and even then only if one is very lucky indeed.

The profile of a good financial asset in normal circumstances in the real world.

A typical rental property (also called a buy-to-let): high initial negative cash flow to buy the property, then rental income most months, but with some months without income or when the cost of repairs exceeds income.

How pensions are supposed to work.

FIGURE 1·4 Some varieties of asset, in terms of cash flow profits

- immunity from prosecution
- rights over property
- trade concessions and
- certain kinds of options in general.

The picture in our example was an asset because cash flows attached to it. The list above starts with gold. Typically gold is kept either in a safe or secreted about one's person. In either case one is not charging the public to see it, as we were in our thought experiment with the picture. If no cash flow attaches to the bars of gold in the bank vaults, then how are they an asset? Keeping your gold in a bank vault costs money: the bank charges a fee for this service. If you keep it in your own safe at home, then there is the cost of the safe, of maintaining the safe and insuring the gold. The reason that gold is an asset is that at some point you or the executors of your will or your descendants will sell the gold, which will in turn create a positive cash flow. We say that gold is a liquid asset.

Liquidity, in this sense, means that the asset can be converted into cash (liquidated) easily. The concept of liquidity is important. If you have only one asset and may need money in a hurry, that asset had better be liquid. You can sell a bag of gold coins almost anywhere in the free world at almost any time for about the same price. In contrast, if you have a buy-to-let house and it is in a rundown area which has a poor reputation, you may not be able to sell it. So when evaluating an asset and making a decision about it, one of the characteristics you may want to understand is its liquidity.

Some of those in the two lists of assets, above, are tangible assets and others are intangible. Tangible means things that you can drop on your foot and it would hurt. Reputation, good friends and intellectual property rights are intangible assets. Houses, gold, and commodities such as oil or wheat are tangible assets. Some of the items in our list cover both tangible and intangible assets. One example is 'Major works of art'. Paul Day's sculpture *Peter's Faith* and Hercules Brabazon Brabazon's painting *The Acropolis* are tangible works of art, and *Peter's Faith* in particular would hurt were one to drop it on one's foot. Bach's music and the songs of Creedence Clearwater Revival are also works of art but are intangible.

Krugerrands – a popular gold coin

Gold coins have been used by mankind for commercial payment
almost since the dawn of civilization. Despite efforts by many governments to prevent citizens from using it or even owning it, it seems
unlikely that mankind will stop trusting in gold in the foreseeable
future. Gold is a liquid asset because it is widely accepted for payment
even in times of war and crisis, it is easy to carry and a small amount
of gold has a high worth. To this day air force pilots, special forces
soldiers and other members of the armed forces and intelligence
services who are deemed 'prone to capture' are issued with gold coins
as a means to try to buy their freedom in the event of capture.

Source: Shutterstock: Chris Curtis

Why does this distinction matter? As the hypothetical example of
our one-painting art gallery showed, assets are prone to theft and
other forms of impairment, such as rotting, rusting, fire, general
wear and tear, and in all countries at some time, government
expropriation. The risks associated with tangible assets are
fundamentally different from those associated with intangible assets.
One protects a tangible asset with physical security, by putting the
picture in a shatterproof glass case, for example, or by chaining the
sculpture to the floor. But there is nothing to be put in a case or
chained to anything where an intangible asset is concerned.

As an example of why this matters, consider another hypothetical example. Despite your setback with the picture business, you decide that you had learnt enough from the experience and the theft to set up all over again and make a profitable business. With the help of a loan from your rich in-laws, you buy ten paintings and house them in a purpose-built gallery, charging £10 a time for visitors to see them. Your art gallery business grows, and becomes famous. You sell out to a venture capital firm and retire on the proceeds. At first things go very well for the venture capital firm. They buy more paintings, they expand the gallery, they spend lavishly on advertising and promoting the business and even hire Tony Blair to be the face of the gallery. Although few people suspect it at the time, this all begins to go wrong when a junior analyst in the venture capital firm takes over, fresh out of an almost impossibly smart university. The analyst reasons as follows: 'we are an art business, paintings are boring, pop music is where it's at, music is art, so we'll become even more successful by adding music to our business'. And so under the zealous and aggressive leadership of the Young Gun, the business spends heavily on buying music. But it turns out that apart from being called 'art', the great paintings in the gallery and the great pop songs bought by the venture capitalists have almost nothing in common, and therefore need to be managed in quite a different way. Thanks to the changes you made after your first painting was stolen, it is now very hard for anyone to steal any of the gallery's pictures. But thanks to the Internet, it is very easy for anyone to steal pop songs. This is, of course, a hypothetical example, but there are many real life examples of previously very successful investors and entrepreneurs who seem to have exactly the problem described in this example. (Just one of many examples is EMI's acquisition by Terra Firma.[2])

The problem of understanding assets and their key characteristics is not a problem limited to high rolling professional financiers. Many ordinary people consider buying holiday homes in pleasant, warm regions, and often these are promoted as an investment, that is as good assets that will produce a steady stream of cash flow. Just as a song and a sculpture, while both works of art, have significantly different characteristics as assets, so there may be significant differences between property in different legal jurisdictions. Physically a house may be almost identical, but the

FIGURE 1·5 An asset – but is it tangible or intangible?

Source: Public domain made available by www.rowy.net

effect of the legal jurisdiction can make it a substantially different kind of asset. The key differences that the particular characteristics of an asset engender fall under the heading of risk and optionality. Both of these ideas are so important in financial literacy that they have their own sections, below.

Some formal definitions of the term 'asset' contain the concept of ownership of that asset, so that it is yours only if as well as having revenue attached to it the thing that might be the asset is in fact yours, either because you own it or because you have some right other than outright ownership to use or enjoy it. Perhaps this refinement of the basic idea of an asset is helpful in some cases or to some people, but it is unnecessary and may be confusing. As we have seen, an asset is an asset for some individual or entity. What is my asset can be your liability. Furthermore, the paramount and defining feature of an asset is that cash flows are associated with it, and unless the concept of an asset is meaningless those cash flows must accrue to the person for whom the asset is an asset.

Some problems with the concept of an asset

The reader will by this point have noticed a problem in the concept of an asset. How an asset can be an asset when its cash flow for the period that it is yours is negative? Why is a picture that halves in value between when you buy it and sell it an asset, but a sports car that does the same is a liability? The simple answer is that the picture is an asset, but a bad one (in that it declines in value) because positive cash flows attach to it after acquisition. This is in contrast to most modern sports cars which cost much to maintain and also decline in value. However, this example, the simplest case of an asset where the only two cash flows are acquisition and purchase, shows that there is a fundamental problem remaining even after this clarification. (If you want to test your bank manager or financial adviser, and if they have not yet read this book, ask them to define the word 'asset' and listen carefully to their answer.)

As we have seen, if Alice Assetbotham takes out a million pound loan from Bank Bourgeois that loan is a liability from Alice's point of view but an asset from the bank's. The point of view matters, and it makes no sense to talk of something being an asset without indicating from whose point of view. Often the context makes it obvious whose point of view it is, so when for example gold is said to be an asset, the obvious implication is from the point of view of whoever owns the gold, and, less obviously, there is an implication

A ballad of two assets

An asset that wasn't: Terra Firma's takeover of EMI

May 2007. Private equity group Terra Firma buys the international music business EMI for £3·2 billion.

September 2008. Terra Firma injects a further £16 million.

March 2009. Terra Firma injects a further £28 million into EMI (*Financial Times*, 16 July 2009). Guy Hands resigns as chief executive of Terra Firma, 'amid anger from his backers over the ill-timed purchase of music company EMI Group Ltd' (*Wall Street, Journal* 18 March 2009).

July 2009. As at July 2009, losses and a wide range of problems at EMI continue. It is not clear how, if at all, the original investment can be recouped.

Assetzilla: Apple's iTunes – virtually the only profitable music store

April 2003. Apple opens its online iTunes store to sell music. It sells more than 1,000,000 tracks in the first five days.

April 2004. iTunes store is profitable.

January 2009. iTunes is the largest legal music retailer, accounting for 70 percent of worldwide online music download sales, and having sold over 6 billion tracks (Wikipedia, 'iTunes Store').

What are the assets in EMI and in iTunes?

If Terra Firma had taken their £3·2 billion in May 2007 and instead of investing it in EMI had invested it in Apple's shares, then those shares would have risen to be worth £5·76 billion (as at 14 August 2009) instead of seeming, at perhaps the most optimistic, to have risen not at all. What exactly is the asset that Terra Firma bought? Essentially, it was the employment contracts of artists and managers in the pop music business, and if those people become upset by a new management style, as apparently EMI's artists and managers did by Terra Firma's, then the risk is that the cash flows will cease to be as reliable as they once were. Apple's iTunes, on the other hand, is an asset of quite a different kind. While it has some people in it – the managers of the iTunes business – its real asset is its online shopfront, the clever technology that the customers find easy to use and the pricing and payments system, which makes people feel that they are paying a fair and reasonable price for the music.

that reasonable and normal assumptions prevail. There will be special cases where gold is a liability and not an asset. If the gold is radioactive, if a gang of murderous pirates know you have the gold and your available firepower and marksmanship skills are inferior to those of the pirates, then gold is a liability from your point of view. So context matters when thinking about and making decisions about assets. One aspect of the context that matters is who is it that owns or has some right or ability to enjoy the asset.

By considering the point of view we also solve the problem of how something can be an asset if it declines in value. Normally we expect to pay for an asset, so the first cash flow associated with it, F_0, is negative. We expect but are not completely certain that over the life of the asset and including its disposal, the cash flows coming in as a result of having the asset will exceed this initial cost. So to say that something is an asset means that we expect this to be the case, but nothing in life is certain, and although we expect it to be the case we also know that there is a chance of the asset becoming worth less than we paid for it. Even if this happens, however, there may still be positive cash flows coming in because of the asset. For practical purposes it is more useful to say that it has turned out that we overpaid for the asset, but that it is still an asset. If instead of cash coming in we instead have to keep paying out, then one can say that the asset has changed into a liability – and we look at liabilities in the next section.

Context is essential: there is no point in thinking about assets (or liabilities) in isolation from the context in which you plan to use them or may need to use or deal with them. It may be that the thing that was the asset has not changed at all, but you or some other part of the context relevant to the asset has. This is normal in life generally, not just financial life. For example, if one day, you go bald, then the comb that you used to use will be less useful to you. It is not the comb that has changed, but the change on your head makes the comb virtually useless to you. This example suggests the notion of utility, the usefulness of something. We have defined a financial asset by the criterion of positive net cash flow attaching to it, but more generally the notion of an asset, rather than the special case of a financial asset, is something that has utility attached to it.

Even experts have problems defining what an asset is

The question of exactly what an asset is has not yet been settled and may never be. Institutions such as the Securities and Exchange Commission, the Financial Accounting Standards Board, the International Accounting Standards Board, and many practitioners, clients and academics in accounting, business and finance have debated what the best definition should be. This question may never be resolved and perhaps, like the question 'What is a work of art?' it is not possible for there to be any objective and final definition, and furthermore perhaps, also like the question of a work of art, the reason may be that the concept of an asset is a human creation of an essentially subjective nature.

One of the roots of the argument is the nature of an asset. Are these primary or secondary qualities? John Locke set out what has become the modern understanding of this problem in the *Essay Concerning Human Understanding* (1690), although the problem was recognized long before him, by Galileo and possibly by the pre-Socratic philosophers.

Primary qualities are those that exist independently of there being an observer, and include extension (size), mass and number (quantity). These qualities may be said to be facts. Secondary qualities, on the other hand, are sensations occurring in observers, such as colour, taste and sound. Secondary qualities may be said not to be facts, but rather opinions or impressions. This is the origin of Berkeley's question of whether if a tree were to fall in a forest and there was no one to hear it, would it have made a sound? The answer is no, because a sound is a secondary quality, and depends on there being an agent in whom the sense-impression (in his case, a sound) is created. The primary qualities associated with a tree falling existed, including the vibrations in the air that, had they reached an ear, would have caused a sound. But in the absence of an ear or something similar, there is no sound.

One of the arguments about what an asset is turns on whether they must exist independently, like primary qualities, or whether they are secondary qualities, and depend on something else. In this book we are fortunate to be concerned only with financial assets, which simplifies the problem. Also, this book aims to be a practical book for those who are not accounting experts. These two factors allow this book the luxury of taking a simple definition of an asset, which is what we have done: a financial asset is something from which future cash flow or flows will come to us and it is reasonable to expect those cash flows to be positive. (In this book assets are like secondary qualities.)

Does all of this matter? If we have a good working definition for the purposes of this book, do you need to know these details of theoretical definitions from Plato all the way through to the FASB and SEC? No, it is not essential. But if one day someone, perhaps a financial adviser or a government spokesman or your boss wants to argue that such-and-such is or is not an asset, and belittles your view on the grounds that your view fails some test of their definition, then it might be useful. One of the problems for even the best educated and hardest working manager or professional who is not a finance specialist is that they have to rely on the advice and guidance of such specialists, and sometimes those advisers fall into the temptation to present things in a way that is not in one's interest. So there are two kinds of financial literacy that this book aims to impart. One kind of financial literacy that is useful because it helps you understand directly your own financial matters so that you can make better decisions; another that is useful because it helps you to judge how much your financial advisers and others who would influence you actually know what they are talking about in a given area, so that you have a better chance of trusting only those who most deserve your trust.

What is a liability?

A liability is the opposite of an asset. After the acquisition of the asset, we expect it to produce a net positive cash flow. In the case of a liability, after acquisition we expect it to produce net negative cash flows, also known as cost or cash outflows. Many of the best things in life are financial liabilities but personal assets. Wine and song are traditional examples of this, and other examples include cars, dining out in restaurants and holidays. Many of these things may be assets in the general sense of being something either good or necessary for life – and a life with no holiday and no song and no meals out would be a very miserable sort of life. So one of the challenges in financial literacy is to be clear when thinking about assets as to whether, besides being assets in the general sense, they are assets or liabilities financially. The point of having money, that is, financial assets, is to be able to support your financial liabilities. The challenge is to keep them in balance as you go through life. Liabilities may be good: they are often the things that make life worth living or things that are necessary to enable you to get other good things. Financial literacy helps one to keep on top of one's liabilities rather than them being on top of you.

Some common examples of liabilities are: taxes, costs of complying with legislation, bills, maintenance and personal dependents. Less obvious examples are: certain kinds of knowledge or opinions, certain kinds of contracts, some friends and personal relationships, reputation, want of energy or drive, liability to prosecution, obligations in relation to property, trade restraints and certain kinds of options in general.

These examples illustrate that what is an asset today can be a liability tomorrow. Suppose you go horseracing and wager. After a good day at the races you are £5000 up. You celebrate by going to the pub with friends who also made money. In the pub you decide to buy a racehorse and hand over your £5000 for your share in ownership of the horse. 'Great, an asset' you think; and indeed the racehorse has a fine record and you have had a professional vet to check it out. Before you can get the racehorse home, however, one of your friends accidentally throws beer over the horse, causing it to bolt. It canters over the flower beds of the local hospital, causes the driver of a brand new Jaguar to crash, and then does a solo re-enactment of the Charge of the Light Brigade through a hospital kitchen, complete with the horse dying as it charged a baklava. Your asset is gone and your share of the liability for repairs is £7500.

What you had judged to be an asset turned out to be a liability, and before you could take steps to try to change it back again, it expired forever.

Transaction costs and taxes

Before we leave the subject of assets and liabilities we must cover transaction costs and taxes. Assets almost invariably never arrive or depart completely alone, like some wallflower at a party, but instead they are much more like rock stars, who have groupies and other hangers-on. In the case of assets these groupies are transaction costs, and often taxes too. Transaction costs are costs associated with the transaction of procuring or disposing of an asset. When buying a house transaction costs include conveyancer's or solicitor's fees, and various kinds of taxes such as land registry fees and stamp duty. When buying art at auction there may be a buyer's premium, which is also a transaction cost. When you are calculating whether something is a worthwhile investment remember to include the transaction costs.

Deprival value as a way to value assets

We have seen that the value of an asset is the sum of all future cash flows accruing to it, discounted for time. In practice this definition is often of little use in valuing an asset. Another way to get to the same answer is by means of *deprival value*. Deprival value is a simple idea and can be thought of as a psychological trick to help us think clearly about the real value of an asset. At the heart of the idea of deprival value is the question 'What would we do if this asset vanished?' Let us explain how deprival value works by way of a hypothetical example, and then give its formula.

Suppose that you own a light engineering workshop, and in this workshop is an old piece of engineering equipment called a screw turning lathe. Your business bought this screw turning lathe many years ago. What is it worth? Imagine that this lathe vanishes overnight. Tomorrow morning you arrive at your engineering works and where the lathe used to stand is bare floor. What do you do? This depends.

If the lathe had not been used for years and there was no likelihood of it ever being used again, then you would do nothing. You would not waste time thinking about the lathe, but instead get on with running your business. The lathe's sudden disappearance may even have saved you money on hiring specialist contractors to dismantle and move it. At the other extreme, suppose that the lathe was in constant use, you had no other equipment that could substitute for it and you were relying on the lathe being there to complete a critical order today. In this case you might not only pay full list price for a replacement, but pay extra to have it installed today. Now imagine a third case, somewhere in between the other two. Imagine that your business does use the lathe, but only rarely, and for low-value work that can be subcontracted to a neighbouring farm equipment repairs business. In this case you would not replace the lathe, but would instead make a deal with the farm equipment repairs business, because that would be much cheaper than buying a new lathe and not using it most of the time. Your lathe thus has three possible values:

1 If not used at all, its scrap value.

2 If lightly used, the value is the cost of contracting with the farm equipment repair business.

3 If heavily used, the cost of replacement as soon as possible.

Our example describes the main features of deprival value, but the full definition of deprival value is a little more extensive.

Formal definition of deprival value

The deprival value of any asset is the lower of:

either its *replacement cost* (if it can in fact be replaced)

or its *recoverable value*

The recoverable value of an asset is defined as the higher of:

either what the company could sell it for, e.g. on eBay.

or the value to the organization created by keeping the asset in use within the business – the asset's *value in use.*

Asset and liability matching

The matching of liabilities and assets is a key principle for insurance companies and other financial institutions, and can also be a useful concept for thinking about your own finances. Suppose you have assets of £1 million and a bill to pay next week for £10,000. Unfortunately all your assets are illiquid and none can be converted into cash in less than a year, at the earliest. In this case you have a liquidity problem. Although you have more than enough assets to cover your liabilities in terms of total value, there is a mismatch in the timing of when you will have cash and when you need it.

Summary

We have seen that assets and liabilities are opposites. The defining characteristic of an asset is that positive cash flows attach to it. The quality of an asset is determined by the size and reliability of these cash flows. Assets can change: their quality as assets may change, or they may cease to exist, or they may become liabilities. A cash flow diagram is a tool to help clarify and understand the cash flows associated with an asset or liability. The value of an asset or liability is the sum of all the cash flows associated with it, adjusted for time. Deprival value is a way to help us value an asset if it is not clear what the cash flows associated with it are.

REVIEW QUESTIONS

1. Is the house or apartment in which you live an asset? Why?

2. An object has a random stream of positive and negative cash flows attached to it. Is this an asset or a liability? Why?

3. Your little brother has a cocaine habit and no job. Is he an asset? Why?

4. Imagine that you buy a house and intend to rent it out at a profit, that the house is dilapidated and that you will borrow money to repair it. Draw a cash flow diagram to represent the cash flows involved.

5. Now imagine that you are the bank that will lend you money in Question 4. Draw a cash flow diagram from the bank's point of view. What are the similarities and differences between the two diagrams?

6. Define deprival value. If you own a car, work out its deprival value for the next week and for the next ten years. If you do not own a car, work out the deprival value of a taxi or bus.

Time

A bird in the hand is worth two in the bush.

Born Free, now I'm expensive

Sasha (pseud.)

The most powerful force in the universe is compound interest.

Albert Einstein

The only reason for time is so that everything doesn't happen at once.

Albert Einstein

Time is the school in which we learn, time is the fire in which we burn.

Delmore Schwartz

Time is fundamental to finance and especially to making decisions about anything to do with finance. How good is an absolutely certain return of 5 percent on an investment? If it takes one day to make 5 percent, it's outstandingly good. If it takes a year, it is reasonably good but could perhaps be better. If you make 5 percent return over 100 years, it's lousy. To make good financial decisions you need to be able to identify the time factors that are relevant to it, and to determine what they mean. This chapter aims to show you how to do that. A complication is that in many cases those selling financial products and those asking you for money or justifying tax rises aim to confuse you by making the time factor hard to understand, so this chapter also shows you how to burn through such confusions and make decisions in your own interest.

The effect of time on financial assets

Time is fundamental to the questions of financial value and financial decision making. Other things being equal, having cash now is better than having cash at some later time. More generally, having an asset now is better than getting the asset at some time in the future, whereas bearing some liability now is worse than the same liability arising later. Let us look at why this is. There are two reasons: one concerns the natural productivity of assets and the other concerns learning about assets.

The natural productivity of assets and interest rates

Natural assets such as fruit trees, crops of wheat and herds of domestic animals have a natural rate of increase from year to year. A stem of wheat grows and produces more than enough seeds to ensure replacement. If unchecked natural assets increase at a certain rate each year. The farmer who has two chickens does not keep those chickens in the expectation of never having any eggs. The farmer expects the chickens to lay eggs and perhaps also to be able to rear new chickens. The concept of interest payable of cash deposits and of return on investments seems to derive from this feature of the natural world.

By extension the time value of money probably came originally from the rate at which crops or domestic animals created surplus from the original stock. It is not a great conceptual leap to the idea that an interest rate payable on a loan should reflect what could be done with the money in a period of time.

When applying time to determine the value of an asset, the starting point is money, and the argument is what else could have been done with that money instead. This is the idea of *opportunity cost*. If we do such-and-such with this money, what are we not doing?

Learning curve effects

Instead of taking money as our starting point, we could take the asset itself, and instead of following the argument of what else we could have done with the money, we can follow the argument of how to get better returns on the asset. This is the notion of the *learning curve* (or experience curve). Suppose that tomorrow you were to wake up and find that by magic you had been given a brand new aircraft factory, with brand new managers and a brand new workforce. At first your factory would be chaos because no one would know what they were doing, but after a few years individuals and the group of employees as a whole would have learnt how to work better.

What the time value of money means in practice

Suppose that the time value of money happens to be 5 percent per year. What this means can be expressed in a number of other ways, all of which mean the same thing:

- If you lend £100 to someone and can be certain of getting your £100 back you should in addition get £5, that is a total of £105, one year after lending it.
- The value of having £100 for one year is £5.
- The cost of not having £100 for one year is £5.
- £100 now is worth £105 in one year's time.
- £105 in one year's time is worth £100 now.

We have seen that opportunity cost and the propensity for natural assets to grow justifies the notion of the time value of money. There are other reasons for requiring more in a year's time than the amount of money you now have, including inflation and compensation for risk. We will explain inflation later in this chapter and risk will be explained in the next chapter, but now let us clarify the notion of the time value of money.

1. Opportunity cost – focus is external, on other uses of cash equivalent of the asset over time

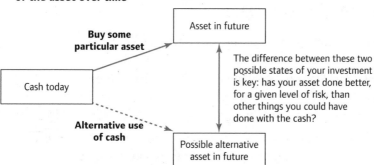

The base case for an alternative use of your cash is to lend it at no risk. (In theory this means lending to your government, in practice it may mean putting it in a deposit account or, if gold it as a historically low price, buying gold.)

2. Learning curve effect – focus is internal, on what you can do with the asset over time

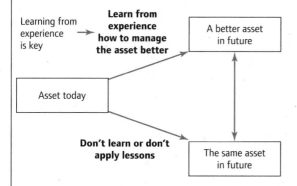

This diagram represents two ways in which time affects value. The most common way to think of time affecting value is in terms of opportunity cost, as shown at the top of the figure. The key question here is 'What better alternative use could I find for my money?' and the base case is to lend the money without risk, i.e. to lend at the risk-free rate of interest. The focus here is an external one, on all the opportunities out there in the world. A less common way to think about time's effect on the value of assets and in particular to learn how to manage them better. If the main problem in the first approach is to predict the future the main problem in the second approach is to ensure that you learn from and apply the lessons of experience over time. These two effects may work together in the same direction, or may work against each other, or may not both apply in any particular case of holding a financial asset.

FIGURE 2·1 Two ways in which time may affect financial value

How to do it – compound interest, present value and net present value

In this section you will see how to calculate the time value of money. There are two types of problem that will make it necessary to do this. One is to calculate the total of interest payments to you (or by you) over time, the other is to adjust future payments for the effects of time – *compound interest* and *present value*, respectively.

TABLE 2·1 The effects of time and compound interest: the number of years taken for money to double at different interest rates

Annual rate of interest	Number of years for the money to double in value, rounded up
1%	70
2%	36
3%	24
4%	18
5%	15
6%	12
7%	11
8%	10
9%	9
10%	8
11%	7
12%	7
13%	6
14%	6
15%	5
16%	5
17%	5
18%	5
19%	4
20%	4

Compound interest

Compound interest is interest on interest. You need to know about it because it is one of the most powerful forces in finance. It can work for you, for example where you reinvest dividends into buying new shares, or it can work against you, for instance where you don't pay off credit card debt.

Table 2·1 shows the power of compound interest. If you get 1 percent per year on your money, you have to wait 70 years for it to double. However, if you can get a few percent more, 5 percent, then you save yourself 55 years, doubling your money in 15 years. Financial institutions make fortunes out of the general public by focusing on exactly what percentage rate of interest to charge because most of their customers don't care about 'a few percent'. If you care about every percent and every hundredth of a percent, you will understand how much you are really handing over to big financial institutions and you will be able to avoid being ripped off.

How do you calculate compound interest? If you understand O level, GCSE or School Leaving Certificate maths, you will have covered this and as a reminder the key mathematical technique is exponentiation. Where:

PV is the present value of an investment,

r is the interest rate,

n is the number of years, and

FV is the future value (i.e. the result of compound interest),

the formula to use is:

$$FV = PV \times (1+r)^n$$

So, if you put £100 into a savings account that pays 5 percent per year for five years, the calculation is:

$$FV = 100 \times (1.05)^5$$
$$= 127.63$$

In a spreadsheet such as Microsoft Excel the formula to use to do this calculation is:

$$PV(1+r)^\wedge n$$

We assume that interest is compounded annually and will explain what this means below.

If your mathematics is a little rusty, fear not! This is a very simple calculation. In essence the trick is to work out interest on interest. So after one year at 5 percent you have your original £100 plus the £5 of interest (5 percent of £100). In the second year you still have the original £100 and the £5 of interest from the first year, as well as a new £5 of interest from year two, but you have in addition one year's interest on the £5 that was interest in the first year. Table 2·2 sets this out in slow time, without using exponentiation. Table 2·2 has been generated on a spreadsheet and Table 2·3 shows the formulae used. There is no shame in not being comfortable with compound interest and how to use it or how to calculate it. For every ten people who say that they understand the concept, probably one in ten is able to calculate compound interest. It is the most important mathematical ability in finance, so if you are a little rusty or if you are unfamiliar with the idea, get out a calculator or a spreadsheet now and work out some compound interest calculations. Start by trying to replicate the one we have just done.

TABLE 2·2 Working out compound interest year by year, at an annual rate of 5 percent compounded annually, for five years

Year	0	1	2	3	4
Deposit (year 0), then opening balance	100·00	105·00	110·25	115·76	121·55
Interest to be paid in year	5%	5%	5%	5%	5%
Interest	5·00	5·25	5·51	5·79	6·08
Balance at end of year	105·00	110·25	115·76	121·55	127·63

TABLE 2·3 The formulae in Microsoft Excel behind the numbers in Table 2·2

Year	0	1	2	3	4
Deposit (year 0), then opening balance	100	=SUM (B31)	=SUM (C31)	=SUM (D31)	=SUM (E31)
Interest to be paid in year	*0·05*	*0·05*	*0·05*	*0·05*	*0·05*
Interest	*5*	*=SUM (C29* C28)*	*=SUM (D29* D28)*	*=SUM (E29* E28)*	*=SUM (F29* F28)*
Balance at end of year	=SUM (B28+ B30)	=SUM (C28+ C30)	=SUM (D28+ D30)	=SUM (E28+ E30)	=SUM (F28+ F30)

Compounding period

In the example above interest is compounded annually, at the end of the year. This means that the rate of interest is calculated once per year, and is applied at the end of the year. There are other ways to compound interest. Suppose that you have a savings account that pays 12 percent per year interest and in the account you have £100. One way to calculate how much interest is payable to you is to apply 12 percent to your £100, which gives you £12 of interest. Another way to apply the 12 percent would be to apply 1 percent twelves times, once each month. You will still have been paid 12 percent, but the 12 percent annual rate is applied split over every month.

TABLE 2·4 Illustration of the effects of different compounding periods

In all cases

Annual rate of interest	12%
Principal	£100,000

Annual compounding over one year	Year 1
Balance at start of period	£100,000
Interest rate for the period	12%
Interest earned in the period	£12,000
Balance at end of period	**£112,000**
Equivalent annually compounded rate	12·00%

Quarterly compounding over one year	1Q01	2Q01	3Q01	4Q01
Balance at start of period	£100,000	£103,000	£106,090	£109,273
Interest rate for the period	3%	3%	3%	3%
Interest earned in the period	£3,000	£3,090	£3,183	£3,278
Balance at end of period	£103,000	£106,090	£109,273	£112,551
Equivalent annually compounded rate				12·55%

	Jan	Feb	Mar	Apr	May	Jun	Jul	Aug	Sep	Oct	Nov	Dec
Monthly compounding over one year												
Balance at start of period	£100,000	£101,000	£102,010	£103,030	£104,060	£105,101	£106,152	£107,214	£108,286	£109,369	£110,462	£111,567
Interest rate for the period	1%	1%	1%	1%	1%	1%	1%	1%	1%	1%	1%	1%
Interest earned in the period	£1,000	£1,010	£1,020	£1,030	£1,041	£1,051	£1,062	£1,072	£1,083	£1,094	£1,105	£1,116
Balance at end of period	£101,000	£102,010	£103,030	£104,060	£105,101	£106,152	£107,214	£108,286	£109,369	£110,462	£111,567	**£112,683**
Equivalent annually compounded rate												12·68%
Daily compounding over one year												
Balance at end of period					(Workings not shown for reasons of space)							£112,747
Equivalent annually compounded rate												12·75%
The difference over ten years												
Annual compounding	£310,585											
Monthly compounding	£326,204											
Daily compounding	£330,039											

Time

Table 2·4 illustrates the effect of different compounding periods. The effect of the different compounding periods is small for small amounts of money, but on mortgages, pension schemes, heavily used credit cards and long-term savings plans the effects can be significant and are worth checking.

Of course the extra interest payable in monthly rather than annual compounding works to your advantage when you are receiving interest and works against you when you are paying interest. Some financial institutions have been known to tend to compound annually in their savings products and monthly or even daily when charging interest. A number of attempts to standardize reporting of interest have been made to prevent retail investors from being misled by such tricks. AER and APR, 'annual equivalent rate' and 'annual percentage rate' are two results of such efforts. Neither is wholly satisfactory, but are a step in the right direction. The definitions of APR, AER and similar terms vary from jurisdiction to jurisdiction, and sometimes allow fees to be excluded. Financial institutions tend to get around the intention of these terms by charging you fees that are described in such as way as not to count as interest, and thus be excluded from APR and AER numbers. This can be grossly misleading

The best way to protect yourself against being misled on what interest rates you are being charged is to do your own calculations, and to include all fees and interest charges, because if you are charged an additional £500, say, as a 'set-up fee' it's still £500 of your money gone. For choosing between different loans, mortgages and savings products, simply treat all fees and interest payments as interest, and calculate interest on the different options on the same basis. This is easy to do with a spreadsheet.

Present value and net present value – adjusting payments for the effects of time

We have used the concept of compound interest to calculate how much money we will get in future, but we know that money tomorrow is less valuable than money today. Net present value, abbreviated to NPV, allows us to adjust for the time.

A hypothetical example can illustrate the idea of NPV. Suppose that four years before the next Olympics you spent £1000 in creating a website about the Olympics with the aim of making money from it. What you spend and get back is as follows:

This year (Year 0)   spend £1000
Next year (Year 1)   gain £100
Year 2   gain £250
Year 3   gain £750

Have we made a profit? We seem to have done, in that after spending £1000 we have made £1100, which looks like a profit of £100. But is it enough of a profit given that money has a time value? We can make a quick check of what the time value of that £1000 is. Let us assume that the time value of money is 5 percent per year in each of the next four years.

Year	Time value of £1000	How time value is calculated (when it is 5 percent)
This year (Year 0)	£1000·00	No adjustment for this year
Next year (Year 1)	£1050·00	Add 5 percent of last year's value
Year 2	£1102·50	Add 5 percent of last year's value
Year 3	£1157·63	Add 5 percent of last year's value

So while we have made a profit, that profit is too small to compensate us for the time value of the money we invested. We invested £1000, the time value of which after four years is £1157·63, but we have only got back £1100. So we are £57·63 worse off than we should be.

Where does this *should* come from? Instead of investing your £1000 in the Olympic website project you could have put it into a deposit account at a bank or you could have lent it to the government by buying £1000 of government bonds. These alternatives would have given you a *risk-free rate* of interest. 'Risk free' means that you would have been in effect virtually guaranteed to get your money back (we say more about the risk-free rate and what it means in the next chapter).

Looking at the table on p.47, we can say that the *present value* of £1050 next year is £1000 (if the risk free rate is 5 percent). Similarly, the present value of £1157·63 after three years is also £1000. The term present value means the value in today's money of a sum of money in the future. The further away in the future a sum of money is, the less its present value is, that is, the less it is worth today. You can think of this like railway sleepers on a railway line stretching into the distance: from where you are standing, the further away the sleeper the shorter it looks.

Calculating net present value (NPV)

You need to be able to calculate the NPV of a series of payments in order to get rid of the distorting effect of time, by working out what they are in terms of money today.

In applying interest and compound interest we saw that £100, say, left to grow annually at a certain interest rate gets bigger every year. NPV is simply doing this calculation in reverse. We know that £100 today will become £105 next year at 5 percent interest. How do we work backwards to find out what £100 next year is worth today? It's not £95. We have seen above that:

$$FV = PV \times (1+r)^n$$

so by rearranging this formula we can see that:

$$PV = FV / (1+r)^n$$

In plain English, this says to divide the future value by one plus the rate of interest, raised to the power of the number of years out to the future that the payment occurs. (This is the most complicated formula in this book. Being able to use it might well save you tens of thousands of pounds over your life.) You can use a spreadsheet to apply this formula, or you can use the built in PV and NPV functions in Excel and other spreadsheets. Table 2·5 shows a calculation of what five annual payments of £100 are worth in today's money, their NPV, when the discount rate is 4·5 percent. The *discount rate* is the rate of interest applied to adjust for the time value of money. This should usually be chosen to reflect the risk of the stream of payments. Table 2·6 shows the Excel commands beneath Table 2·5.

TABLE 2·5 How to calculate net present value

Year	0	1	2	3	4
Payment	100·00	100·00	100·00	100·00	100·00
Discount to be applied	0·0%	4·5%	9·2%	14·1%	19·3%
Interest	5·00	4·50	9·20	14·12	19·25
Present value	100·00	95·69	91·57	87·63	83·86

TABLE 2·6 The Excel codes behind Table 2·5 for calculating NPV

Year	0	1	2	3	4
Payment	100	100	100	100	100
Discount to be applied	=SUM($B19+1)^B12-1	=SUM($B19+1)^C12-1	=SUM($B19+1)^D12-1	=SUM($B19+1)^E12-1	=SUM($B19+1)^F12-1
Interest	5·00	=SUM(C14*C13)	=SUM(D14*D13)	=SUM(E14*E13)	=SUM(F14*F13)
Present value	=SUM(B13/(B14+1))	=SUM(C13/(C14+1))	=SUM(D13/(D14+1))	=SUM(E13/(E14+1))	=SUM(F13/(F14+1))

Time

The present value (PV) is the value of each year's payment in today's term. Adding these together gives the NPV.

NPV is one of the most important tools in finance. It is like a motorcyclist's crash helmet or a sailor's lifejacket. It is your personal protective equipment in the jungle of finance. Use NPV whenever you are deciding:

- whether to invest
- choosing between investments
- deciding how to pay over time
- choosing between loans or between mortgages
- and in general comparing streams of payments or income over time.

Using NPV to make decisions

Although Table 2·4 shows NPV calculated for payments to you (positive cash flow) it works in exactly the same way for payments from you (negative cash flow) – simply put a minus in front of the number. A great advantage of using NPV is that it can take account of positive and negative cash flows in a project. For example, a property investment has an initial outflow, perhaps over several years, followed by inflows of cash. The golden rule is not to invest if the NPV is negative, and when choosing between alternatives choose that which has the highest NPV.

Risk and the time value of money

Remember the hypothetical example in the last chapter of you buying a horse? Suppose that you were very unlucky with your horse and it bolted right after you had just bought it. How probable was that? It depends on the nature of the horse. We can imagine that most people would say that you would have been far unluckier if the horse had never bolted before than if it had had a history of bolting several times a day. Why? The idea behind this claim is that if something is hardly likely to happen at all, and it happens immediately, that is much worse luck than if that something had been likely to happen. It is a simple and straightforward idea, and we agree with it. We cover risk in the next chapter, which is the main element in what we call have just called luck in this example of the horse bolting right after you bought it. But notice that this idea also includes the notion of time. If there is some particular chance that something will happen, then it is more likely to happen the more time that passes. If your new horse is a bolter, then as time passes it is more likely to bolt (for the first time). This is common sense, but again the effect of time on finances is so important and fundamental that it is vital to be clear about it.

Conversely, suppose that your brand new horse is not a bolter but an amazingly fast horse that wins almost any race it enters. At the moment you buy the animal you may hope that this is the case, but you do not know. After its first race, you still do not know that it is a real winner because it might have just been lucky, but after a couple of seasons of racing you know that your horse is special, and very valuable. So time matters.

Consider now the case of two horses. Suppose one horse has a small chance of winning a race, the other a large chance. You have just bought both these horses and are entering them in the same race. Suppose, furthermore, that the winner is your horse with the small chance of winning. It was not likely that that horse would win, but it did. Of course you would not know with much certainty how likely each horse was to win. Horses, and all financial assets, have a probability of winning or of making a high return on investment, but this is a characteristic which is not knowable directly. Characteristics such as colour, mass, girth and height are such that we can measure them directly: the characteristic of how likely a horse is to win a race, although it exists as a statistical fact in the world, is not something that we can measure directly. Some things we can ensure directly may probably tell us something about this which we cannot measure directly; for example a very short, very fat horse is unlikely to be a winner, but this is indirect and uncertain knowledge.

More formally, we can say that the further into the future we try to predict, the less certain we can be about the future. I am quite certain what I am going to be doing for the three hours until my aircraft lands, I have a fairly good idea of what I will get up to tonight, I have some idea of what I will be doing next week, but I have no idea what I will be doing in ten year's time. I may even, heaven forfend, be dead. It turns out that everyone in the world faces the same problem of uncertainty, not just individually but collectively. As time passes we gain a better understanding of the risks in an asset.

The short overview of some aspects of risk given above show how as time passes one can gain a better understanding of the risk profile of an asset and that this improvement in such understanding is valuable. In return for bearing risk we demand a risk premium or payment to compensate for bearing this risk. Except for inflation, which we cover in this chapter, money has none of the kinds of risks that we have just described, so there is no risk premium except for inflation, in the case of money, that is, cash. This chapter is concerned with the time value of money, and we will leave non-inflationary risks for the next chapter.

Inflation

Suppose that there is a hospital where there are three senior surgeons, nine junior surgeons, twelve trainee surgeons and twelve administrators. In this hospital to be a senior surgeon means having at least 20 years' experience of doing surgery and being able to complete difficult operations successfully, from the patient's point of view. Junior surgeons are competent to operate on their own, except in the most difficult cases. Trainee surgeons show potential to be able to operate on their own, but are not yet able to do so safely. And administrators have no surgical skill, not least because they are not trying to be surgeons but are trying to be good administrators (which is important, in any organization including hospitals.) Now suppose that one day the government, which controls this hospital, in order to prove that it cares about the health service wants to prove that it is creating more surgeons than before. There are two quite different things the government might do. It might raise taxes and spend the extra money to produce more surgeons, which means either finding and training more suitable people to be surgeons or importing ready-trained surgeons from other countries. The first of these courses is expensive and takes time, the second of these is even more expensive but takes less time. What if the government wanted to be able to claim an immediate improvement? Neither training more people to be surgeons nor importing them would produce an immediate result, but there is another course of action for our government: at the stroke of a bureaucrat's pen, those who yesterday were surgeons could today be deemed to be senior surgeons, and trainee surgeons could be deemed junior surgeons, and, if the government was particularly desperate, administrators could be deemed to be trainee surgeons. This is inflation. Nothing has changed except the labels.

The example above is a type of qualitative inflation known as title inflation. Title inflation is commonplace, although not yet affecting surgeons. In finance we are concerned with quantitative inflation. In finance the term *inflation* refers to the money itself becoming worth less over time. (Its opposite is *deflation*.) The main cause of this is the government printing more currency, or taking effectively equivalent actions. If you slice a cake into four slices and then next year you slice a cake of exactly the same size and density into five slices, what was one slice last year will this year be less than one slice (20 percent less, in this example). The expression *printing money* is now so well known to refer to a bad thing that governments now use the term *quantitative easing* instead. But whatever you may decide to call the new smaller slice, it is still smaller.

The cake analogy explains the problem of inflation. In finance the formal concept we use if purchasing power. How much can you buy with a unit of currency – with a pound or a euro or a dollar? The effect of inflation is to reduce the purchasing power of the capital. In a sense what we today might call £100 is a year hence called £105, if inflation is running at 5 percent. If you think that because you have kept your £100 intact over the year and are therefore no poorer, you are mistaken. The £100 that you have a year hence is less than the £100 you have now. It is just like the cake: what you have is still called a slice, exactly as before, but it is smaller. So when you make financial decisions about the future you need to take account of inflation. You need to be concerned primarily about the amount of cake, not whether it is called a slice or a slice-and-a-fifth.

Inflation should not be confused with opportunity cost or interest payments. These three things are quite different. However, inflation can obscure what is really happening in finance.

Real versus nominal rates

In finance the terms *real* and *nominal* are used to mark whether inflation has been taken into account. A rate of interest or a monetary value is said to be real if the effects of inflation have been removed, or nominal if they have not been removed.

Suppose you are offered an investment that returns 20 percent over the next year. If this is a real rate of 20 percent, it means that on top of whatever the inflation rate is, you get 20 percent. If it is a nominal 20 percent, then it is a great return if inflation is 5 percent but unspectacular if inflation is 15 percent.

When comparing possible uses of your money, or in business when comparing possible projects, it does not matter whether you use nominal or real rates to make your decisions, but always compare like with like. So ensure that all your workings and all the cases you are looking at are either completely in nominal form or completely in real form.

Summary

Time has an effect on money in the same way that distance has an effect on the size of things we see. A pound today is worth more than a pound tomorrow, therefore we must adjust for the effects of time. The compounding of interest is a powerful multiplier of the value of money over time, and also of the size of debt. Some lenders and financial providers use compounding periods other than annual ones to confuse customers. You can protect yourself from this by making your own calculations of interest or returns, and the key tool is NPV. When choosing between possible uses of money chose the greatest NPV, or between possible loans the lowest. Inflation is another potential distortion. When examining a financial problem either work entirely with the numbers adjusted for inflation, in which case there are real values, or excluding inflation, in which case they are called nominal values.

REVIEW QUESTIONS

1 (a) Calculate the compound interest on £3000 at 4·5 percent over ten years, compounded annually.

(b) Calculate the compound interest on £10,000 over three years at an annual rate of interest of 5 percent, compounded annually.

(c) Repeat (b) but compounding monthly instead of annually.

2 If your boss offers you a choice between a rise of 10 percent now or 6 percent in six months' time and another 6 percent in a year's time, which will make you richer over the next two years, assuming no other pay rises?

3 You see a headline stating that the government has spent more than any predecessor on the nation's health. Generally speaking, is this kind of headline based on real or nominal data?

4 What is the NPV (in nominal terms) of payments if you own a rental property that pays £6000 per year, and your discount rate is 8 percent? Use a ten-year time horizon.

5 A politician promises to spend 5 percent more on something next year. Is this kind of promise real or nominal, typically? Why does this matter?

6 Do you want to know your projected pension entitlement in real or nominal terms? Why?

Risk

Most people ignore very low probability risks of catastrophic outcomes.

> Robert Rubin (in Philip Delves Broughton, *Ahead of the Curve*)

Human beings are flawed creatures who live in constant peril of falling into disasters caused by their own passions. Artificial systems have to be created to balance and restrain their desires.

> David Brookes, *New York Times*, 7 July 2009

Trust, but verify.

> Ronald Reagan

He that resteth upon gains certain, shall hardly grow to great riches; and he that puts all upon adventures, doth oftentimes break and come to poverty: it is good, therefore, to guard adventures with certainties, that may uphold losses.

> Francis Bacon

When you cross the road or swallow food or greet a stranger you take and manage risk. We all know roughly what risk is and how to manage risk to some extent. There is a risk when crossing the road that you will get run over. There is also a risk that if you do not cross the road some other terrible fate, perhaps starvation, will befall you. There is a risk when you swallow food that you will choke. And there is a risk when you meet someone new for the first time that you will create the wrong impression. Risk pervades our world. Managing risk is as normal an activity for us as eating, breathing and sleeping. At the same time, risk is an elusive concept, hard to define precisely, and just as we have seen in the case of assets, even experts are unclear about how to measure and manage risk. Does anyone know exactly what risk is? There are precise mathematical definitions of risk and these are used widely in modern finance, but as we shall see they are defective.

The aim of this chapter is to help you develop your understanding of the risks inherent in making financial decisions and to reduce those risks, wherever your current level of ability in personal financial risk management. The structure of this chapter is:

- What is financial risk?
- Why risk matters in financial thinking?
- How to think about risk.
- Mistakes in how the finance sector thinks about risk.
- The risk-free rate of interest.

What is financial risk?

In Chapter 1 we imagined that you bought a share of a horse, a leg as it's termed in the betting world. In the imaginary case of your horse you were quite justified in categorizing the horse as an asset. Through no reasonably foreseeable chain of events, owning a share of the horse changed from being an asset into being a liability, because the horse ran amok and caused damage for which you as owner were liable. This is an example of risk. Risk can be defined as the possibility or probability that the quality of an asset will change. To put it more bluntly, financial risk is the possibility that part or all of your financial affairs goes bad. So risk is the combination of how probable it is that the quality of the asset will change together with the magnitude of that change. In accounting the term used is the impairment of an asset, meaning a degradation of its quality. One of the tests that auditors of public companies are required to make is an impairment test, to check whether the quality of the assets reported in the accounts of the company has fallen since the last report. Let us look more closely at the notions of the quality of an asset and the probability of an asset being impaired.

Risk is about the impairment of assets

We saw in Chapter 2 that assets are assets because cash flow attaches to them or is reasonably expected to do so. The value of an asset is determined by how much cash will flow. If the asset has a cash flow worth £100 attached to it and no resale value, then it is worth £100. How much would you pay for a lottery ticket? Normally one would pay whatever tickets are sold for by the official resellers, say £1, but suppose that you have the opportunity to buy a ticket that you know is the winning ticket (never mind how you know, but assume that for some reason you know for a fact this is the winning ticket). For this particular ticket, you would be prepared to pay rather more than the £1. The quality of the lottery ticket is its chance of winning, because that is the expected future cash flow. This ticket you now want to buy has undergone improvement, the opposite of impairment. Initially it had the same chance of winning as every other ticket had – say one in a million or 0·001 percent – but now it it has a 100 percent chance of winning, it is certain to win. In financial terms we say that the quality of the lottery ticket has changed, and because the change is for the better, that is the cash flow expected from the asset is increased.

Note that the quality of an asset is a matter of opinion. In many important areas of life such as parts of the fields of medicine, criminal law, engineering and all of science, there are sometimes objective tests. If you want to know the quality of a piece of steel or the purity of a bottle of water or the active ingredients of a medicine, a laboratory will conduct a test and produce an answer that is hard fact. Laws of nature and scientific laws are also matters of fact. For example, it is a fact that in free space the speed of light is exactly 299,792,458 metres per second. And if you doubt it, you may conduct your own experiment to test whether this is true. One of the features of finance is that the subject contains few laws of nature. Finance is first of all about human nature, and this has two implications for managing financial risk. Even in accounting, which may be regarded as a branch of finance, some of the most important variables such as profit and fair value are matters of opinion rather than objective matters. (The current trend in accounting is away from objectivity towards even greater subjectivity.)[1]

- Risk comprises the probability of impairment together with the size of that probable impairment.
- Impairment means a reduction in the quality of the asset.
- The quality of an asset means the net total of cash flows that will derive from it.

Financial risk is a fundamentally human construct

One implication is that financial risks are fundamentally human, which means that while there is much that must be done with maths and statistics to understand and manage financial risk, to ignore the human element is likely to lead to failure in financial risk management. This is a lesson that the human race seems to re-learn every financial cycle. The second consequence is that absent objective measures, much of what we need to do in finance and especially in risk management requires a person to estimate or guess the answer to critical questions. Part of being financially literate is to be able to make better guesses yourself or to understand why an adviser or expert has estimated in a certain way so that you can form your own view and, if you think fit, modify or even reject their view. Terrifying? You are not alone: many people are a little shocked when they first discover this.

The numbers that appear so crisply in the report and accounts of a company or in government statistics about the economy are for the most part guesses and no more. That is all they can be. Risk management is about knowing how to make the best guesses, recognizing where and why your guesses might be wrong, and protecting yourself to a reasonable extent against the consequences if you are wrong. What does 'to a reasonable extent' mean? That too we must guess. But there are tools for making these guesses and, more generally, for risk management, that despite the recent financial crisis have stood the test of time and work well, if one does not forget to use them.

Why risk matters in financial thinking

Risk matters because it is exactly what causes your financial plans to fail to reach their objectives. Put in this way, this assertion seems obvious and trivial. It also hints at, even if it does not point to, some of the fundamental problems in financial risk management. Put in this bald way we might well ask why have risk management as a separate subject within finance if risk is in effect an umbrella term for everything that can frustrate our financial plans? What is risk as a subject doing apart from reminding us that we need to plan carefully and execute our plans carefully? There are two parts to the answer to this question. One is that yes, it is a good point, there are some reasons to feel that it is a waste of time treating financial risk management as a separate subject within finance. Lehman Brothers, Barclays Bank, AIG and all the rest of the financial institutions that failed or came so close to bankruptcy as to need massive injections of emergency funding in the financial crisis after 2007 all had highly paid risk managers and sophisticated risk-management techniques, which clearly failed abysmally in the task of risk management. However, this line of thinking is a little unfair because the proper comparator is not an ideal state of the world in which no banks failed but some unknown state of the world in which there were no risk management functions in these financial institutions. The other part of the answer to this question is a more practical one. A range of techniques for trying to think about and manage risk in finance have been developed over centuries and they form a coherent body of knowledge within the field of finance. This way of thinking and set of techniques is useful not because it is called risk management but because of what it does.

Risk management will not tell you what you should do, it will not come up with investment ideas for you. What good risk management will do is help you, along with other tools and techniques, to prioritize and select those ideas, and help you to execute them safely.

Risk management is a distinct body of knowledge in most fields of human endeavour. In factories and mechanical things it is best known as health and safety. In catering and cooking it is known as food hygiene, and so on. Just as industrial accidents in the Western world are a fraction of what they were a century ago as a result of great improvements in health and safety, and the same is true of food poisoning, so financial risk management has created an almost unrecognizably safer and more enjoyable society in which to live compared to a century ago. Much of this improvement has been as a result of thinking specifically about risk management.

While as an individual or family your personal finances are much smaller than the finances of a large insurance company or bank, many of the problems of financial risk management exist just the same for you as for large institutions. Examples include the problems of credit control, process errors, payment risk, concentration of risk in too few assets, and possibly litigation risk. Thus the principles of risk management also apply to you and your family.

Our approach in this chapter is the same as the overall approach in the book. We will give you tools and techniques for managing risk, but more important is that you get a good grasp of the concept of financial risk, because once you understand that and can develop your own thinking, the tools and techniques for risk management will be easy to understand and use.

How to think about risk

Diversification, the fundamental principle in risk management

There are two opposite approaches to financial risk: one is 'don't put all your eggs in one basket' and the other is 'put all your eggs in one basket and watch that basket'. History shows that the first approach is much safer than the second. Diversification is the term used in finance for not putting all your eggs in one basket, and diversification should permeate your thinking about risk.

Diversification is a good protection against risk, but like insurance or safety measures in other fields, you can have too much of it. Your aim should be to get as much diversification in your portfolio of financial assets as you need and no more. Excess diversification imposes costs for no benefit. For example if you are investing in ordinary shares of listed companies, then once you hold shares in 20 dissimilar companies there is little benefit in terms of diversification as protection against risk to holding any more companies' shares.

A three-step plan for managing your financial risk

This section sets out a simple three-step plan for you to manage your financial risk:

1 Understand your own circumstances and in particular work out how much you can afford to lose, if anything.

2 Identify and review the risks in your current financial assets and liabilities.

3 Focus on the risks in the decision you are making.

There is also a fourth, more general step, which you are doing by reading this book, which is to build up your financial risk management knowledge and capability over your life by lifelong learning about it. Keeping a diary of your financial decision making and the consequences as seen from the longer term afterwards is a great way to improve your ability to manage financial risk.

Understand your own circumstances and in particular work out how much you can afford to lose

The starting point for thinking about risk in financial matters is how much can you afford to lose? If you are retired and unlikely to be able to get back into paid work without a struggle, and have slender financial means, then you can afford to lose very little. If you are young, fit, healthy, highly qualified for lucrative work and free of dependents then losing your entire savings would be much less catastrophic.

Understanding your own circumstances is vital for you because there is a difference between taking on some financial risk and seeing or not foreseeing the likely consequences. For example, if you were to quit a steady job to set up your own company, running into financial problems when in one case you had foreseen roughly how that would be likely to affect your dependents and your own mind, and in the other case the reactions of your dependents and the chaos in your own mind came as another surprise shock on top of the financial shock itself.

Remember that your financial risks change with time. If you marry, change jobs, move house, suffer a death of a close family member, make or lose a large amount of money, or have a child then your risk profile changes. External factors can also change your risk profile – a general deterioration in your industry or the economy for example. And your own mind may change over time. So if you have not reviewed your risk profile for a couple of years, you should give some thought to it before making your next big financial decision. Above all get a feel for yourself and your own taste and aversions in risk.

Identify and review the risks in your current financial assets and liabilities

Once you have understood your own circumstances, the next step in thinking about risk is to understand the risk in your finances, which means your investment portfolio together with your non-investment financial assets. These include:

- your current job,

- your home and any other assets that are not financial assets but which if lost would hurt you,

- any relationships that would be likely to be altered by a change in your financial circumstances – e.g. children and their schooling, your dependents and their expectations, your own mental health,

- the ease with which you could get a new job at the same or better level of pay and prospects if you were to lose your current job.

Identifying risk is partly a problem of perception and experience

Written down on paper as above it is simple to say that you should identify risks. One of the main difficulties is seeing something that you have not seen before. It is not only in finance that unfamiliar things bear you greater risk than things with which you are already familiar. In some cases this is learning to apply your existing way of seeing things more carefully. An illustration of this type of problem is Figure 3·1, in which there is at least one very dangerous wild animal – how long does it take you to see the dangerous animal(s)? In other cases the problem is to get your mind to adjust to seeing the same thing in a new way, rather as if you were trying to see how the animal could look like something completely different because of an optical illusion. Figure 3·2 is an illustration of this type of problem. Is this exercise far fetched? Is it relevant to finance? In 2004 mortgages were considered by investment bankers as boring, low risk assets. Within five years some of the most common mortgages had nearly brought down the entire world financial system and many governments. The nature of these financial assets had not changed, it simply had not been seen for what it was.

In 1999 mainstream finance experts saw gold as a bad investment with high risks and no use to retail investors. But if you had bought gold on 4 October 2001 you would have paid £210 per ounce, and on 27 June 2010 you could have sold it for £740[2] per ounce, an annualized return of over 15 percent. Seen through the lens of conventional wisdom at the time gold was a risky, perhaps even foolish investment. However, for the person who had taken time to understand the risks not only in gold but in the main alternative investment options such as index trackers, high-interest savings accounts and property, gold did not appear particularly risky: governments were obviously going to have to start printing money to cover unsustainable spending, because government spending was crowding out private investment, which was also facing fierce price competition from China and elsewhere, and because property investment was reaching dangerously high levels.

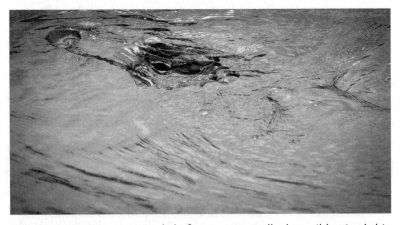

Figure 3·1 How many seconds before you can tell what wild animal this is? Is that long enough to survive?

Source: Shutterstock: Twisted Shots

Focus on the risks in the decision you are making

The third and final step is to focus on the risks in the investment or other financial decision that you are considering, if there is one. You may well be able to identify the likely risks yourself, and search engines such as Google can help you ensure you have covered the main known risks. For example, typing in 'risks in mortgage for customers' to Google throws up a number of specific

FIGURE 3·2 How many animals (living things) are there in this image?

risks. Some questions which may be useful in prompting your thinking about risks specific to a financial decision that you are making include:

- What is the worst that could go wrong? What would have to happen – what would be the chain of events leading up to it – for the worst to happen?
- What are the risks of not going ahead?
- What is the next best course of action to this one, and what are the risks in that? Are they worse than the ones associated with this course of action?
- Who is involved in this decision? Who has helped persuade me into considering it, who will be vital to executing it? What are their incentives to look after my interests? What recourse am I likely to have against them if things go wrong?
- If things go wrong, then looking back on where I am now, what might I wish I had done differently now?

- If this goes wrong, what are the other risks elsewhere in my life that could make it even worse? How are they connected?

- How can I protect against this risk? Diversify? Insure against it? Talk to someone who has taken the same decision and succeeded? Join an Internet discussion group?

You might like to write down your thinking about risk, but usually it is enough to go through it in your mind. Spending 5 percent of your income a month on a low-risk savings product is not the kind of decision where much thought about risk is needed. (Low risk here are such things as a low-cost index tracker or an additional payment into a good pension scheme or repaying your mortgage early.) Choosing a pension scheme, a financial adviser, changing job, setting up a business, or investing large sums are the kinds of financial decisions where some time and effort thinking about risk as such is worthwhile.

If you are investing in a new asset class or undertaking a type of financial decision that is new to you, you may want to allow some time for learning about the risks as you go. Suppose you are serious about investing in, say, shares, and right now you have no experience. Allow yourself one to two years to learn by doing, i.e. by investing in shares. Accept that you will make mistakes in this period and may lose much of what you invest. Budget and manage your risk accordingly.

In Chapter 8 you will find a list of rules of thumb for making better investment decisions. These are specific rules for better risk management.

The Five Whys as a risk-management technique

Another risk-management technique is a variant of the Five Whys from quality management. The principle is to ask 'Why?' five times in succession, as a way to ensure that you get to the bottom of a problem. This technique can be illustrated by means of a hypothetical example:

The example is of a risk assessment for a bridging loan. A bridging loan is a loan, often very large, taken out by someone moving house to pay for the new house before the old house is sold. You may think of it as a temporary mortgage.

Why? 1 The risk is that having doubled your mortgage, something happens that prevents you from paying off the bridging loan.

Why? 2 The most obvious risk is that for some reason you cannot sell your old house.

Why? 3 Perhaps there is something wrong with it that you don't know about but that the buyers' surveyors find out?

Why? 4 You have not had a survey done and although you feel that you know your house is OK, you are not really certain, because you were not expecting to need a bridging loan.

Why? 5 The housing market has experienced a downturn since you embarked on selling your house.

So ... what?

- Get a survey of your old house, to minimize the risk of finding out too late that it is unsellable.

- Do more research into how severe the downturn in the market is likely to be. What drop in price can you not afford, and how likely is this now?

Classical responses to risk

There are four traditional responses to risks. These are useful and are reproduced below for those not already familiar with them:

1. Do nothing – accept the risk and the probability of its consequences.

2. Mitigate the risk – take steps to reduce the damage that the consequences of the risk crystallizing will do to your interests.

3. Transfer the risk to someone else (insuring against the risk) – someone else will bear the consequences of the risk.

4. Diversify – do nothing about that particular risk but do other things that at least partially neutralize its consequences.

Mistakes in how the finance sector thinks about risk

The great financial crisis that began in the last quarter of 2007 and engulfed Lehman Brothers, Northern Rock, RBS, Barclays, Goldman Sachs and many other famous names in finance shows that there is great weakness in how the finance sector as a whole thinks about risk. Some banks were notable for having managed the risks well enough to survive without emergency funding, including National Australia Group (which includes Clydesdale Bank in the UK), HSBC, Standard Chartered, Wells Fargo and many Canadian, Australian and New Zealand banks. While a minority of financial institutions managed risk well, the scale of the financial catastrophe suggests that in general the finance sector operates on a fundamentally flawed model of what risk is and how to manage it. This argument has been set out well by others, especially Nassim Nicholas Taleb.[3] The purpose of this section is to give you an overview of some of the main features of how the mainstream finance industry thinks about risk and to point out some of the problems. The rationale is to help you develop your own thinking about financial risk, and to help you get started in understanding where the professionals' strengths and weaknesses lie so that you can avoid problems created by their weaknesses and can profit from their strengths. This section is by no means comprehensive, and we focus on just three weaknesses and one overall strength.

- The overall strength – financial and political firepower.
- Black swans: financial catastrophe is not normally distributed.
- Moral hazard.
- Large, established organizations are unlikely to be original.

The overall strength – financial and political firepower

On the whole, large, conventional financial institutions have failed utterly since 2007. However, most of those that actually failed have a few great strengths from the point of view of a saver's self-interest (i.e. from your point of view.) Northern Rock was incompetently managed and was a financial disaster in every respect, to take one of many examples. However, it had the supreme advantage that politically the government responsible for it was not going to let it fail. There have been many far worthier cases for taxpayer bailouts and many institutions who have got into less trouble by means of far less incompetence than Northern Rock but which have not been bailed out. Unfair? That's not the point. When picking a financial institution with which to trust your money in risky times, pick one that the government will most probably not allow to go under.

Black swans: financial catastrophe is not normally distributed

David Hume[4] (1711–1776) formulated the problem of induction, which is that merely because something has happened reliably until now that does not mean that it is going to go on happening, nor that it is a universal rule. The fact that the sun has risen every morning is not obviously a reliable reason to believe that it will go on doing so. John Stuart Mill (1806–1873) and others have since used the term *black swan* to illustrate the problem.

Consider this question: before anyone (in Europe) had seen a black swan, how likely was it that black swans existed? From the viewpoint of today, we can say that they were just as likely to exist as they do now, i.e, that they did in fact exist. But the force of the question is at that time, before anyone (in Europe) had ever seen a black swan, how reasonable was it to believe that such things existed? We might say how *probable* was it that black swans existed? We might, and one half of the subject that is probability would agree with us.

There are two main concepts of probability (in the sense of a branch of statistics). One has it that probability is a reasonable degree of belief. The problem here is that the question of what is probability gets pushed back into the questions of what is reasonable. The other half of probability as a discipline has it that probability means something only in situations which are in principle testable, in a way that alternative histories (possible states of the world other than its actual state at any time). Does this matter to you? Leaving aside the wider question of whether the statistics on which the finance industry is based is fit for purpose, it does not take much thought to see that these two contrasting schemas for probability may in practice give widely different numbers for the probability of any event. Much of the work done in investment houses, insurance companies and financial regulators uses the science of probability in a way that is effective and beneficial to the ordinary investor, but there are problems with the underpinning sciences used. Two specific defects are the definition of risk and the use of the normal distribution.

The finance sector's definition of risk is defective

Suppose you invest £100,000 in a business and you expect to get £200,000 back in total after two years. There is a risk that you will instead lose £100,000 and get nothing, i.e. a loss of 100 percent. Finance theory sees this as a risk, and you surely do too. Suppose that instead of getting your expected £200,000 total return you instead get double the profit, i.e. a total return of £300,000. Finance theory treats this as just as much a risk as getting nothing. This is unhelpful. Since when has getting too much money been a problem? The only problem about it is that this turn of events does not happen often enough. The reason that finance theory treats an unexpectedly large gain as representing exactly the same risk as a corresponding degree of disappointment in return on investment is that this is the only way that the maths and statistics used by mainstream finance professionals and risk managers can be made to work. The maths and statistics used by the finance sector to manage risk puts it in the position of the drunk looking for his keys one dark night. The drunk was walking around a lamp post peering intently at the ground. 'Where did you lose your keys?' you ask him. 'A hundred yards over there' he replies, pointing a long way away from where he is looking. 'Why aren't you looking over there?' you ask trying to be helpful. 'Because it's dark over there and where I am looking there is light.'

If you have the energy and drive to learn about one area of finance or investing in depth, you may well be able to do much better than many institutions by not being constrained by their limitations.

The finance sector's use of the normal distribution curve is a problem

A normal distribution curve is shown in Figure 3·3. The normal curve when used in probability shows the probability of an event occurring for a range of events. The vertical axis is the probability, the horizontal axis is a range that represents the range of possible events such that a numerical scale makes sense. Taking our last example, the highest point on the curve, the most likely event might be that you get a total return of £200,000. The left and right extremes would be respectively the cases that you get nothing back and that you get £300,000. The normal curve aims to show the probability of any return. Some of the essential features of the normal curve are that:

- there is one value in the range of outcomes that is most probable
- all other values are progressively less likely the further they lie from this one value
- the probabilities for upside and downside relative to this one value are the same for the same gap on the upside as on the downside
- the overall curve may be flatter or deeper, but otherwise its shape is always the same.

Many things in the world do follow the normal distribution sufficiently closely for it to be a reliable tool. However, many things in finance don't.

Moral hazard

Moral hazard is the risk that someone will behave differently if they have a safeguard from how they would behave had they no safeguard. If the director of a bank knows that the government will bail him out if his rash bet with the bank's money on the financial markets goes wrong, but that he will get a large bonus if the rash bet comes off, perhaps he will be less careful in evaluating the best than if he stood to lose his shirt if the bet went wrong. Moral hazard is a type of risk that pervades the financial system. There is probably little you can do to make the financial system more honest, but you can steer clear of moral hazard where you see it and where it is likely to work against your interests.

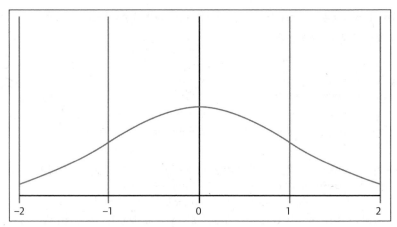

FIGURE 3·3 The normal distribution curve

Large, established organizations are unlikely to be innovative

The central challenge in growing your wealth is to get a greater return than average. This is difficult because so many other people are trying to do the same thing. Superior returns depend fundamentally on innovation, but over time the advantages created by successful innovation get competed away in the market. Getting superior financial returns therefore depends fundamentally on being able to exploit successful innovation, which means either being an innovator yourself or investing in a business or person who is likely to reap rewards from successful innovation and give you a share of it. A problem for large organizations is that for many reasons they find it hard to innovate. The processes and culture within large organizations conspire to suppress innovation. There are exceptions to this rule, such as 3M and Apple in the USA, Astra Zeneca and Clydesdale bank in the UK, but it is a general rule. One reason for this is that large, established organizations have more to gain from things staying the same than from change, and much besides to lose from change. Another reason is that the power structure and hierarchy that is essential to running a large organization by its nature suppresses new young managers with new ideas. And a third reason is that it is simply harder to get a large, complex system to change, unless it is under extreme pressure, and even then change tends to cease once the immediate threat has been ameliorated.

The risk free rate of interest

It is useful to have some firm reference point when thinking about financial risk. The most common reference point is the risk-free rate of interest, otherwise known as the risk-free rate or r_f. In finance theory this is the rate at which you can lend to the government in the short-term government bond market. In practice for the ordinary investor it is the rate you can get if you deposit funds with a bank guaranteed by your government. 'Risk free' means 'risk free for all probable eventualities'. However, you can also lend to the government by buying government bonds, which in the UK are known as gilts (for gilt-edged securities).

How can you use the idea of the risk-free rate in making financial decisions? The main ramification of the notion of the risk-free rate is that any investment you make should return more than the risk-free rate, or else why take on risk? It further follows that not only should the return on an investment that has greater than zero risk be greater than the risk-free rate but that it should be greater in proportion to the degree of risk.

In theory this means that we want to be able to calculate that because the risk-free rate is x percent, an investment with a level R of risk should return $(x + y)$ percent. There is a well-developed body of theory that does precisely this – *modern portfolio theory*.

Modern portfolio theory

This theory is widely used by professional investors. Returns from different types of investment are measured and used to help decide (guess) what levels of risk there are in possible future investments, and what degree of return must be required. It is useful in that it prioritizes investments and enables the fund manager to decide what to invest in and how to monitor investments. It suffers from two problems. One is that it implicitly assumes that the future will look like the past, and secondly, in most implementations it explicitly assumes that the normal curve describes the universe of investment instruments more closely than is the case.

Summary

There is no complete and consistent definition of risk. This makes risk hard to manage, and you should be sceptical of claims by finance professionals about the reliability of risk management. Nonetheless, defective though the efforts of the finance industry are in regard to risk management, they are far better than making no effort, and they point to the difficult nature of the problem. They also provide opportunities for the private investor to compete effectively in the global financial markets, if you specialize and invest time and effort in learning about finance and risk management in a particular area.

There is a number of tools for managing financial risk that have stood the test of time. These include the notion of the risk-free rate and the four standard choices in the face of risk: acceptance, mitigation, transfer (e.g. by insurance) and diversification. These also include the Five Whys approach. This chapter also gave a three-step method for managing your financial risk. Good as these tools are, two problems remain. Part of the difficulty in managing risk lies in perceiving it, and we used two visual analogies to illustrate the two different ways this problem meets us. Part of the problem is that the underpinning probability theory and other maths and statistics are simply not fit for purpose, as in the case of the notion of risk used in the financial world and in the case of the normal curve. In the end, risk is risky. Keeping an investment diary is a great way to improve your risk management capability.

1. Go to a website or newspaper and find today's risk-free rate in two different countries.

2. Is the risk-free rate completely free of risk? Why?

3. Define financial risk (a) as the financial services industry uses the term and (b) as you use it.

4. The government decides to spend 70 percent of gross domestic product (GDP) in bailing out banks and investment banks, and claims that this is low risk because it is temporary and the government will get its money back. (a) Is this really low risk? (b) what else could the government have done with 70 percent of GDP that would have given the same or better return for less risk?

5. What is moral hazard? List three cases of moral hazard in the past three years.

6. A great friend suggests to you that you invest in a holiday property that he saw in Croatia last year when he went there with his family. Spend five minutes considering risk. Write down two questions to ask your friend when you next see him aimed at improving your understanding of the risks.

7. Should you invest in things where you do not understand the risks. (Yes or no.)

8. Write down the top three financial risks in your life, and also write down the financial risks in your main investment asset and your main financial liability.

9. Do you trust the CEO of your bank to tell the truth? (Yes or no.)

10. List the advantages and disadvantages of the normal distribution curve as a way of thinking about the probabilities of financial events.

Who? Whom? Interests and character

The main criterion for lending is character – before the money or property of the borrower or anything else.

J. P. Morgan, in his testimony to Congress

How much of the experience of managing money is emotional and how much is analytical [?] ... the emotional content is not more than 90%, in our experience.

James Grant, *Mr Market Miscalculates*

No matter how hard it tries, business can never escape the fact that it is the practice of potentially thieving, treacherous, lying human beings.

Quoted in Philip Delves Broughton, *Ahead of the Curve*

It is impossible for a man to learn what he thinks he already knows.

Epictetus

One lies to oneself more than to anyone else.

Lord Byron

AIM OF THIS CHAPTER

The aim of this chapter is to enable you to understand and use the factors of people's interests and also of their character when making financial decisions. In order to do this the specific aims of this chapter are to help you to:

1. Recognize the two central problems around truth in the financial world.

2. Understand what an interest is and why interests are important, be able to identify or make reasonable guesses about interests, and use them to make better financial decisions.

3. Understand how the character of a person affects their financial performance and their impact on your finances.

4. Understand your own character as it affects the quality of your own financial decision making.

5. Get better at finding out things that other people do not want you to know about their interests in your finances.

6. Know about winner's and loser's games, the framing bias and the sunk cost fallacy and understand their implications for your decision making and how others are likely to behave in ways that affect your finances.

The two central problems of truth in the financial world

Have you ever felt that in business someone you trusted has lied to you? Or perhaps the other party did not actually lie but chose their words very carefully, and allowed you to come to believe something that is not true. One of the problems in finance is that many people you deal with are quite happy for you to be deceived, even if they pride themselves on not lying. The solution is to develop your skill at recognizing when there is a risk of becoming deceived, and asking questions to find out what is really going on. You need to understand interests and character to do this.

> **Harvard Business School on professional deceit**
>
> While it is true that most people go to great lengths not to lie, many are happy to allow others to become deceived.
>
> Harvard Negotiation Programme, Harvard Business School

Consider this real-life experiment. A woman dressed in a gorilla suit walks through a basketball game, passing right between the players in full view. You ask someone who was watching the game intently if there was a person in a gorilla suit anywhere in the game and they reply that no there wasn't. What is going on here? This was a real experiment[1] and 46 percent of people watching the game failed to notice the woman in the gorilla suit. The reason is that those watching had been asked to count the number of passes of the ball between the players. Being focused on counting passes made 46 percent of people blind to the woman in the gorilla suit walking right through the middle of the game. Had they been told to look for a person in a gorilla suit then they would all have seen her. This effect stems from what psychologists have termed _inattentional blindness_.

Sometimes a huge opportunity or a massive risk wanders into your portfolio of assets, and you must ensure that either you or your advisers can see the risk or opportunity in the gorilla suit. The finance industry and its practitioners are not above using inattentional blindness and other weaknesses of the human mind to persuade you to do things against your interests.

Are psychological factors such as inattentional blindness part of financial literacy? We have treated this as a practical question, i.e. is it something that makes people lose large amounts of money? Every finance professional interviewed when writing this book felt that this is one of the most important subjects in finance.

The second central problem relating to truth in financial matters is seeing that there is a problem or an opportunity when there is one. The woman in the gorilla suit is there, but can you see her? This can often be one of the biggest problems in making financial decisions.[2] A key part of preserving your wealth and making good strategic investment decisions is simply to avoid the major known risks, which are sometimes like gorillas wandering through the room – invisible unless you remind yourself to look for them.

What are interests and why are they important?

The definition of an interest is _the advantage or benefit of a person or group_.[3] Very often people will not tell you what their interests are, but one can make a reasonable guess. In financial decision making you must identify all the people who stand to gain or lose from your decision, or who can block your decision or who are advising you. Consider what each person or group of people or organization stands to gain or lose; that is to say, consider their interests.

Character

The challenge is to guess what is going on in another person's mind. Understanding character is a vast subject but you do not need to become an expert in it in order to make better financial decisions. You need at least to see how to apply what you already know about judging people's character to some of your financial affairs. In routine financial decisions you may not need to consider the question of character, but in some decisions it does matter, for example in choosing a lawyer, accountant, private banker or an independent financial adviser.

Your own character is a factor in whether a risky investment will cause you sleepless nights or not. The character of those who advise you can determine whether you get good or bad advice. The character of the directors of the companies in which you invest influence the prices of shares and bonds issued by those companies. The three steps to assessing character and using this assessment to improve your financial decision are:

1 Know your own character.

2 Understand the decision and how the character of those involved might affect it.

3 Learn as much as you need to about the characters of the key people in the decision, subject to practical constraints of time and cost.

You must know yourself. In financial decisions you must understand how your feelings and biases work in different kinds of situations. An investment that makes one person happy can give another sleepless nights. Keeping an investment diary is a good way to improve your knowledge of your own financial character. When keeping an investment diary write down how your different investments made you feel. This may not make much difference over two or three years, but ten years later when you re-read it you will be able to recognize patterns and avoid certain kinds of investments that make you feel bad.

Figure 4·1 is a flow chart for how to assess character in a financial decision. This is a simple 12-step process that should be applied in any of your major financial decisions where character matters. It assumes that you know your own character. An example of this 12-step process in use is shown at Figure 4·2. It illustrates a hypothetical case in which you want to buy a house for your daughter to live in while she is at university. You want a mortgage because you do not have the cash to pay for the whole price of the house. You started to look for mortgages on the Internet but decided to use a mortgage broker because you realize that you do not understand the special types of mortgage for this type of situation, and also you would rather pay a reasonable fee than spend a large amount of time doing research and learning about this kind of mortgage.

Note the interplay of character and interests. The interests of each person determine what aspects of their character matters. In this hypothetical example, it matters if the mortgage broker is lazy because they are then less likely to know about all the mortgages available to you and to have bothered to think hard about exactly which one is best for you.

Asking questions

How do you size up a financial adviser? Can you tell when someone is lying or simply being misleading? Far more of us think we can do this than actually can. Experiments show that only one in four hundred of us can judge this right at least 80 percent of the time. However, with practice anyone can improve their score.[4.] The way to improve is to ask questions carefully. Consider the following dialogues:

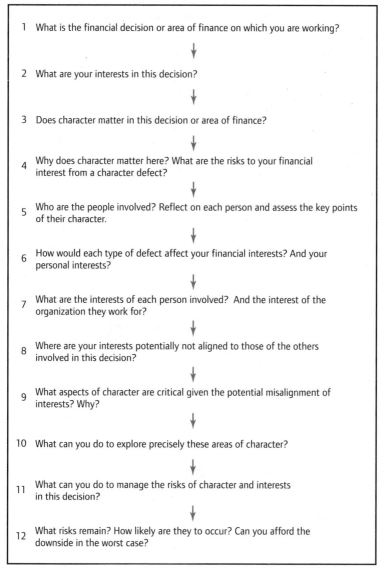

1   What is the financial decision or area of finance on which you are working?

2   What are your interests in this decision?

3   Does character matter in this decision or area of finance?

4   Why does character matter here? What are the risks to your financial interest from a character defect?

5   Who are the people involved? Reflect on each person and assess the key points of their character.

6   How would each type of defect affect your financial interests? And your personal interests?

7   What are the interests of each person involved? And the interest of the organization they work for?

8   Where are your interests potentially not aligned to those of the others involved in this decision?

9   What aspects of character are critical given the potential misalignment of interests? Why?

10   What can you do to explore precisely these areas of character?

11   What can you do to manage the risks of character and interests in this decision?

12   What risks remain? How likely are they to occur? Can you afford the downside in the worst case?

FIGURE 4·1 A flow chart for assessing character and thus making better financial decisions

1 What is the financial decision or area of finance on which you are working?

Whether to take out a mortgage to buy a house for your daughter to live in while she is at university.

2 What are your interests in this decision?

(1) To ensure that your daughter has somewhere to live at university that is safe and allows her to study effectively, (2) to preserve your hard-earned wealth by diversifying your portfolio into property, (3) if possible, after preserving wealth, to increase your capital.

3 Does character matter in this decision or area of finance?

Yes, because you are using a mortgage broker and the broker is a source of risk of your mortgage being more expensive than you need, or being unsuitable in some other way. The character of your daughter also matters, because it will affect how well she looks after the property, whether she gets

4 Why does character matter here? What are the risks to your financial interest from a character defect?

reliable sub-tenants and whether she collects their rent regularly.

5 Who are the people involved? Reflect on each person and assess the key points of their character.

1. The mortgage broker.
2. Your daughter.
3. Any tenants who will share the house with your daughter.

6 How would each type of defect affect your financial interests? And your personal interests?

If the mortgage broker is dishonest, lazy, disorganized or narrow minded there is a higher risk that you will pay too much for a mortgage. The same is true in the case of your daughter. Additionally if your daughter is too nice then she may not be goodat collecting rent from any sub-tenants in the house, and you will end up subsidizing her friends.

7	What are the interests of each person involved? And the interests of the organization they work for?	Your daughter: (1) having a safe plave to live, (2) being able to study effectively, (3) having a reasonable social life, (4) being away from home. The mortgage broker: (1) making money, either from a fee based on the time spent advising you, or more likely, from a commission from the mortgage recommended, (2) preserving and enhancing their reputation.

↓

8	Where are your interests potentially not aligned to those of the others involved in this decision?	Mortgage broker – you are interested in lowest cost mortgage, they may be more interested in their fee. Your daughter – may be more interested in her quality of life than in preserving or enhancing your capital.

↓

9	What aspects of character are critical given the potential misalignment of interests? Why?	Mortgage broker: integrity, so that they resist the temptation to put their interest in a fee in front of their duty to advise you. Your daughter: (1) self-discipline so that she will look after the property and manage her budget, (2) ability to read people, so that she ends up with good housemates, (3) ability to be firm, so that she collects rent from housemates.

↓

10	What can you do to explore precisely these areas of character?	Mortgage broker: (1) find out how they make money and if a commission, its basis, (2) talk to other clients of theirs, preferably people you know well, check for regulatory infringements, see what the press say about them. Your daughter: from your own knowledge of what she has done in the past. (Assume that she will not change.)

↓

11	What can you do to manage the risks of character and interests in this decision?	Mortgage broker: (1) negotiate a fee arrangement that aligns your interests better, or find a new broker with a better fee arrangement, (2) confirm your understanding of the deal and of their fee arrangements in writing. Your daughter: (1) talk to her and explain exactly what this investment means to you personally, and what she must do to help you, (2) put in writing to your daughter what her responsibilities are, perhaps as a formal contract, (3) give your daughter some incentive, financial or otherwise, to manage the property well and to collect rents in full and on time.

↓

12	What risks remain? How likely are they to occur? Can you afford the downside in the worst case?	Two risks that remain are (a) that the mortgage broker does not give you the best mortgage, despite seeming to be diligent and honest and perhaps even being so, and (b) that your daughter goes off the rails at university. The probability of these and whether you can afford their consequences is for you to decide.

FIGURE 4·2 A flow chart for assessing character and thus making better financial decisions – a worked example finding a mortgage to buy a house for your daughter while she is at university

You:	Is this financial product a good choice for me?
Financial Adviser:	Yes. We expect it to deliver a good return, it is are putable brand and many other investors like you are very happy with it.

A different way to ask the question is:

You:	I'm interested in whether this financial product is a good choice for me. I would like to know what you think the next best product is, the conditions under which it may not work out well for me, and how much commission you get paid on it. Let's start with your commission?
Financial Adviser:	I receive 5 percent per year on all the payments you make on this. But if you wish, I can rebate 2 percent to you, which will mean my commission is 3 percent per year.
You:	Are you aware of other financial products similar to this on which you receive a lower commission?
Financial Adviser:	There are a number of other roughly similar products available. In this firm we sell only two of them, and we also take between 3 percent and 5 percent on those.
You:	What in your opinion is the next best product, and why is it not as suitable for me as the one you recommend?
Financial Adviser:	MegaPlanetFinance does a similar product, which we have sold in the past, but recently they implemented a new back office and enterprise resource planning system which seems to have degraded their level of customer service. The product is about as good as the one I recommend, but I am worried about their customer service. There is no material difference in price or fees.

Other people's interests in your finances

The 2009 political scandal of the expenses of UK Members of Parliament (MPs) demonstrates how far even the most successful and respected people will go to cover up embarrassing knowledge. People will do this even when it means that they will let down those they are meant to look after or when it requires them to break the law. What was going on here? What are the implications for your personal financial decision making?

If British MPs can't be trusted in financial matters and preferred to break the law rather than come clean on financial information, what can you do about finance professionals with whom you have to deal? The risk is that the sort of behaviour exhibited by British MPs will make

Source: Shutterstock: stocker1970

you the next victim of a Bernard Madoff or an Equitable Life. It does no harm to start with the assumption that people will not tell you some of the key things you need to know or have a right to know. Let us take as an example insurance salesmen selling insurance investment products.

Insurance salesmen are often paid a commission, so if you buy an insurance-related savings product from them part of what you pay does not get invested in the insurance product but goes to the salesman as commission. Suppose you agree with an insurance salesman to buy a product that costs £100,000, to be paid in ten annual instalments of £10,000. Suppose that the salesman is on a 5 percent commission. Three of many ways of the commission being taken off your payment are for the commission to be paid up front, in arrears, or spread evenly throughout the life of the product. Table 4·1 shows particular instances of these three ways of paying commission. The problem with commissions is the way in which they are implemented. Does the salesperson care about how the product they have sold you performs? This depends on the character of the salesman and on how and when commission is paid.

Table 4·1 Three different commission structures on a financial product

Year	1	2	3	4	5	6	7	8	9	10
You pay, £	10,000	10,000	10,000	10,000	10,000	10,000	10,000	10,000	10,000	10,000
Commission A	500	500	500	500	500	500	500	500	500	500
Commission B	£3,750	£1,250	0	0	0	0	0	0	0	0
Commission C	0	0	0	0	0	0	0	0	0	£5,000

Now consider the three different commission scenarios, A, B and C in Table 4·1. The salesman might get a commission only if you are completely satisfied with the performance of the product that he has sold you, which is Commission C in the table. While this might sound ideal from your point of view the salesman would have to wait ten years to get paid. This type of commission structure is rarely seen in retail financial products.

Commission B is the sort of structure that is most common for insurance-related savings products. A large part of your first few payments goes in commission. This means that correspondingly little of what you invest in the early days of your insurance policy goes into an investment. In B, the salesman has little financial interest after the first two years in ensuring that your product is performing well. He has his commission and needs to look elsewhere for new commissions. In this example you are relying from the end of year two on the man's conscience and professionalism to look after your interests.

Commission A is a common arrangement in non-insurance savings products such as managed funds. While it solves some of the problems in B it is not without problems. The relatively small commission in the first year may not be much compensation for the time and effort spent selling you the product, and it may be a better use of the salesman's time, from his point of view, to sell other products with higher commissions.

These three examples illustrate that how commissions are paid matters. When you are dealing with salesmen or brokers or anyone else who earns their pay from your decisions you must find out how they are paid and if it is by commission, on what basis. Ask them whether they are paid a flat salary or a commission. If a commission, ask how it is calculated and whether they get it up front or over the life of the investment you make. Many salesmen are reluctant to give this information, and you can read into that reluctance what you will. The honest, capable and diligent advisor who takes a commission has nothing to hide by setting out clearly exactly how they are compensated.

An alternative to commission-based payment is a time-based fee. Typically people tend to buy more insurance when they pay hidden or largely hidden commissions than when they pay for advice separately from insurance. For most people this is because it feels expensive to pay, say, £200 per hour for two or three hours of advice than to pay a few percent commission. And for some people writing a separate cheque for £600 feels more expensive than paying £1000 per year by standing order of which the first £750 is commission. Such biases seems to be natural human traits, but you can overcome them by finding out how your advisers are making money out of you and then working out the cash cost to you. Compare that to the cost of financial advice charged on a time basis. Some questions to ask are:

- What is your personal interest in this matter?

- What is X's interest in this matter, so far as you know or can guess?

- If you were in my position, what would you be asking me about my interests in this decision, and why?

- Have you been involved in this kind of decision before? What kinds of things have you seen go wrong that stem from conflicts of interest?

- If there were a million dollars here on the table, what do you think each of us could or should do differently?

- If this deal went ahead and then had to be cancelled early, how should we set the interests of the parties involved now so that the termination would be smooth and as painless as possible for everyone?

- What would make this deal go really badly wrong? How do we stop each of those things from happening?
- Why can't you give me the information for which I am asking?

Three psychological quirks of character and what they mean for your financial decision making

There is a whole field of behavioural finance that looks at experiments such as *Gorillas in our Midst* and investigates what they mean for financial decision making. You don't need to become an expert in financial psychology and there is not time in most people's lives to do so anyway, but it is worth thinking about the role of psychology and how human character matters in finance. Understanding the key points of some of the major experiments is a good way to do this.

1. Winner's games and loser's games

You have to be very good at playing tennis to win Wimbledon. This is hardly a remarkable claim. But what about the rest of us in our ordinary games of tennis with friends and neighbours? That kind of tennis, the sort that most of us play, turns out to be in a sense a different kind of game to top level professional tennis. The rules of the game are the same, but the rules for winning are quite different. Top level professional tennis is a winner's game. The sort of tennis that most of the rest of us play, recreational tennis, is called a loser's game.

A winner's game is one in which in order to win a player must focus their effort on winning and as part of this must develop advanced tactics and skills. In order to win in a loser's game, by contrast, a player must focus on not losing, for example on not making basic mistakes. In a loser's game you merely need to avoid making simple mistakes and the chances are that everyone else will, especially if they try to play an advanced technique or to deploy advanced skills. In a loser's game having mastery of basic skills is usually sufficient to win. In a winner's game having a mastery of the same basic skills is necessary to stay in the game, but is not sufficient to win.

Retail investing is a loser's game. The message is to prioritize on avoiding basic mistakes when making financial decisions, unless you are an expert in that area of finance.

2. Framing bias

This effect is similar to anchoring, although not identical. How you frame a question or how you frame your thinking affects what you perceive and how you see it. In Holborn in London there has been a church on the site of what is now the church of St Giles-in-the-Fields for over a thousand years. One of the longest serving rectors of this church used to pose the following question to women who were planning their weddings at the church. 'Would you like a modern wedding with the very new language, or would you like the language that you already know and that your mother and grandmother had at their weddings?' This framing of the question ensured that most brides-to-be opted for the wedding service largely as set out in the 1662 *Book of Common Prayer*. This paragraph uses the same technique. Had the church in question not been described as a thousand years old and in the middle of an ancient City, but as a Richard Rogers or Le Corbusier structure in, say, Milton Keynes or Schipol airport, what preconception about the preferences of the priest would have been set up?

The framing bias is widely used in marketing, negotiating, politics and much of finance. In the USA, the argument about abortion is between camps who describe themselves as 'Pro-choice' and 'Pro-life.' 'Pro-life' is a much more appealing framing of that group's position than 'Anti-choice'. How a question is framed is important because it exerts a powerful sway over which answer people choose. Life insurance salesmen have long known that to sell their product it is much more effective to ask 'Do you want to make sure that if anything happened to you, your family would not be thrown out of their home and have to struggle to survive?' than it is to ask 'Do you want life insurance?'

The countermeasure to use against the risk of adverse framing working against your interests is very simple. Frame the same question in a number of different ways. This simple technique can help to develop your insight into the problem. And having selected the best way to frame the question to suit your own interests, keep using that frame.

The Eurobond market: framing, a small change in the law and the creation of one of the world's biggest financial markets

Today one of the biggest financial markets in the world is the Eurobond market, and it is centred in London. This market came about because of a few changes in the laws of the UK and USA between 1956 and 1963. The US banned British bank deposits in the US, a year later the British government made it illegal to finance trade for non-UK residents with sterling, and subsequently the US government made a new law requiring some depositors to be paid lower-than-market rates of interest. The consequence of these laws was a very high-growth new market in Eurobonds based in London. Had US lawmakers framed the situation differently, might they have made a different decision?

In 2005 the size of the Eurobond market was US$400 billion.

---

3. The sunk cost fallacy

The sunk cost fallacy is the fallacy of continuing with some course of action when there is no advantage in doing so because one has invested a large and unrecoverable sum in it already. As an example, imagine someone who has bought a movie on DVD. This person has watched half of the movie and it is truly dreadful – the plot is non-existent, the characters are as wooden as a rotting tree, and the jokes are dire. Some people in this situation will watch the movie to the end. Their reasoning is that they have paid their money and watch it they will, because they have already paid and cannot get their money back. The cost of the DVD is sunk. Of course you are not such a person. People who behave this way ignore the full analysis of their situation: while it is true that the cost is sunk, they have a choice, of either to do something more enjoyable or productive with their time instead of watching the rest of the movie, or to watch the rest of the movie which they know beyond any reasonable doubt will be tedious and a waste of their time. The sunk cost fallacy is a challenge in business.

In the case of investments, a bad investment where the value of your investment falls and is not realistically likely to recover is a sunk cost. It is a mistake to hold on to your investment simply because you invested heavily in it. You may need to accept that you have lost the money, get what little of your money is left out of the investment and do something else with it. Invested gone wrong provide many instances of the sunk cost fallacy. As they say on the trading desks of major financial institutions: 'The first cut is the cheapest'. So if you see a sunk cost, stop throwing good money after bad.

A trend – but how to make money from it?

Source: Shutterstock: Brian A Jackson

The sunk cost fallacy is also known as *loss aversion*.

Summary

This chapter may be summarized in four ideas:

1. *Recognize the two central problems around truth in the financial world.* We saw that these were: (1) being deceived, especially when someone else allows you to deceive yourself; and (2) being able to see problems and opportunities in the first place.

2. *Understand how other people's interests and character affect your finances.* Many routine financial decisions can be taken without considering interests and character, but in major decisions and in all decisions where you take someone's advice, you need to assess the interests and character of those involved. This is not in order to restrict your dealings to saints, but in order to understand where the risks are in the decision and what you might do about them.

3. *Understand your own character as it affects the quality of your own financial decision making.* Understanding your own

character is important. An investment that suits one person very well, for example, may affect another person of the same age, wealth, abilities and general circumstance very badly if it keeps them awake at night. One of many ways to improve your knowledge of your own financial character is to think back over financial decisions you have made and review them and how your feelings changed over time.

4 *Get better at finding out things that other people do not want you to know about their interests in your finances.* People will go to great lengths to avoid revealing their interests and position, and this includes their interests in your financial decisions. Further to the previous three points, you should develop your skills at finding out what others do not want you to know about their interests in your affairs.

These four ideas are related and you can use them as a checklist when making financial decisions.

REVIEW QUESTIONS

1 How do you assess someone else's character? Which parts of their character matter in financial decisions?

2 What is a sunk cost?

3 You are considering investing in two businesses, both run by different cousins of yours. They are both restaurant businesses, about the same size. The only investors will be you and the entrepreneur, one of your cousins. Each restaurant business needs £300,000. One cousin, Chloe, is offering a deal where you put in £20,000 and she puts in £80,000, which is her entire savings, and she mortgages her house to raise a further £200,000. The other cousin, Delilah, offers you a deal where you put in £100,000, she puts in her time which she values at £80,000 and also £20,000 of her total of £80,000 savings, and the remaining money needed will come from a government grant (she has shown you solid evidence that the grant exists and she will get it). What is the difference between the interests of your cousins? Which is more closely aligned to yours? If you have a total of £120,000 to invest this year, what would you say to each cousin?

4 What is the anchoring effect? How does it influence financial decisions?

5 List three recent fashions in investing. Why are they popular, and will they make good investments? Why?

5 Options and their value

When a person acts without knowledge of what he thinks, feels, needs or wants, he does not yet have the option of choosing to act differently.

Clark Moustakas, Michigan School of Professional Psychology

Derivatives are financial weapons of mass destruction.

Warren Buffett

Choice of aim is clearly a matter of clarification of values, especially on the choice between possible options.

W. Edwards Deming

To enable the reader to:

1 Understand what an option is and why it is important.

2 Identify or make reasonable guesses about where options are and what factors are relevant when valuing them.

3 Identify the component parts of the the options that you identify.

4 Understand how the options are likely to change if circumstances change.

5 Draw an options tree.

6 Use an options tree to value an option.

7 Use options to make better financial decisions and as part of one's portfolio to reduce risk and increase returns.

Options may at first seem difficult but are an essential concept in finance. However as you will soon see, the key ideas in options are ones you use in everyday life. An option is the right but not the obligation over some asset or act. It is a choice that you can make if you so wish, but are not obliged to make. Sometimes options come labelled as such but often options are hidden and require some work to be seen for what they are.

Some people see options as risky or even a great danger to civilization. The caricature Wall Street options trader with loud braces is seen by some as a leading cause of the world's ills. However, this is misleading. Options are as much a natural part of the world as the air we breathe and can be used to reduce risk and make your savings safer.

Anyone who wants to make good investment decisions must understand the basics of options. While it is not necessary to trade options in order to run your personal or business finances, once you learn to see options in everyday business and investing decisions you can use them to reduce your risks.

Some finance specialists complicate the subject of options, and sometimes there is a need for advanced mathematics when trading options professionally. However, one of the lessons from the great financial crisis that began in 2007 is that being able to do advanced options mathematics is pointless and often very expensive for society at large if you do not understand the qualitative principles behind them. The fact that most of the West's biggest financial institutions employed many mathematicians on very high salaries to run their options desks and yet still imploded because their options trades went wrong proves this, although not many members of the financial establishment like to admit it. As a private investor or manager you do not need to know advanced maths to understand and use the concept of options, and even with no maths you can profit from the concept.

What is an option?

An option is the right, but not the obligation, to obtain something or to perform some act, including to avoid something or to get some other person to perform or refrain from some act. Living in the town of High Wycombe in Buckinghamshire gives you an option to send your children to the Royal Grammar School in that town if they pass the entrance exam, but you are free to send them elsewhere. This is a valuable option because this school is an excellent school but low cost.

Options can be assets, and nearly always are from someone's point of view. The option to send your children to a good school free of charge is a valuable asset – if you have children.

Options are a kind of derivative instrument, so called because their value and utility derives from something else. Five pound notes used to be derivatives in the days when the bearer of a note could go to the Bank of England and exchange it for five pounds worth of gold.

Derivatives now have a dubious reputation because of their role in the great financial crisis that began in 2007. However, options and other derivatives are not in themselves bad, nor are they new.

How do options work?

If you hold (own) an option, then somewhere another person or organization is subject to the obligation corresponding to the option. So an option is a special kind of contract. If you have the right to buy 100 IBM shares at US$100, then someone else has the obligation to sell them to you at that price. You might want to have such an option because it gives you an upside and no downside. But why would anyone want to be on the other side of such a deal? Perhaps you can get a high enough price to compensate you for the risks and inconvenience that you take on as a result of writing an option. So just like any other market a market for options arises when the price of options is such that some people are willing to sell and others are willing to buy.

Some options are incompatible. Suppose that you have two rich aunts, one in Barbados and one in Brisbane, and suppose further that both have invited you to spend new year's eve with them entirely at their expense, including flights. It is not possible to exercise both of these options.

In personal finance one of the most common options is an insurance policy. This is an option because you have the right but not the obligation to compensation in certain circumstances. An insurance contract will have certain conditions restricting the insured's right to compensation. Typically you will not be able to claim if you have deliberately or recklessly created damage.

Some options occur naturally, such as the option to turn left or right for a walk along the beach or the option to grow vegetables in your garden. These are trivial options but illustrate that life is a vast set of options. Most of the options that matter in financial decision making are man-made and carry such exercise conditions as the option writer may choose.

Sellers, buyers and writers

In the language of options, the person who buys an option is the buyer, and the person who first sells the option is a writer, which term derives from the idea that they write the contract specifying the terms of the option.

Taking up one of our previous examples, suppose you live in High Wycombe. You have an option to send your children to school at the Royal Grammar School in High Wycombe, but you cannot sell this option to anyone else. Just because you have an option does not automatically mean you can sell it.

Suppose that you have planning permission from High Wycombe Borough Council to build an extension to your house. This is an option that you can sell, if you sell it with your house. This option is valuable because houses with planning permission sell for more than houses without it where planning permission is rare. In the language of options, the local council has written the option to build an extension on your house, and you have bought the option. If you sell the house with planning permission then you will have sold the option and the new buyer will have bought the option. Note that the seller of the option may not be the same person as the writer, and that the obligation in the option lies with the writer, who may not be the seller.

Financial options

Let us now return to financial options. Let's consider in more detail the option to buy shares in IBM. The writer sells the option to buy shares. Suppose that person p takes up this option, in other words p buys the right to buy shares. Why would anyone do that? An alternative is to simply buy the shares in the stock market. If p wants the shares now, then there is no point buying an option. Creating an option (writing it) costs the writer something. Even if the option is given to p free of charge p incurs more costs in time and effort in exercising it than in simply buying the share on the stock market, in that he has higher transaction costs (paperwork and time) than if he bought the shares. In addition, p takes on the risk that the option may be invalid, that is, the risk that whoever has written the option cannot actually deliver the shares.

p will be willing to pay more for an option exercisable in the future than one exercisable right now. This is because the future is uncertain, and it is more uncertain the further out it is. We should therefore expect options to cost more the longer they last.

Suppose that IBM shares are trading at US$ 100 now, and p believes that in three month's time they will be trading at double this price, i.e. US$200. If p can get an option to buy the shares for US$100 in three months' time and the shares are at US$200 then, p will make a profit of US$100 less the cost of the option, per share. Why not just buy the shares now at US$100, hang on to them and sell them in three months time? Usually the cost of the option will be much less than the cost of the share, which means a greater profit for the same amount invested, provided the shares do in fact rise. Suppose this option, i.e. to buy a share in IBM at today's price of US$100 in three months' time, costs US$10 today. If p has US$100 to risk on IBM going up, then there are two things that p can do to try to take advantage of this:

- Buy one share of IBM and wait for three months, which, if IBM shares do rise by then to US$200 will give p a return of US$100. The cost to p will be not having the US$100 for three months plus the risk of the share price falling below US$100.

- Buy ten options and wait. In this case if the share price is at US$200 in three month's time then p will have made 10 × US$100 − 10 × US$10 = US$900 (i.e. ten times the pay-off of US$100 profit per share on ten shares, less the cost of buying the ten options).

In this scenario the rationale for buying options rather than buying the shares is that the pay-off will be nine times greater, if p is right in predicting the rise in IBM share prices. There is a substantial downside. Suppose the shares do not rise to US$200 but stay right where they started, at US$100? If p had bought the share in IBM, it would still be worth US$100 and p would be no worse off. If on the other hand p had bought the option, then as we have just seen, the option will be worthless and p will have lost the entire US$100.

Fundamental factors in pricing options

A question left open in this example is at what price should the writer of the option sell it? The price of the option matters because whether you are buying or selling options it will make a difference to your profit, perhaps the difference between profit and loss. The price of an option on shares should relate to the probability that the shares will move up, down or stay flat. More specifically it should relate to the probable pay-off. We can look at how to price an option in two ways, from the point of view of the buyer and the option writer.

The buyer of the option, p in our example, always has the alternative of buying the shares and holding them. So the value to p of the option to buy the shares is less than the current price, but more than zero, assuming that p believes that the shares are likely to rise.

$$0 < \text{Value of option} < \text{Current price of shares}$$

Suppose that p somehow knew that IBM shares were going to rise to US$200, for certain. Because the pay-off in that case from buying options is US$100 per share before the cost of buying the options, p should be willing to pay any amount less than US$100 per share.

Strictly speaking p should be willing to pay anything less than the US$1,000 minus the cost of not having the use of the money tied up in buying the options for three months. Suppose interest rates are 12 percent and p knows for certain that IBM shares will reach US$200. The cost to p of not having the US$100 for three months is US$4 (being $3/12 \times 12$ percent $\times$ US$100). p should be willing to pay any price less than US$96, because this will make a profit.

Indulgences as options and the market for indulgences

From at least the twelfth century until the end of the medieval period the Roman Catholic church sold indulgences as a kind of option. An indulgence is a forgiveness of sin by the Roman Catholic church. This mattered in medieval Europe because people believed that sin meant eternal damnation of their souls, unless God forgave them. The forgiveness of sins was in those days regarded much as pension rights are regarded today, and just as today there is a thriving market for pensions and the bonds and shares that back them, there was once a thriving market for indulgences. The price of the indulgence varied according to the sin.

Professional dealers in indulgences set up to take advantage of the demand for them, and it became a significant sector of the economy with some parallels to today's bond market. In 1517 the Roman Catholic church sent a Dominican monk, John Tetzel, to sell indulgences in central Europe. Tetzel and his indulgences prompted Martin Luther to write his ninety-five theses and thus begin the Reformation and the rise of protestantism.

Source: Shutterstock: Andrejs Pidjass

The scenario just given is of course unrealistic. p will never know the future price of IBM shares for certain. Let us suppose instead that p believes that there is a 50 percent chance of the shares rising

to US$200 and a 50 percent chance of the shares remaining at
US$100, and no chance of any other share price. This is equivalent
to believing that there is a 50 percent chance of a US$100 per share
return and a 50 per cent chance of no return. Ignoring the cost of p's
money being tied up in the options for three months for the sake of
simplicity, p might value this option in this circumstance as

$$50 \text{ percent} \times US\$0 + 50 \text{ percent} \times US\$100 = US\$50$$

What does this value of US$50 mean, and what does the arithmetic
that gives it mean? The arithmetic is another way of saying what p
believes about the likely outcome of the IBM share price, which we
could write as follows:

$$\left(\begin{array}{c} \text{probability of shares} \\ \text{going to US\$0} \times \text{nil} \end{array} \right) + \left(\begin{array}{c} \text{probability of shares going to} \\ \text{US\$100} \times US\$100 = US\$50 \end{array} \right)$$

Note that p does not believe that the shares will ever be worth
US$50. The US$50 is the average of the US$0 and the US$100,
and that is the value of the option. (To be precise, the US$50 is
not simply the average but is the average adjusted for likeliness;
as there is an evens chance in this example, there is no adjustment
to be made.) All of this can be drawn as a simple tree diagram, as
in Figure 5·1. Such tree diagrams are also called option trees. It is
useful to draw an option tree when you are making an investment
decision in which an option is a key factor, because doing this
helps you to clarify exactly what is going on.

All option pricing is based on the principle of identifying the
possible outcomes, valuing each outcome, and then weighting
each of those values by the probability of that outcome. There is
a mystique about valuing options and the Black–Scholes formula
used by professional traders for option pricing.[1] The Black–Scholes
formula is named after its inventors Fischer Black and Myron
Scholes. Mr Scholes was awarded an Economics Nobel prize for
this work (Mr Black being ineligible because he had died before the
prize was awarded). However, all that advanced maths is simply
elaborating on this basic principle. What tends to cause disasters
in options trading is not getting the advanced maths wrong but
failing to understand the set of outcomes possible in the real world.
For example, the financial crisis around mortgage derivatives in

the USA that began in 2007 arose because some derivatives traders excluded from their models the possibility that people who had borrowed more than they could afford would not be able to repay their loans.

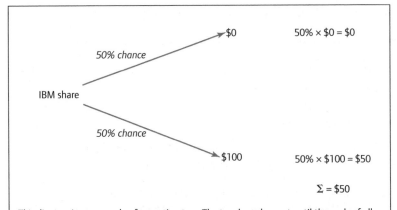

50% chance

IBM share

50% chance

$0

$100

50% × $0 = $0

50% × $100 = $50

Σ = $50

This diagram is an example of an option tree. The tree branches out until the ends of all the branches show all the possible outcomes. Each branch of the tree shows the probability associated with that branch. This example is simple, in that there is only one level of branching (there are no branches-off-branches) and there are only two outcomes. The way that option trees are used in valuing options is to multiply the value of each outcome by the probability of the branch or branches that lead to it, and then adding the resultant sums together. This grand total is the value of the option.

FIGURE 5·1 Pricing of an option for an IBM share

Option pricing is not inherently difficult

It is important to understand that pricing options is as simple as has just been explained. Option pricing is not something that is fundamentally difficult or that is impossible to understand without advanced maths. It suits many people in finance who are highly paid to have you think that it is. It is important that you see and feel that the main problems that arise in options, such as the great financial crisis that began in 2007, have nothing to do with mathematics and everything to do with a failure of people who should know better to think carefully about the fundamental principles. It is not option pricing itself that is difficult, but rather forecasting the future or identifying possible outcomes of some particular choice.

Deprival value in option pricing

Let us now price a more everyday option than an IBM share in order to get into some of the key details of options. Consider a voucher for a buy-one-get-one-free (BOGOF) coupon for a pizza. Suppose that the pizza you normally order costs you £10. What is this BOGOF voucher worth? Its maximum value is £10, because that it is the cost of the second pizza, which is free if you use the coupon. Its minimum value is nil, because it cannot be worth less than that. Its actual value lies somewhere between £0 and £10. We can use the notion of *deprival value* (explained in Chapter 1) to find out where in this range the true value of the BOGOF voucher lies.

Suppose that you were deprived of this coupon, that it suddenly vanished into thin air – how much worse off, if at all, would you be? A few possible scenarios are:

- Rather than being worse off, you are slightly better off because you hate junk mail and merely receiving this coupon had irritated you.

- No worse off, because you don't eat pizza and all of your friends who do have similar vouchers.

- £10 worse off, because you are taking your best friend out to lunch for pizza.

- Slightly worse off, because Friday is pizza day at the office, and while your employer pays for take-away pizzas, your boss always appreciates contributions, in cash or vouchers, towards the cost to the department. In the past when you have chipped in with your voucher your boss has given you a bottle of beer from the company's entertainment store. You like beer and those bottles save you £2 each time.

- Slightly worse off, because although you do not like pizza and nor do any of your friends, your next door neighbour does who will always swap one of your £10 pizza vouchers for one of her £10 Chinese meal vouchers, which you always use. However, swapping the pizza vouchers with your neighbour involves having tea with her in her kitchen, which always takes much longer than you have time for. The cost of your wasted time is £5, so the deprival value in this case of the pizza voucher is £5.

Valuing a BOGOF pizza coupon under time constraints

We can apply exactly the same method of valuing the pizza coupon as we applied to the share in IBM. Suppose it is a Thursday and you have one pizza coupon which expires at 4 p.m. tomorrow, Friday. Further suppose that your choices are similar to the last three bullet points above. Normally you work from home on a Friday, but your boss has told you that there is a 50 percent chance that you will be needed in the office tomorrow, in which case the pizzas are on him, as is usual on Friday. If you don't go into the office, then either you will see your neighbour and swap the pizza voucher for the Chinese meal voucher or you will take your friend to lunch, both of which eventualities are equally likely at 25 percent. Figure 5·2 shows the maths of this valuation, the result of which is that in these circumstances the voucher is worth £4·75 to you. There are several points to note from this valuation:

■ There is no outcome in which the value of the voucher is £4·75. This is a number that serves a specific purpose and does not represent an actual state of the world, in the same way that no family has 2·2 children even if the average number of children per family is 2·2.

■ The valuation is a best guess, and is sensitive to the probabilities we assign to each outcome. Whereas we know the value of the voucher in each outcome with a high degree of certainty, we probably do not have anything like the same degree of certainty in our knowledge of the probabilities of each outcome happening.

■ Although we have not looked at them yet, there are costs associated with exercising some of the options; going to work as required by your boss may not entail any additional cost on your part, but spending time with your boring neighbour is a cost.

■ There are non-financial benefits, and costs, which are not captured in the numbers, and these may override a decision based on the numbers. There is something about having lunch with your best friend that simply cannot and should not be turned into a monetary valuation.

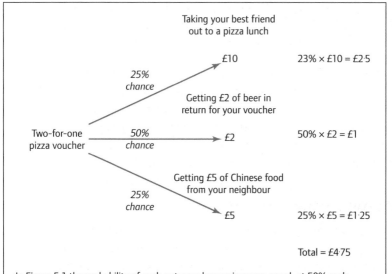

In Figure 5.1 the probability of each outcome happening were equal, at 50% each. In this example, valuing a two-for-one pizza coupon in certain circumstances, there are three possible outcomes but they are not equally likely. Multiplying the probability of each outcome by its value and summing up gives the value of this option, which is £4·75.

FIGURE 5·2 Valuing the two-for-one pizza option

We have valued the option given by the pizza coupon at £4·75. A question we should perhaps have asked before doing this is – why are we valuing it?

Valuation is not blind to purpose

What is the purpose of the valuation? We should ask this question before performing any valuation. Suppose a colleague at work offers to buy your coupon for £6·00. The valuation tells you that if you wish to maximize your financial gains then you are better off, by £1·25, selling the coupon to your colleague. But what if things change? Just before you accept the emailed offer from your colleague at work you get a call from your boss. Now, instead of the probabilities being 25, 50 and 25 percent that you will tomorrow take your friend to lunch, go to work, or meet your neighbour respectively these probabilities have changed. Your boss called to say that it is now unlikely you will have to come in, and rates it only a 10 percent chance; your chance of taking your friend for lunch is 50 percent, and if neither of those things happen – 40 percent likely – you will see your neighbour. Figure 5·3 shows the new calculation, which gives the value of your option over a second pizza free as being £7·20.

Should you still accept the emailed offer from your colleague? This is not a question that numbers alone can answer. Ultimately, it depends on your tastes. The crux of the matter is whether you prefer the certainty of £6 to the melange of possibilities that averages to £7·20. Note that your chance of getting more than £6 if you reject your colleague's offer is 50 percent.

Spotting hidden options

A key part of being financially literate is to be able to spot the options hidden in a decision or in a business or situation. If it is true that public sector workers are able to award themselves extra holiday more easily than private sector workers, then the option for extra holiday is an embedded option, and it is embedded in the employment at the public sector bodies concerned. Common decisions in business that include options include:

- Buying more space (warehouse, factory, shop or office space), which gives you options to use it to raise productivity, to rent it out, or to hold on to it in the hope of selling it on at a profit later.

- Hiring more people, which creates the option of producing more or selling more.

- Closing the business down, which creates the option of liquidating the assets.

- Increasing the training of employees, which should create options associated with having a more capable or a more flexible workforce.

- Buying a new business.

Valuing a business opportunity with options theory

Suppose now that the problem you face is to decide whether to buy out your main competitor to double the size of your business and the pay-offs are £100,000, £20,000 or £50,000 respectively. The cost of buying your main competitor is £45,000 and if you do not sell it immediately to someone else you will have to pay an extra £5,000 of employment tax due, making your costs £50,000. There are three possible outcomes having the same probabilities as in the pizza BOGOF case. You have first refusal on buying the business, that is you have an option. By the same maths as in Figure 5·3 the value of this option is £72,000 and a former colleague emails you offering £60,000 for the business. After deducting the £45,000 cost of buying your competitor, you face a choice between making a certain profit of £15,000, if you accept your former colleague's offer, or ending up with a business that has an option value of £72,000 – £50,000 = £22,000. Some people will prefer to take the certainty of £15,000, others will prefer the 50 percent possibility of doubling their money (£100,000 – £50,000 = £50,000) without being too worried by the other possibilities, one of which involves losing £30,000 and the other break-even. One way of posing the question is whether you can sleep at night knowing you may lose £30,000. If not, then it's unwise to proceed. The numbers are useful but often they do not provide you with an answer on their own. They are necessary but not sufficient for making a management decision.

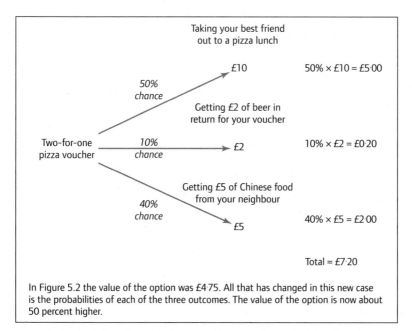

In Figure 5.2 the value of the option was £4·75. All that has changed in this new case is the probabilities of each of the three outcomes. The value of the option is now about 50 percent higher.

FIGURE 5·3 Valuing the two-for-one pizza option – revised for changed circumstances

Right of first refusal as an option

Now consider a slightly different example. The owner of your main competitor has not offered to sell you his business but approaches you and offers you the right of first refusal to buy it when he puts it up for sale next month. You ask him how much he wants for giving you that right – which is another option, in fact an option on a set of options – and he replies that it's up to you to make an offer. How much should you offer him? Figure 5·4 shows how you might start to work out what you are prepared to offer: it calculates the value of the option on offer by considering not only the three possible outcomes if you roll the new business into your own, but also the other outcome of selling it on. The option is worth £17,200. You are in effect being offered an option to get £17,200 of free money. The most that you would pay, therefore, and leaving non-financial factors aside (maybe your daughter needs a business to practice on before she takes over your business from you) is just under £17,200, say £17,199. Of course in real life you would want some margin of safety, and you would also take account of the non-financial costs to you, especially the work and disruption involved in a deal. But the figure of £17,200 is useful in decision making in that it gives you some hard data to help you make your decision.

Embedded options

In real life we would not normally bother to value a pizza coupon but the principle of how we might value one applies to valuing any option. We have just seen how this principle applies to valuing a business acquisition. In business the most important decisions tend to have an option in them somewhere. Financiers talk of 'embedded options'. Suppose that the business you are considering buying in the example above happens to include a showroom that has been converted out of a former casino. If the planning laws allow you to continue to use the property as a casino then your new business has the embedded option of entering the casino market. One of things that successful entrepreneurs do is to find options where others ignore them. Many airlines had the option to fly aircraft between unglamorous airports in Europe, but only Michael O'Leary and Sir Stelios Haji-Ioannou saw and exploited the option to create a profitable businesses in European low-cost airlines, with Ryanair and easyJet respectively. Isn't this merely ordinary business? Do we need complicated theories like options pricing before we can set up a new business even if we are not aiming as high as easyJet or Ryanair? Thinking in terms of options may help you do three things better: see risks and opportunities, understand what these options are made of, and price them.

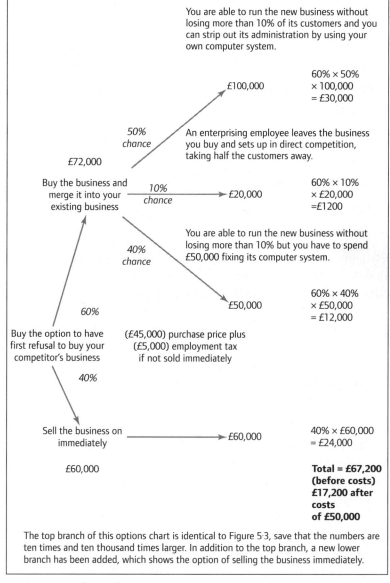

You are able to run the new business without losing more than 10% of its customers and you can strip out its administration by using your own computer system.

£100,000

60% × 50%
× 100,000
= £30,000

50%
chance

£72,000

An enterprising employee leaves the business you buy and sets up in direct competition, taking half the customers away.

Buy the business and merge it into your existing business

10%
chance

£20,000

60% × 10%
× £20,000
=£1200

40%
chance

You are able to run the new business without losing more than 10% but you have to spend £50,000 fixing its computer system.

£50,000

60% × 40%
× £50,000
= £12,000

60%

Buy the option to have first refusal to buy your competitor's business

(£45,000) purchase price plus
(£5,000) employment tax
if not sold immediately

40%

Sell the business on immediately

£60,000

40% × £60,000
= £24,000

£60,000

Total = £67,200
(before costs)
£17,200 after
costs
of £50,000

The top branch of this options chart is identical to Figure 5·3, save that the numbers are ten times and ten thousand times larger. In addition to the top branch, a new lower branch has been added, which shows the option of selling the business immediately.

FIGURE 5·4 Valuing the options to buy your main competitor's business

Key terminology in options

The key terms used when specifying an option are listed below, with an explanation after the list:

- Underlying asset
- Real options
- Financial options
- Premium/option premium
- Expiration/expiration time
- Strike price/exercise price
- Settlement terms
- Exercise
- Holder/option holder
- Writer/option writer
- Time decay.

Underlying asset. The underlying asset is that over which the option is a right. In the example of the option on an ordinary share in IBM the underlying asset is an ordinary share in IBM. In the BOGOF voucher for a pizza, the underlying asset is a pizza. The underlying asset can be another option. Generally, a distinction is made between real options and financial options. In a *real option* there is a real asset as the underlying asset, such as a pizza. In a *financial option* there is a financial instrument, such as a share in IBM, as the underlying asset.

Premium/option premium. The price of buying the option. In the BOGOF voucher for a pizza, the voucher is free, so the option premium is nil. In the example where the seller is asking you how much you would be prepared to pay for the right of first refusal (i.e. the option) to buy his business, he is asking you to decide what the premium should be. Another word for 'premium' is 'price'. Suppose you sell-on the BOGOF pizza voucher to someone else. What they pay you is the price of the option, and if they sell it on again they may do so at a different price. The price of an option can change and usually does as events change and as the expiration approaches.

Options become less valuable as their expiration approaches, so the option premium declines with time. See *time decay*, below.

Expiration/expiration time. The time at which the option ceases to exist, that is, it no longer confers rights. In the two-for-the-price-of-one voucher for a pizza, the expiration is the last day on which the voucher is valid.

Strike price/exercise price. This is the price to be paid to gain control of the underlying asset at the point when the option is exercised. In the two-for-the-price-of-one voucher for a pizza, the strike price is complex: it is nil conditional upon you paying for the first pizza. In the example of the option to buy your main competitor's business, the strike price is £45,000.

Settlement terms. Does your main competitor require a banker's draft to be presented for the full £45,000 on the day you buy the business, or is a staged payment over three months of £15,000 per month acceptable, or perhaps some other terms? These are examples of the settlement terms. In commodity futures, for example soya beans, oil or cocoa futures, an options contract might specify physical delivery or a cash equivalent. The settlement terms are not trivial and you must understand them. Suppose you make a great profit on your cocoa options, will you be given the cash price of the underlying cocoa when your gain crystallizes, in which case it can simply be wired into your bank account, or will you have to accept several tons, possibly hundreds of tons, of cocoa beans?

Exercise. To take up the right inhering in an option. In the example given above of having a BOGOF pizza voucher you exercise that option when you say to the waiter or waitress 'Here is my coupon, please may I have my free second pizza' or words to that effect.

Holder/option holder. The holder is the person who has the option, in contrast to the writer. In the BOGOF voucher for a pizza the holder is literally the person who holds the voucher. (The voucher is a *bearer instrument*, because whoever bears it has the right to it. Banknotes are usually bearer instruments, share certificates used to be but this is no longer the case in the UK, as ownership is now determined by an entry in a central registry.)

Writer/option writer. The writer is the person on whom the liability falls to deliver on the right held by the option holder. In the BOGOF pizza voucher the writer is the pizza company. Writing options is risky.

Time decay. The value of an option declines as its expiration approaches. It decays with time. This is because options are valuable because they give the holder power to change the future, and the closer to expiry the less power there is to exercise. This can be illustrated by considering an option on a share, say an IBM share. We do not know what the price of shares in IBM will be tomorrow or in a year from tomorrow, but we do know that tomorrow's price is likely to be closer to today's price than next year's price. We know what today's price is, so we can make a probably more accurate estimate of tomorrow's price than the price a year from tomorrow. An option with expiry tomorrow to buy the shares at today's price is not as big a risk for the writer as an option to buy the shares in a years' time, by when we expect they will have gone up. In brief, the longer until expiry, the more valuable the option.

Putting the key terminology to use

When you are evaluating a decision in terms of options make sure you are clear about the elements of the option using the list above. For example, if you are offered an option to make a sequel of a film, what is it that you are really being offered? We know that sequels can be highly profitable in the film business. The first Harry Potter film, for example, *Harry Potter and the Philosopher's Stone*, has generated sales of US$974 million worldwide, on a cost of US$125 million to produce. The sequel, *Harry Potter and the Chamber of Secrets*, has generated sales of US$878 million, on costs of US$100 million. All the six Harry Potter films together have generated sales of US$5,412 million on costs of US$905 million between them. Sequels can be lucrative. Suppose you were offered a contract that was the option for the next Harry Potter film – how valuable is it? To answer this we need to understand what this option is. What are the ingredients of a successful film? Is having the contractual right to make the sequel enough, or are there ingredients such as the mood of the actors and the goodwill of the whole film crew that makes a critical difference? The problem with film rights is that you have no control over whether the right actors sign up and whether they really put their heart into it. You can try to influence them, but your influence at best is not full control. The problem with the idea of a market for selling the rights (options) to sequels of films is that the option is not an option on some of the most critical underlying assets.

When examining real options in business or in your personal financial affairs, start by asking what the underlying asset is, and check that you really understand it. Next, as was illustrated above in the example of possibly having to take physical delivery of tons of cocoa, understand the exercise conditions.

Puts and calls

So far in this chapter we have only described one of the two classes of option, a call option. A call option is the right but not the obligation to receive something. The BOGOF voucher for a pizza is a call option. A put option is the opposite of a call option in the sense that it gives you the right, but not the obligation, to dispose of something. A call option on pizza would be the right to sell a pizza to the pizza company. Put options on pizzas don't exist, not least because there are hygiene laws governing what pizza retailers must know about the pizzas that they sell. However, the wholesalers and grain merchants who supply raw ingredients to large pizza companies may well buy or write put options as a way of managing their inventory.

Puts or put options are so called because they give you the right to put something onto someone else, as we have just seen with the example of literally putting your children into a school. Call options are so-called because they give you the option to call or call for something.

Options in personal finance

One way to use options your personal finance is to trade options. This is a high-risk for investing and you will be up against professional traders and their back-up teams. Nonetheless some private investors are able to make good profits from it. This book has not given you enough of a basis to set out on this sort of trading.[2]

Options as insurance

Rather than investing in options as a way of trading, options, and especially options on indices, can be part of your portfolio to insure against risks. Suppose you have a portfolio of £1,000,000 invested in a wide range of shares. You fear that the stock market is going to fall but you don't want to sell because to do so would trigger capital gains tax; in any case although you expect that the market is likely to fall you are not certain. You could protect your portfolio against a fall by buying a put option on an index of shares. This way your option will pay off if the index goes down. If your portfolio is at all diversified, it will track the index to some extent, and so you will have some protection. Alternatively you could buy put options on some of the shares you own. Or you could try to boost the returns to your portfolio by writing call options against the shares you own, that is, selling to others the right to buy your shares. You hope that you will collect the premium for writing these options but that the buyer, the option holder, will never exercise them. If he does, you get paid for your shares but lose any upside profit.

Knowledge in itself is power

For most retail investors the most important thing to do with your knowledge of options is to look out for financial options hidden in retail financial products. This is not quite the same as embedded options. What we mean is retail financial products that have in their ingredients options or other derivatives. An example is a financial product that claims to track a share index but not to go down. In the past there have been a number of such products, most of which had two notable and in our view undesirable features. First, the product never went up as much as the index, if adjusted for fees and other charges; and secondly, downside protection was limited to only relatively small falls in the index. If the stock exchange index fell by, say, 50 percent, then the protection did not apply. On the other side of such a transaction is a professional derivatives trading desk. What is often going on when you buy this type of retail product is that you, the retail punter, are taking on the brightest and best of the City of London or of Wall Street in a specialized derivatives product that they trade every day, backed up by massive computing power and other support. Would they be taking on your trade if they expected to lose? If you are offered this kind of product (anything with 'guaranteed return' or 'downside protection' or 'potential losses are limited') and it is not a simple bank savings account, make sure you understand exactly how its magic operates and exactly what the fees are and exactly when the downside protection will and will not operate.

Options theory and general management

Finally, a key use of options theory in general management and business decision making is to gain a better understanding of the likely value of different business choices than a straight application of net present value (NPV) gives. Like so much in options theory, this is no more than an orderly application of common sense decision making. We have seen in Chapter 2 that NPV is the best means of determining the value of a business asset or initiative. NPV on its own however does not capture very well the uncertainties of real life. Using the idea of options and drawing out options diagrams to describe the factors in the decision you are making overcomes this drawback of NPV. (It applies just as much to other methods such as internal rate of return and break-even analysis.) Figure 5·4 illustrates how to use options theory in this way. What drawing out the options and decision points does is to make clear the *option to abandon* at each stage of the proceedings. An NPV calculation would show the cost and revenue of the whole project to completion. What a diagram like Figure 5·4 shows is all the points at which you can abandon the initiative, and it also gives you a way of adjusting the value of the project to factor in the undesirable outcomes. The advantage of options theory over NPV on its own is that you can see how far you can afford to proceed at each stage, so that you can initiate more projects than would otherwise be the case, provided you are willing to abandon them if they become unfavourable.

Graphical representations of options

The options diagrams presented so far, Figures 5·1 to 5·4, make a number of simplifying assumptions. For real life problems you will need to simplify. Include the main factors, the most probable and the most dangerous outcomes in your diagram. Ignore detail. In a complicated decision the very task of drawing out an options tree is itself real work and clarifies your thinking.

So far we have drawn one type of options diagram. Another graphical representation that is useful is a pay-off diagram. Consider again the ordinary share of IBM. Figure 5·5 is perhaps baffling in its simplicity, and shows that the share is worth its price. Now consider an option on an IBM share, specifically a call option with a strike price of US$60. As we have seen, this option gives you the right to buy a share in IBM for US$60, irrespective of what the share is actually trading at in the stock market. Figure 5·6 shows what this call option is worth. The option is worth nothing when you can buy the underlying share on the stock market for less than US$60, because you will save money by buying the share on the stockmarket rather than paying for the right to buy it at US$60.

Figure 5·7 shows the pay-off to you for holding a put option. This is at its most valuable if shares in IBM are at zero because holding this option means you can sell a share in IBM for US$60 whatever it is actually trading at.

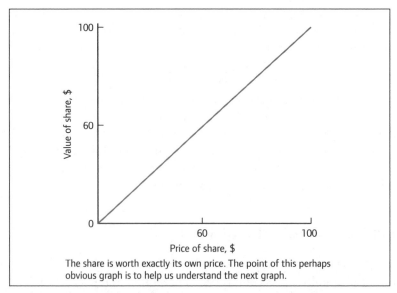

The share is worth exactly its own price. The point of this perhaps obvious graph is to help us understand the next graph.

FIGURE 5·5 Pay-off to owning an ordinary share in IBM, showing how the value of the share changes with its price

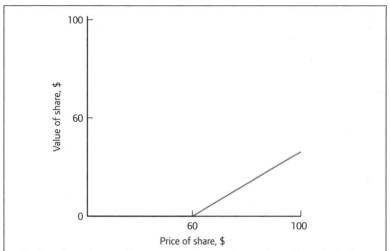

This chart shows the pay-off to owning a call option on an ordinary share of IBM that has a strike price of $60. This option gives you the right, but not the obligation, to pay $60 to buy an ordinary share in IBM. When these shares are less then $60, there is no point paying $60 for them, so this option is worthless. But as soon as the shares trade above $60, your right to get one for only $60 starts to be worth something.

FIGURE 5·6 Pay-off to owning a call option on an ordinary share in IBM that has a strike price of US$60

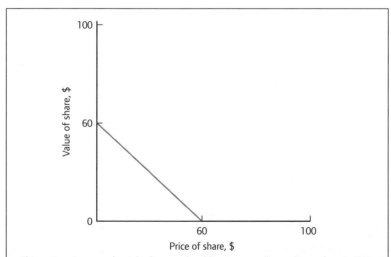

This option gives you the right, but not the obligation, to sell an ordinary share in IBM at a price of $60. This option has value only when the shares are worth less than $60. At the $60 point these options are worthless because then you can sell shares for a price greater than $60.

FIGURE 5·7 Pay-off to owning a put option on an ordinary share in IBM that has a strike price of US$60

It declines in value as the share price increases, until it becomes worthless when the share price is US$60 because after that point you can get more than US$60 for selling an IBM share by selling it in the stock market.

These diagrams are known as pay-off diagrams and are used to clarify what an option gives you, especially where options are combined with each other or with shares or other underlying assets. Figure 5·8 is an example of this, and it shows the effect of holding together both a share in IBM and a put option on it with a strike price of US$60. The effect is that it is impossible to lose money: you will always have in this pair of assets US$60 of value, and sometimes more. Such protection comes at a price, which is why share options, unlike two-for-one pizza vouchers, are not handed out free of charge. (The pricing and exercise conditions of the two-for-one pizza vouchers does give an indication of the profit margin on pizza.)

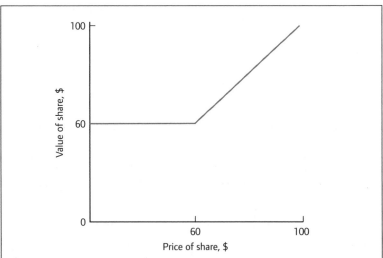

Holding both a share and a put on it gives you downside protection, i.e. insurance against the price of the share falling. Of course there is a price to pay, which is the cost of buying the put option. Retail financial products that claim to guarantee against a fall in the market will usually use some sort of put option in this way, often a put option on index. The curve on this chart is the sum of the two curves in the charts in Figures 5·5 and 5·7.

FIGURE 5·8 Pay-off to owning a both option on an ordinary share in IBM that has a strike price of US$60

Writing options – a risky business

For you to be able to buy options someone must be prepared to write that option. The key difference between the option holder and the writer is that the choice of whether to exercise the option lies with the holder. The writer is obliged to do something if the holder chooses. Often the holder gets to choose also the timing of exercise. This makes options risky for the writer. Options are risky for the writer, not for the holder. If you write a put option with a strike price of US$60 on a share in IBM how much can you lose? If the shares are at US$100 when the option holder wants to exercise the option, then you will have lost US$40. Either you will already own a share in IBM, which will be worth US$100, and you will have to sell it for US$40 less than it is worth, i.e. the US$60 strike price; or if you don't own a share you will have to buy it at US$100 in order to sell it at US$60. (In fact in share options trading and in many but not all other kinds of options trading, you are not normally required to deliver the shares but can settle in the cash equivalent.) However, if the shares go to US$600 or US$1,000, your losses are much greater. Theoretically the price of a share can go up an almost unlimited amount, which means that the writer of a call option who does not own the underlying share can lose a practically unlimited amount. Options are therefore priced to reflect this additional risk to the writer.

Why does anyone write options if they are so risky? Options are risky in the way that many human endeavours are risky, but humans undertake them nonetheless because they feel the ends are worth the risks. Those who write options try to charge enough to make a decent profit after adjusting for risks.

Covered options versus naked options

Some retail investors write options but usually they write covered rather than naked options. Writing a naked option is writing an option without owning the underlying asset. One day the holder of that option may call you on the option and then you will have to buy it. If there are none for sale you will be in trouble. If you have to buy a large number of shares this may force up the price you pay. Even if settlement of the trade is in cash rather than shares settlement is off the market price, so you will still be in trouble. It is safer for retail investors to write options to boost their income from shares they already hold than to write naked options.

Suppose you own £100,000 of shares in a company. You get some dividend from these shares, but if you write options on them you may get some additional income. Suppose that the shares are trading at £10 a share, and the highest you believe they will go is £13·90. You could write options on some or all of your shares at a strike price of £14 with a three month exercise. Suppose you receive 10p for writing the put on each share, you will receive £1,000 each quarter. This is 4 percent of extra yield. The risk you face is that the shares go higher than £13·90, confounding your expectation, and the holder calls your shares away. Of course the holder pays you £14 per share, so you will not have lost money on the trade, but you will have capped your upside on the shares.

Options as a substitute for shares

If call options give you all the benefits of shares going up and none of the downsides when shares fall, is it a good investment strategy to buy options instead of shares? Not unless you are skilled in options trading, for three reasons. First, there is a price to pay, the options premium, for getting this advantage. The premium is designed so as to take away this apparent advantage. As we have seen option writers need compensation for the extra risk that they take on. Secondly, shares exist for as long as the company does or until it gets taken over, which can be for decades. Options on shares generally last for no more than two years. Longer expiry options are sometimes possible (they are called warrants) but are correspondingly more expensive. So shares can be long-term investments whereas options are not. Thirdly, options pay no dividends. Holding shares gives you dividends, which most ordinary shares in well-established companies pay most of the time. Dividend payments are a major portion of the total return from owning shares, and if you swap your shareholding for options over the same shares you will be giving up much of your expected investment returns.

There is a fundamental reason why options are not a substitute for shares as a long-term investment. The pay-offs from holding shares and from holding options are fundamentally related, as are their costs. We show how in the next section. Options are more complicated and unless you are skilled in options trading the price of this complexity is greater than the probable returns.

Option replication

Any share call option can be replicated by borrowing money and buying the share. Suppose that you can borrow money at 10 percent and that one share of IBM pays a dividend of US$6 per year and that IBM shares are trading at US$60. Further suppose that you borrow US$60 and with it buy one share in IBM. What you have just done gives you the pay-off shown in Figure 5·6, which is the same pay-off as holding a call option. It is costing you US$6 per year in interest charges but you are receiving the same amount in dividend from IBM, so borrowing is effectively not costing you anything. If the share rises above US$60, however, you are in profit, because you can sell the share, pay off the US$60 bank loan and keep the profit. You can make your position worth less than nothing by selling the share at below US$60 if it falls in price, but you are not compelled to, you can sit there and keep on taking the US$6 dividend and paying it in interest. On the other hand, if the share falls below US$60, your position is worth only zero. It is not negative because you keep receiving the US$6 per year and you keep paying that in interest. (The example assumes that you can borrow forever, which in the context of options in practice means a few years, so is not such an unreasonable assumption. It also assumes that dividends do not change.)

The fact that any option can be replicated by a mix of borrowing and holding the underlying asset provides a way to value options. It also provides a way for an investor to replicate the pay-off of holding an option if those options cannot be bought. And for those whose business is trading options, it provides an arbitrage opportunity between the price in the options market and the price in the stock market or other market in the underlying asset.

Summary

We have seen in this chapter how options can create benefits that are not easy to show in other types of financial analysis such as NPV. Options can also create non-financial benefits. Options are a feature of the world and many financial decisions must consider options, especially the option to abandon. Use option charts to draw the chain of options in a decision or plan, and to understand the pay-offs in options. If you are not already familiar with options, start to think in terms of options in financial decisions. Look for options, and understand the pay-offs and risks.

1 List four embedded options that are part of your trade or profession.

2 Identify an option facing you at work or your employer. State what the option is. Draw an options diagram (Figure 5·2 is an example), assign probabilities to each outcome occurring and a value to each outcome. Work out the value of the option.

3 You receive an email from BrownGordon LLP offering to sell you at a price of £1 a voucher that gives you the right but not the obligation to buy a former prime minister for £5. What is the strike price of this option? Is it a put or a call? What is the underlying asset? What legal and practical problems should you expect to encounter if you were to buy this option? (For extra points, draw an options tree and try to value this option.)

4 Your son has an exceptionally fine singing voice and perfect pitch. List some options embedded in him.

5 Draw a pay-off diagram for a call option on an ordinary share in Rio Tinto that has a strike price of £30. Look up today's share price. What will you charge for writing this option? Draw a pay-off diagram for you as the writer. What is your risk as the writer? How could you manage your risk? Does this change your initial thoughts on what you should charge for writing this option?

Pensions

People are delighted to accept pensions and gratuities, for which they hire out their labour or their support or their services. But nobody works out the value of their time: men use it lavishly as if it costs nothing.

> Seneca (in Philip Delves Broughton, *Ahead of the Curve*)

Capital formation is shifting from the entrepreneur who invests in the future to the pension trustee who invests in the past.

> Peter Drucker

Gordon Brown is more responsible for that than any other politician including Tony Blair.

> George Osborne

Employers who do not run occupational pension schemes are now required to offer Stakeholder Pensions to their workers. Pension professionals find this structure complex; non-experts find it impenetrable. In the words of Dr Deborah Cooper (Retirement Research Unit, Mercer Human Resource Consulting Ltd) 'a huge obstacle to saving at the moment is not a lack of incentive, it is just the maze that you have to go through in order to make the decisions, and it is just too difficult. It is difficult for us to understand exactly what it all means so I dread to think what the ordinary lay person thinks'.

> House of Lords, Report of the Select Committee on Economic Affairs: Aspects of the Economics of an Ageing Population, Vol. I, Session 2002–03

AIM OF THIS CHAPTER

Your pension is probably your biggest financial asset. If your pension is your largest financial asset it follows that this is where being financially literate can make the biggest difference to your wealth. As will be explained in more detail in this chapter, your pension need not mean only your formal pension scheme, it can instead include property or other investments that you intend to use to pay for your retirement. However, your property investments do not include the property in which you live: that is not an investment because it does not return an income. For most people in the West their pension, formal or informal, is the largest financial asset they have.

The aims of this chapter are:

1 To increase your understanding of what a pension is.

2 To help you choose the right pension.

3 To ensure that you understand the main sources of risk in the different arrangements that you can make for your pension, and how to think about and manage that risk.

4 To help you ask the right questions of those selling or administering your pension and to understand their answers, so that once you are in a pension scheme you can satisfy yourself that it is being run well, and if you have doubts about this, you can formulate a good plan to investigate and if necessary correct problems.

Pensions – an overview

Pensions are complicated and difficult to understand, even for the experts. One way to understand pensions better is to learn about them in detail. This is not the approach we will take in this chapter, because pensions are so complicated that even experts get lost in the detail. Another way to understand pensions better is to understand their key features, so that in effect you have a map and can then home in on the detail that is relevant to you. This is the approach that we take in this chapter, because we believe that it is a more effective way to help you make better decisions about your pension.

A conceptual map of the pensions problem

A pension is a special case of saving. However, it differs from ordinary saving because of the great risk if things go wrong. If you save for a holiday or a new house or to send your children to public school and your plans for savings go awry it may be a disappointment but will not be a complete disaster. You can put off the holiday, stay in your existing house or send your children to state school. But to be destitute in old age is a disaster rather than a disappointment. If you have understood the book thus far reasonably well, then you already know everything you need in order to plan how to save for retirement. Figure 6·1 is the conceptual map of the pensions landscape – of the factors that complicate pensions planning and make pensions more complicated than other decisions about how to save. With this map you can identify the factors that are most relevant to your situation and so focus your existing knowledge of finance on the factors that matter. You will be able to cut through the jargon and irrelevant detail that complicates pensions.

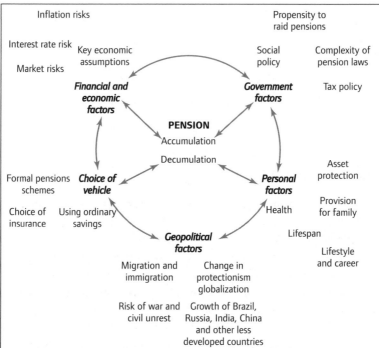

Inflation risks

Interest rate risk

Market risks

Key economic assumptions

Financial and economic factors

Propensity to raid pensions

Social policy

Complexity of pension laws

Government factors

Tax policy

PENSION

Accumulation

Decumulation

Formal pensions schemes

Choice of vehicle

Choice of insurance

Using ordinary savings

Personal factors

Health

Asset protection

Provision for family

Lifespan

Lifestyle and career

Geopolitical factors

Migration and immigration

Change in protectionism globalization

Risk of war and civil unrest

Growth of Brazil, Russia, India, China and other less developed countries

This conceptual map shows a way to think about pensions. A large number of factors affect pensions. What it is in a pension that is affected is either the accumulation phase of the pension of the decumulation phase, or both. The factors can be grouped into four sets: those controlled by government, your own personal factors, the choice of pension vehicle available to you, and the financial and economic factors within these groups interact with other factors. A change in government policy on immigration may over time affect the key economic assumptions such as the demographic balance, which may then lead to a change in tax law and pension regulation. Similarly, your health and how you want to provide for your spouse or family through your own pension arrangements will affect your choice of vehicle and what sort of insurance to have included in your pension scheme. One way to use this conceptual map is as an aid to thinking through the factors that are relevant to you.

FIGURE 6·1 A conceptual map of the pensions landscape showing the principal sources of complexity, risk and tension

Pensions – first principles

What is a pension?

The first principle, and something always to remember when in the weeds and complexity of pensions, is that a pension is a form of saving, specifically saving for retirement. All the principles of finance that have been covered in this book so far apply to pensions. They are no more and no less than a kind of savings.

The word 'pension' as it is used in personal finance has two meanings, and the first thing you need to know is that most people who make a living by selling or regulating or talking about pensions have no interest in being clear about the two different meanings. These are:

1. The means to a regular payment in retirement. A pension is a regular payment after the end of your working life (or towards the end of your working life) that ensures you have enough money to live on.

2. A regular payment in retirement subject to great complexity and heavy regulation. A pension is a heavily regulated financial product with many rules and laws about who can invest, how they can invest and how money can be taken out of it, which promises everything in the first definition, and which usually promises and often has many tax advantages. However, the regulations which govern a pension in this sense are of great complexity, which can baffle even the UK's House of Lords.[1]

The important distinction here is the heavy regulation that characterizes the second meaning. However, it is the first of these definitions that matters; the second is the one that is usually behind what is sold and discussed, and the second is also the one that most politicians and some company directors find it almost irresistible not to interfere with, which creates a source of significant risk to those who hold them. The point of having a pension is shown in the first definition, which is simple and clear. What makes pensions complicated lies in the second definition, the bureaucracy and complex laws and tax regulations that surround some types of pension, and the political and business risks that attach in consequence.

It does not matter whether the regular payment that you get in retirement is from property, a business that you started, your employer's pension scheme, a private pension, selling your stamp collection, selling your wine collection or any other source. What matters is not where the money comes from, but that it does come, regularly and reliably, so that in your old age you have financial security, and if you have dependents, that they share in that security. While it does not matter where the money for the regular payments comes from, the sale of a stamp collection is for most people less likely to ensure reliability of payments than a company pension scheme. On the other hand, if you have been fortunate enough to become a senior employee of an investment bank or a partner in one of the world's top law firms, your investments accumulated during the course of your career will be enough to provide regular pension payouts in your retirement.

Accumulation and decumulation phases of pensions

Although the word 'pension' in one sense, and originally, means a series of payments, usually in retirement, it is sometimes used to refer to the entire cycle of a pension scheme. In this sense a pension or pension scheme has two phases, an accumulation phase which comes first, and then a decumulation[2] phase. The decumulation phase is the pension proper, that is the phase in which you the pensioner get regular payments. This stream of regular payments has to be paid for, and the accumulation phase is the phase in which you or someone else accumulates (saves) enough to be able to make the pension payments in the decumulation phase.

Funded and unfunded pension schemes

What we have just described is a funded pension scheme, because the payments to the pensioner are made from a fund, and moreover the fund is specifically for the purpose of making such payments. Unfunded pension schemes also exist. Anyone can write a contract to pay someone else a stream of income in retirement. The question is will that contract be honoured? If the contract is written by a large, wealthy, law-abiding government of a politically stable country it is more likely to be; *per contra* if the contract is written by a feckless and dissolute organization or individual, probably not, and even an organization who wants to deliver on its obligations may have suffered some misfortune beyond its control by the time those obligations fall due and will simply be unable to pay. Most unfunded pension schemes lie somewhere well between these two extremes. The obvious risks of unfunded schemes have led to a trend towards funded pension schemes, especially in the private sector. As part of this trend, pension legislation has increasingly required pensions run by private sector organizations to be funded. In many developed countries, however, state sector pensions remain unfunded. For example, the UK's unfunded public sector schemes' rate of annual payout was £25·4 billion in 2010.[3]

Defined benefit and defined contribution pensions

The terms *defined benefit* and *defined contribution* are among the most important to understand in pensions. The terms seem designed to confuse and mislead, because governments and large companies wanted language that would hide the fact that they are replacing good, valuable pension schemes that have defined benefit, with an inferior arrangement, defined contribution. What matters to pensioners is the benefits of a pension scheme: undefined benefits in a pension scheme sounds bad, which is why the term 'defined contribution' is used instead. However, there is nothing defined about the contributions in real terms. Notwithstanding the mendacity of the terminology, the labels seem to be here to stay and we will use them.

■ *Defined benefits (DB) schemes.* A defined benefit pension scheme is one in which each member is entitled to a certain level of pensions benefit, under the terms and conditions of the scheme. Once you qualify for the pensions benefit your entitlement is absolute, and does not depend on how the investments or other assets backing the scheme perform. The risk that the assets may fall short of what is needed to pay your pension is real, but it is not something you have to worry about. That is the pension scheme's problem, and ultimately your employer's problem. This fact, that the risk that the assets in the pension scheme do not meet the liabilities given that the liabilities are predefined (i.e. the defined benefits) is the great advantage to the member of the defined benefits scheme. However, it is also the main disadvantage to employers, which is why so many of these schemes are being closed.

- *Index-linked defined benefits pensions.* This is a kind of defined benefits scheme where the pension payment is linked to inflation. In other words, the pension is guaranteed in real terms in this kind of scheme, whereas in ordinary defined benefits schemes the pension is guaranteed in nominal terms only. One of the main financial risks to an asset and especially to pensions is inflation. Index-linking means that the pension is much more likely not to have this risk and thus to hold its real value. In this type of defined-benefits scheme not only is the problem of how to ensure the payments keep being paid the pension provider's, the problem of protecting against inflation is theirs too.

- *Defined contribution (DC) scheme.* A pension is a regular payment. This means that behind the pension payment there is an asset producing the payment. Suppose that the asset suffers impairment and is unable to produce the full pension payment. In the defined benefit scheme the problem of paying to repair the asset or to buy a new one lay with the pension scheme; it was not the pensioner's problem. The term 'defined contribution scheme' sounds similar to 'defined benefit scheme' but this particular risk now lies with the pensioner, not the employer. If the pension payments cannot be met, there is no one to top them up. Note in passing the way that the pensions industry uses language. 'Defined contribution' sounds bland and safe, almost like 'defined benefit'. Alternative names for these schemes might be 'employee's risk' and 'employer's risk' respectively.

How much must you save to get a decent pension?

What 'decent' means depends on how much you want to draw from your pension per month, and for what length of time. This latter factor depends on when you stop working and when you die. Barring ill-health, you control when you stop working, but when you will die is not known exactly. It is, however, known on average.

Actuaries calculate the probable average age at death for the population, and variances by sex and by other major differentiating characteristics, such as whether the individual smokes or not and whether they are married or not. By looking up your expected lifespan in an actuarial table and deducting the age at which you wish to retire, the length of time for which you will need to draw your pension can be calculated. (Actuarial tables or mortality tables are available on the Internet, often from government actuarial departments.) Although the science of predicting statistically the average age at which people like you will die is accurate it is only an *average*, and you may in fact live far longer or far shorter than the average. If you intend to live off your savings in retirement and you plan to have used up your savings at exactly the time on average that people like you die, you have a 50 percent chance, approximately, of living longer and thus being destitute. On the other hand you also have a 50 percent chance, approximately, of dying before that date, so leaving unused at your death funds which you could otherwise have enjoyed in this life. There are two ways to deal with this problem: either save enough to cover the risk of living longer than your average life expectancy – this is an effective solution, but it means you are buying very expensive insurance. The other option is to buy an annuity.

An annuity is a contract with a large financial company, typically a life insurance company, that promises to pay out a fixed amount until you die, or until whichever of you or your wife is last to die. The lower half of Table 6·1 (see page 153) is the kind that a life insurance company uses, adjusted to allow them a profit, to work out what annuity rates to offer.

Three fundamental types of pension

There are three types of pension scheme, which may be mixed together in various ways and to which various insurance products can be added, which means the actual pensions on offer to you are likely to be complicated and widely varied. If you understand the three fundamental types, then you will be able to cut through the jargon and complexity of what is being sold to you and understand what is on offer so that you can make a good choice. These are:

1. *Plain vanilla*: an ordinary investment (e.g. property or a portfolio of shares or bonds) from which you intend to draw a pension.

2. *Someone else's promise*: a promise by someone else, typically a government or employer, to pay a pension in the future provided that you meet certain conditions, typically working for a certain period of time on a certain salary.

3. *An annuity*: which is a contract between you and an insurance company, under which you pay the insurance company a single large lump sum and then they pay you a series of regular smaller payments until you die.

The first two of these can either be within the regulatory wrapper described above as the second meaning of the word 'pension' or can stand outside such wrappers. In practice, however, someone else's promise will for most people be in the form of a regulated pension product.

The individual problems that pensions aim to solve

Problem 1 – you can't work in old age

The paramount problem that pensions aim to solve is that in old age people lose the ability to work to earn money to support themselves. An old person must therefore have enough money stashed away to meet all their needs from the point at which they stop working until the day they die. A complication here is that while we know on average how long we are likely to live, there is wide variance around that average, so it is impossible to predict how long a particular person will live, and therefore impossible to predict how much money they will need. There are two further complications to the problem of having enough to live on in old age. One is the risk of inflation. Pensions, of all three kinds, are typically denominated and contracted in nominal amounts, but the pensioner has needs that must be met in real amounts. (See page 54 in Chapter 2 for the difference between nominal and real – this is vital for understanding pensions.) Another complication is the risk of illness and infirmity. As people age, so our tendency to become seriously ill or infirm increases, and illness and infirmity usually raise the cost of living; you need a larger pension if you are infirm or ill than if you are old and healthy. Again, it is currently largely impossible to predict the onset of infirmity or disease in individual cases, but the averages are well understood and the facts are bleak: on average we need to provide for expensive healthcare and modification of our homes during retirement.

Problem 2 – people find it difficult or impossible to save directly a sufficient sum to fund their retirement

Because you are likely to be unable to work in old age, it is essential to have some financial provision for old age so that you can avoid penury. Ultimately this means that the individual has to save directly or indirectly for their retirement. Indirect savings include methods such as a pension scheme based on taxation, often of a special kind called a national insurance tax or a social security tax, or a scheme where an employer builds up a fund. Whether it is the state taxing the individual or the employer diverting some portion of money that would otherwise have been paid to the employee as wages or salary, these schemes are based on compulsion.

At first it might seem that an alternative to a compulsory scheme is for the individual to make their own arrangements, but the overwhelming evidence is that most people are unable to save enough for retirement if left to their own initiative. The Consumer Association of the UK, for example, found in 1992 that 65 percent of people either felt they were not saving enough for retirement or simply did not know if they were saving enough, but 65 percent of people also felt unable to save any more.[4] The problem is that most people, for whatever reason, are unable by themselves to save enough for their retirement. One solution to this problem is compulsion, as we have just described. Another is to make it easier for people to save and to give them incentives to do so, for example by giving tax breaks on the contributions to a pension scheme. (The tax may be deferred; that is, paid when the pension is drawn.) Countries such as the UK and USA use a mix of these approaches to try to solve this problem. Unfortunately, the cost of doing so is great complexity in the pensions system, a problem we will consider in a moment.

Problem 3 – the problem of long-term control and loyalty of workers

The first two problems we have looked at are, ultimately, those of the individual. This third is a problem for employers. Pay and bonuses, even deferred bonuses, are a short- and medium-term incentive and control mechanism. They do little for the long term. All significant organizations such as large corporations, universities and government departments depend on a cadre of career employees remaining in the profession if not within the same organization for the long term, and behaving well in the long term, even in the face of career disappointment and the usual vicissitudes of life. A decent pension scheme is a prime control and incentive mechanism for employers to deploy over their employees. In the context of defined benefit (DB) pension schemes the pension as a solution to this problem has been characterized as follows, but the principle is general and applies in much the same way to defined contribution schemes if the employer supplements the employee's contribution generously:

> in theories of deferred compensation, DB pensions solve a contracting problem between workers and firms . . . For example, firms may want to deter shirking but cannot perfectly monitor workers. Deferred pension accruals induce workers to devote optimal effort so that they do not lose their job and pension, and perhaps further to retire at an appropriate age. Similar motives for deferred compensation arise if firm-specific training or hiring is costly.[5]

The role of pension arrangements in the Western world as a peaceful but subtle and powerful mechanism of social control is interesting and not well researched, but it is beyond the scope of this book.

Complexity, concentration and agency problems – the terrific triple risks that come with pensions

Pensions are always boring, almost always complicated, and far too often risky. Although pensions exist to solve the most important problems of human existence, namely how to be secure and fear-free in the last part of one's life, pensions are far from perfect and come with three great risks.

First of all, pensions of the regulated kind are highly complex and therefore difficult for most people to understand. This has a number of unwelcome ramifications: complexity puts people off pensions; complexity also makes it harder for you to check that you are not being swindled in your pension or that you are not the victim of simple laziness and incompetence; complexity is widely recognized as a great problem and is the focus of much government attention, but the complexity in regulated pensions is such that so far governments have not been able to do much about it.[6] This is what the UK's House of Lords had to say about the complexity of pensions when it investigated the problem:

> The United Kingdom pension system is complex – arguably the most complex of any industrialized economy ... Dr Deborah Cooper (Retirement Research Unit, Mercer Human Resource Consulting Ltd), speaking on behalf of the Actuarial Profession, 'a huge obstacle to saving at the moment is not a lack of incentive, it is just the maze that you have to go through in order to make the decisions, and it is just too difficult. It is difficult for us to understand exactly what it all means so I dread to think what the ordinary lay person thinks.'[7]

Secondly, pensions are risky because they concentrate large pools of value. As Willie Sutton is reputed to have said in reply to the question of why he robbed banks, 'Because that's where the money is', so pension funds are a natural target for those looking for easy money. Those who are regularly tempted to raid pensions schemes include simple fraudsters, agents of the pension scheme who are lazy or crooked or incompetent, governments and politicians, and those involved in dealing in investments on behalf of the scheme. One of the things you should do if you have a pension scheme (and you ought to have one) is to understand what the risks in your pension scheme are and how to manage them. Many of the risks come from those who administer the scheme or are involved with the administrators in some way. The regulations that make pensions so complicated are largely designed to protect you from these risks, but unfortunately are only partly successful in doing so.

The third problem is related to the second: it is the agency problem. How can you as principal (that is, beneficiary of your pension scheme) ensure that your agent (the pension scheme administrator and others involved in running the pension) act in your best interests? As we have seen previously in this book, the agency problem is one of the central problems in financial affairs, and because pensions offer such attractive targets to delinquent agents the agency problem is severe in pensions.

What should you do about these problems? Fortunately, you can avoid them, but it does require being financially literate, being interested in your pension, and a certain amount of work. What exactly to do depends on the type of pension you have. For example, if you are in a defined benefits scheme the main risk is that the scheme fails, whereas if you are in a defined contributions scheme the main risk is that the level of fees or the choice of investments is poor. The rest of this chapter explains how to choose a pension and what the risks in each type are: understanding the risk characteristics of your scheme, together with the preceding chapters of this book and the final chapter, on financial strategy and decision making, will enable you to safeguard your pension.

To put some perspective on it, the risk of real hardship from a failed pension scheme is probably now less than 1 in 250 (i.e. less than 0.4 percent) if you work in the private sector in the UK, and may be similar elsewhere in the developed world.[8] The risk of your pension not performing as well as it could, which means anything from slight financial hardship to having to drink non-vintage instead of vintage champagne on birthdays, may be somewhat higher. Nonetheless, a 1/500 risk, say, of your pension being wiped out is not negligible. If you have a public sector pension scheme, this kind of risk does not affect you.

Your key decision: how to save for retirement

For most people there is a choice between one or several of the following three options, although not each of these is available to everyone:

- rely on the national or state pension scheme, if there is one,
- participate in your employer's pension scheme,

- setup your own pension scheme,

- create your own pension, outside of any formal pension scheme,

- do nothing.

Large organizations provide pension schemes for their employees. These are either defined benefits or, increasingly these days, defined contributions. A defined benefits scheme may even be index-linked, especially if you are a government employee. For various reasons, some unrelated to each other, the risks of pensions and the responsibility for managing them is being shifted away from the state and the employer and onto the individual. In large companies this means a trend of defined benefits schemes being closed and employees shifted into defined contributions schemes. For individuals not part of a company scheme, it means that the state pension can no longer be relied upon to provide a modest but tolerable retirement.

Even if you already know that a certain type of pension is not available to you now, we recommend that you at least skim read through each of the descriptions of different types below. This is for three reasons. First, each type of pension is a solution that is a different compromise in the face of the set of problems that pensions are designed to solve, and by understanding these different solutions and their trade-offs you may come to a better understanding of which are best in your particular case, even if that type of pension is not best for you. Secondly, circumstances change. Whatever politicians and governments promise, it is certain that in your lifetime pensions laws and regulations will change, so a pension that looks irrelevant to you today may one day become highly relevant, and you will be better positioned for such changes if you are already familiar with the key issues. Finally, some types of pension such as the index-linked defined benefit are in many countries such as the UK a massive hidden cost to taxpayers, and as a voter you may want to know about them, especially as the civil servants who benefit often prefer you not to do so.

Rely on the state or national pension scheme

In some countries such as the UK, New Zealand, Australia and much of Europe, the state provides a basic minimum pension. Entitlement to this pension may be based on citizenship, as the UK scheme was when it was created, or on contributions through a form of tax on employment, as the UK scheme now is. Some schemes are based or partly based on residency, such as the Swiss.[9] If there is a state pension available to you, it is unlikely to be sufficient to cover your financial needs in retirement, but it is also likely to be sufficiently large not to ignore. In the UK besides the choice you have about making additional voluntary contributions, you may also have a choice about opting back into the State Second Pension Scheme.[10] The point is that if a state pension scheme applies to you, even if the benefit is relatively small, you should understand what it offers you and gain sufficient understanding to be able to make a good choice.

If you move from one country to another a whole new order of complexity arises in your state pension entitlement. If you do move to a new country then your entitlement to the pension accrued in your old country may be complex. Don't let this put you off what to do to secure your entitlement in both countries. It is after all free money, backed by a state guarantee, and possibly two state guarantees.

Participate in your employer's pension scheme

This will either be defined benefit (DB) or, more likely today, defined contribution (DC), as we have seen above. If you are eligible for an employer's pension scheme you need to know which of these two types is on offer to you and the key features of the scheme. If you are very lucky, you will be offered an index-linked defined benefits scheme. This is the best possible scheme on offer, and thus the most expensive to your employer. More common is the ordinary defined benefits (DB) scheme. Normally in a defined benefits scheme the annual pension given to a scheme member once they become a pensioner is a fraction of the final salary of the member, depending on the length of their employment. In the UK this is often up to $^{40}/_{60}$ths of the pensioner's salary for the final year, $^{1}/_{60}$th for every full year of employment.

Set-up your own pension scheme

These have different names in different jurisdictions and may also vary depending on whether you are setting up a scheme as an individual or as the owner of a small company. In the UK this option includes Self-Invested Personal Pensions (SIPPS) and Insured Personal Pensions, which together are the two types of personal pension scheme available. In the US this option is realized in the Individual Retirement Account (IRA), of which there are several types.

What is the difference between setting up your own pension scheme, which is what this section is about, and simply saving for retirement, which is what the next section 'create your own pension, outside of any formal pension scheme' means? There are four differences, related to each other. These are:

- tax treatment
- degree of bureaucracy involved
- portability
- protection from creditors.

By setting up a formal pension scheme (such as a SIPP or Personal Pension in the UK) your payments into the scheme receive special tax treatment. Exactly what this treatment is and what the benefits are changes frequently and also may depend on your age and other circumstances. In general, you are allowed to make payments into such a scheme free of income tax. So, if you are taxed at a marginal rate of 50 percent, then for every £100 you earn you may be able to pay into your pension the full £100; whereas if you took the money as wages or salary you would receive only £50, the other £50 going in tax. This means that your full £100 is available to invest within the pension scheme. If on the other hand you simply save for retirement, you pay tax first and then can save only what is left after tax (assuming that you are a taxpayer), so in this example you would have only £50 to invest. You are, however, taxed on what you draw from a pension scheme, at the tax rates then prevailing. If you draw £100 as a pensioner, you would have to pay £50 tax on that drawing if your tax rate was still at 50 percent. There are two reasons why, despite being taxed on what you draw from a pension, you may nonetheless be better off. First, your tax rate may be lower. If the government has not increased tax rates in general, which is by no means guaranteed, you are likely to be drawing less in pension once you retire than you were earning before you retired, so your tax rate is likely to be lower. For example, if your tax rate falls from 50 percent to 40 percent when you retire then instead of getting only £50 of the £100 drawn you get £60. The second reason is that while the money temporarily saved from tax is in your pension fund, it is working for you by earning a return. Over 40 years 5 percent annual interest on £50 is £302. Even after deducting tax, that is free money.

Free money is not entirely free, and the second difference between setting up your own pension scheme and simply saving for retirement is the bureaucracy involved. There are tax and pension scheme forms to complete, rules to follow, and a great volume of paperwork. (One of the mysteries of pensions providers is that they are very keen to use IT and electronic communication internally, in their own organizations, to reduce their costs, but they flatly refuse to communicate electronically with their clients, insisting on reams of paper. Is a financial institution that behaves this way really honest? By what standard?)

Portability is a third difference. You can simply move your ordinary savings from one country to another. This holds for most major countries at the time of writing. The movement of financial assets is subject to any exchange controls that may be in force. Until 1979 it was illegal to take more than £20 out of the UK, and all British passports contained a special page in which, upon crossing a UK border, an immigration official had to record how much sterling currency the passport holder had with them. It is possible given the great problems facing the euro and the indebtedness of European governments that the UK and EU may introduce exchange controls, although at the time of writing it seems improbable. Were this to happen, however, you would stand a much better chance of getting ordinary savings out of the restricted countries than getting a pension scheme out.

If you emigrate and wish to take your pension fund with you the rules are complex and change frequently, and often the tax authorities in the country you are leaving impose severe financial penalties, although sometimes these can be minimized with careful planning and forethought.

The fourth and final difference between setting up your own pension scheme and simply saving for retirement is protection from creditors. In most jurisdictions including the UK and USA, your creditors have no rights over your pension scheme. This means that if you go bankrupt and your creditors apply to the courts to take over your assets, you may lose your savings even if you could show that you had intended them to be your pension, whereas were those assets held in a pension scheme, including one that you had set up yourself, they would be safe from creditors.

Odysseus lashes himself to the mast

Source: Shutterstock: Paul B. Moore

In Greek mythology, Odysseus had to sail through seas infested with a troupe of dangerous bird-women called the sirens. The sirens charmed any sailor who looked upon them or heard their voices to their doom by shipwreck. Odysseus wanted to hear what the Sirens sounded like and so he ordered his sailors to plug their ears with wax and to lash him to the mast of their ship. He ordered them, further, to leave him tied to the mast, no matter how much he might beg, until after the danger of the sirens had passed. Odysseus' action in having himself bound to the mast is an allegory of the human condition and the problems of self-discipline and temptation.

Create your own pension, outside any formal pension scheme

By this we mean simply saving for retirement using any combination of assets and means of saving but keeping those outside a pension scheme. This has a number of advantages and disadvantages. We've just seen the disadvantages compared to a formal pension scheme – lack of protection against creditors and different tax treatment. Another disadvantage is the self-discipline required, which is beyond many people, even those who exhibit great self-discipline in all other walks of life. A formal pension scheme thus acts against the siren of spending money now in the way that being lashed to the mast acted for Odysseus. A freedom that simple savings give you in retirement that a formal pension plan cannot is to do with your money what you will. Even if you run your own pension scheme (i.e. a formal pension scheme) you will usually face great restrictions on what you can do with the money. In the UK, for example, you must spend most of the accumulated fund on buying an annuity. Annuities cease at your death or sometimes at the later of your death or the death of your spouse or other legal beneficiary, which means that your children and your other beneficiaries cannot benefit from your lifelong savings after you are gone. You may well have much greater flexibility from ordinary savings.

Do nothing

Doing nothing about a pension is an option but not a good one.

Key questions to ask yourself about your pension

When beginning to decide what to do about your pension there are four key questions:[11]

- is a drop in your standard of living acceptable when you retire?
- when do you want to retire?
- how much do you want to save?
- what minimum proportion of your final salary do you wish to have as a pension?

A common assumption is that people do not want to see a fall in their living standard when they retire.[12] People may not want their disposable income to drop, but often are quite happy to experience a limited real drop in standard of living, for example giving up a large house in the centre of a capital city such as London and either moving to the country, or keeping on a much smaller property in the capital.

These four questions are linked. How much you save determines how much you can draw in terms of today's money in total, and that sets constraints on when you can retire and how much you can draw each year. (How to calculate in terms of today's money is explained in the section on 'Calculating net present value (NPV)' in Chapter 2 of this book.)

The fundamental problem for most people regarding pensions is that there is a large gap between what we save and what we hope to be able to draw as a pension in retirement. The first thing to do, therefore, is to be clear and honest with yourself in answering these four questions. Table 6·1 illustrates the trade-off between how much you save and what level of pension you will get. Table 6·1 does make a number of simplifying assumptions, chief of which are that return on investment will be a constant 5 percent annually and that you will draw a pension for exactly 30 years. The pension calculation is highly sensitive to variance in the interest rate, and is also sensitive to the length of time over which you draw your pension.

When a pension adviser or financial adviser recommends a pension to you, behind their advice will be a version of Table 6·1 tailored to your circumstances. If you can, you should learn to use a spreadsheet or other computer program to make your own calculations, because this will give you confidence and a greater ability to understand your adviser or provider and if necessary to question their assumptions and calculations.

TABLE 6·1 Illustration of how much you must save for a pension
Accumulation table: showing nominal capital sum accumulated by regular monthly savings at 5% annual interest, compounded.

Remaining years of employment

Monthly contribution	1	5	10	15	20	25	30	35	40
100	1,200	6,631	15,093	25,894	39,679	57,273	79,727	108,384	144,960
200	2,400	13,262	30,187	51,789	79,358	114,545	159,453	216,769	289,919
300	3,600	19,892	45,280	77,683	119,037	171,818	239,180	325,153	434,879
400	4,800	26,523	60,374	103,577	158,717	229,090	318,906	433,537	579,839
500	6,000	33,154	75,467	129,471	198,396	286,363	398,633	541,922	724,799
600	7,200	39,785	90,561	155,366	238,075	343,635	478,360	650,306	869,758
700	8,400	46,415	105,654	181,260	277,754	400,908	558,086	758,691	1,014,718
800	9,600	53,046	120,748	207,154	317,433	458,180	637,813	867,075	1,159,678
900	10,800	59,677	135,841	233,048	357,112	515,453	717,540	975,459	1,304,638

Decumulation table: showing for each amount in the accumulation table the monthly nominal pension for a fixed period of 30 years.

	1	5	10	15	20	25	30	35	40
100	7	36	82	140	215	310	432	588	786
200	13	72	164	281	430	621	864	1,175	1,572
300	20	108	245	421	645	931	1,297	1,763	2,357
400	26	144	327	561	860	1,242	1,729	2,350	3,143
500	33	180	409	702	1,075	1,552	2,161	2,938	3,929
600	39	216	491	842	1,291	1,863	2,593	3,525	4,715
700	46	252	573	983	1,506	2,173	3,025	4,113	5,501
800	52	288	655	1,123	1,721	2,484	3,458	4,700	6,287
900	59	324	736	1,263	1,936	2,794	3,890	5,288	7,072

These two tables together illustrate what pension is produced by differing amounts of monthly savings over differing periods. To use the table select from the top half of the table, the accumulation phase, along the top of the table the number of years until you retire, and then down the table the amount per month that you plan to save until then, to read off the capital sum that you will accumulate. Both halves of this table assume a steady return of 5 percent annually, and show nominal amounts. You should therefore increase the amount you save each year in line with inflation, and should pick an investment that returns 5 percent after allowing for inflation. (An index tracker is very likely to do this, over the long term, but may not do so for a period of less than about 15 years.) Then go to the corresponding figure in lower half, the decumulation table. (By 'corresponding' is meant the same x–y coordinate, or the same relative position.) This number in the lower half of the table is the monthly pension that you will get assuming that you live for exactly 30 years and that interest rates remain constant at 5 percent. (The labels on the columns and rows in the lower table have no meaning, they are provided merely to assist in finding the value corresponding to the upper table.) The aim of this table is to illustrate the level of savings needed to achieve a certain level of pension.

(A number of simplifying assumptions have been made, and the effects of tax, management fees and insurances against illness are not included.)

What sort of person you are and how this may affect pension choice

Different people have different characters and preferences, and these may affect which kind of pension provision is best for you. A person who prefers predictable, steady work and has the right qualifications and temperament to work for a large, bureaucratic organization is quite different in terms of pension needs from an entrepreneurial character. The first person has a steady and reliable cash flow and also easy access to a good pension scheme. The entrepreneur on the other hand may well not have access to a good pension scheme and is likely to need every penny to invest in their business venture. For an entrepreneur their business venture is their pension; and venture capitalists, when providing funding to an entrepreneur, often want the entrepreneur not to have a safety net, so as to ensure first of all that the entrepreneur is intently focused on the venture and secondly so that they have greater control over him. While this pairing of corporate man and entrepreneur represents the extreme ends of the spectrum, it makes the point that what is a good pension for one person may simply not be feasible for another. This means that you must take time to work out who you are, in terms of your pension needs, which pension options are available to you and which of these is best. Also, beware of financial advisers who assume that you are one particular sort of person.

Often financial advisers simply fail to understand that the person they are advising is different from the kind they want to deal with. If you are using an advisor of any sort to help you in pension matters, do spend time at the beginning to check that they really understand what sort of person you are and what that means for your pension. You may have to turn down ten or more advisers in order to get one who does understand your actual situation. Pension advisers tend to make money from following a process closely, and if you do not fit their process then they won't have the time and rarely the nous to work out what to do for you.

Asset protection, insurance and passing on your pension savings

Pension schemes may offer insurance and other protection against key risks. Risks can be divided into those that affect the accumulation phase and those that affect the decumulation phase of your pension. An example of the risk affecting the accumulation phase is an illness that prevents you from continuing to earn and so from paying into your pension scheme. Effective insurance against this risk means being able to top up your pension or being able to draw what is in there, or both, depending on how long you have to live after the misfortune. An example of a risk that affects the decumulation phase is if you die soon after your retirement and cannot provide for your dependents from your own pension. Pension schemes often provide a payment to you and your spouse or other beneficiary jointly, until the last one of you dies. There are of course other kinds of risk, and the pensions industry has evolved a range of what are in effect insurance measures against many risks facing scheme members. If you create your own pension (i.e. use ordinary savings) you should identify the key risks, such as ill-health, and consider buying the appropriate insurance cover.

We have already seen that pensions tend to have greater protection from creditors than ordinary assets. However, a pension is treated as a joint asset by divorce courts in many jurisdictions, because even if a pension is in your name only it is treated in law as a joint asset.

If you wish your family to benefit after you have died from what you have saved in your pension then you will need to save outside the formal pension schemes. That is, you will need to save into ordinary savings vehicles, and it is easier in these to make provision for a spouse, although you should examine carefully death duties and how they will affect your plans.

A macroeconomic perspective on pensions and their problems[13]

Our survey of pensions is incomplete without covering three macroeconomic points. (Macroeconomics is economics that affects large numbers of people, as opposed to microeconomics, which is the economics of the lives of individuals, families, and individual organizations.) These will enable you to understand and manage the risks facing your pension better. One factor is population growth disparity: will the developing world pay the pensions of the developed world? The second point is intergenerational transfer of wealth. The third is economic rents – to what extent do pensions depend on rents, especially in the West, and what risks accrue alongside rents in pension schemes? Although this chapter opened with the claim that geopolitical factors are significant in pensions, most of the chapter so far has said little about what these are and why they matter to your pension. This section addresses these points, which are further reasons why pensions are a complicated subject. However, if you understand the principles that give rise to the complexity, at least you will be able to navigate the complexity rather than be at its mercy.

Population growth disparity and intergenerational transfers

Imagine an isolated island, populated by just two people, an old man and a young man. No one including them knows how they got there or where they came from. As the old man gets older, he wants to retire, and agrees with the young man to give him his main house, in return for the young man providing food and water. This arrangement suits both men, the old man retires to his second, smaller house by the sea, and no longer needs to spend time working, gathering plants and hunting the local delicacy, the sausage vole, because the young man brings these things to him every week. The young man is happy because instead of spending years building a magnificent house in the middle of prime sausage-vole territory, he gets a magnificent house immediately, and given that he is hunting and gathering anyway, collecting food for the owner of the house is an easily manageable extra task.

This imaginary island illustrates how pensions work, but it also illustrates one of their risks. Pensions work by someone with an asset swapping that asset today for a promise of future payments. (This is how the decumulation phase of pensions works. Building up the asset is also important, and we can imagine that the older man spent years building his magnificent house.) This story also illustrates the risks: the younger man might turn out to have a bad character and renege on his promise to deliver food to the old man. Even if the young man is of unimpeachably good character, there may be some environmental disaster or pestilence that destroys the fauna and flora of the island, rendering him unable to provide his own food, let alone food for the old pensioner. Or the young man may suddenly die.

Suppose that none of these things happens, and the island continues idyllically for many years, until the old man passes away peacefully in his sleep. The remaining life on the island continues as before, if a little lonelier, and the young man ages until he too would like to retire. There are no younger men on the island, so its one inhabitant cannot benefit from the deal that the older man and he once entered into all those years ago. At this point a cruise ship, SS Beagle, arrives, and Mr Darius Winston, a retired hedge fund manager with a good natured but spoilt and moderately delinquent son in need of a short sharp dose of growing up arrive on the island and meet the islander. Darius Winston admires the magnificent home of the islander, and offers him a deal. The deal is either that his son should come and spend the next 25 years on the island, or else he will buy the magnificent home of the islander and ship it back home to Greenwich. If Darius' son moves onto the island, he will need somewhere to live and could rent the magnificent house, thus giving the islander the pension he needs under the same arrangements as before. If the magnificent house is sold and taken away, the islander will have enough money to be able to buy food and have it delivered by ship every week for the rest of his life. (Darius Winston was a very successful hedge fund manager.)

What our islander faces is a choice between exporting his capital or importing labour. This is the same choice, for the same reasons, that a country with an ageing population faces. As the population (citizens) of the US ages, the US has been very successful at importing labour and assimilating the immigrants as US citizens. In the early twentieth century the UK exported its capital to achieve the same result in terms of being able to fund the retirement of its population.

One of the central questions in pensions in the developed world today, especially in Europe and the UK, is how to fund the retirement of an ageing workforce. Immigration is one possible solution; the risk in this strategy is whether the immigrants can be assimilated into the economy as successfully as the US has been able to do. Export of capital to countries with a young population is another solution; and the risk in this strategy is whether the countries importing the capital will pay for it, or whether they will default. Both these strategies and the risks associated with them are political questions at least as much as they are financial or economic ones. Do they matter to you, the would-be pensioner? While no one individual can influence such international political questions, however powerful they be, it is worth understanding the assumptions and risks underlying the pension options available to you.

Our story of the two-man island illustrates the complex and fragile web of assumptions on which a safe pension depends. The idea that you can retire and live reasonably comfortably for a further 10, 20 or 30 years without working is a new one. It has obvious attractions. But what if more and more people try to arrange their affairs so as to be able to do this, that is, to have a large pension? Suppose our island had not one retiree but an increasing number, but still only one young man. At first the old retiree is joined by another man, or woman, who arrives washed up on the shore in the dead of night. Perhaps the young man does not mind gathering extra food for one more person. But suppose more of these aged night-time arrivals wash up and soon a colony of old people exists. At what point would the one man begin to feel that he was being taken advantage of in having to look after an increasing number of older people? Or suppose that no additional old age pensioners wash up on the beach, but instead a number of young immigrants arrive, men and women, all hard working, but their number puts a strain on the island's natural ecology and soon the number of sausage voles declines, and it becomes harder to hunt and gather food for everyone. At the same time the young men and women have reproduced, and there are now babies to feed and look after, as well as the old age pensioner. The working people of the island ask whether it is only fair to cut the pension paid to the old man by, say, 10 percent, or perhaps even 50 percent? After all, times have changed, and no one foresaw the new circumstances.

As our imaginary island fills up with more people, the old man in his seaside cottage becomes a legend, and everyone aspires to have such a peaceful and pleasant retirement. However, just as their aspirations to such a retirement grow and ripen in their minds, the possibility of realizing that retirement is withering in their economy. Times have indeed changed, the plentiful fauna and flora of his youth are no more, and everyone is having to work harder to survive. Nonetheless, people's will to believe that they will have such a retirement is undimmed, and from the fertile soil of this desire springs a new profession on the island, which is the pensions industry, in the form of the Island Pension Company.

The Island Pension Company charges a fee to belong to its pension scheme, and its officers live comfortable lives, in effect charging a fee for sustaining the hopes and dreams of comfortable retirement for the island's population. Despite this there is nothing the Island Pension Company can do to ensure that when the time comes to pay out pensions there will be enough young people willing to pay for the old people to do nothing. The risk of that being the case is too much of a nightmare for anyone to contemplate, so the idea goes uncontemplated, which is probably wise because there is nothing anyone can do about it. On the other hand, as long as the population does not shrink or as long as the island can export capital, pensions look reasonably secure. Either way, the officers of the Island Pension Company have secured their own retirement by using the fees paid to them for arranging other pensions by buying the best hunting land and the best retirement plots along the seashore.

The final few lines of our island story illustrate that pensions may be the new gold rush. In the California gold rush that began in 1849 it is said that those who made most money most reliably were not the gold prospectors, but those who sold vital tools and clothing to the gold prospectors. Each of the 300,000 gold prospectors might or might not find gold, but each one had to buy a pick and a pan and to buy clothes and provisions. In the early years many gold prospectors got rich or at least made a decent living, but as the gold rush wore on returns diminished. It is possible that today's enthusiasm for pension schemes is a new gold rush, in that those who entered the schemes early, today's pensioners, will have done very well, but the rest of us are possibly doing little more than enriching those who sell pension schemes.

Economic rents

In economics, the term 'rent' means a payment for something that
is beyond the level of payment necessary to secure the supply of
that thing. This is a subtle but important concept, and is closely
related to the much woollier notion of excess profits. Suppose
you own a boat and you ferry foot passengers across a river for £1
per trip per person. This level of fee for your services as ferryman
covers all your costs of maintaining the boat, paying off the loan
with which you bought the boat, and gives you as much income
after those costs as you could get from plumbing or from being a
carpenter, which are the two other trades you have. You cannot
raise your price for ferrying people because you have a competitor,
who charges the same as you do. Now suppose that your
competitor retires and you buy his boat. You are now able to charge
£5 per trip, and your customers have to make the journey because
there is no other way across. Of your new £5 fee, £4 is economic
rent. It is a 'return over and above opportunity cost, or the normal
return necessary to keep a resource in its current use'.[14]

Economic rents are attractive because rent is free money, in that
you do not have to work nearly as hard for it as you would have
done for the same amount of money. Economists talk of rent-
seeking behaviour, which means the tendency of people to focus
their energies on finding or creating economic rents instead of
focusing their efforts on competing in the market and accepting
the lower, market rate for one's energies. In the imaginary case
just described when you had one of the two ferry boats, you
had a choice of how to secure your wealth in the long term. You
could on the one hand compete with the other ferryman, perhaps
making your boat more attractive to passengers or advertising your
services, or rowing harder to make a slightly faster crossing. On the
other hand you could instead focus your energy into persuading
him to retire so that you could buy his boat.

What have rents got to do with pensions? Three things. First, the
ideal pension from an individual's point of view is a rent, a way
of getting the rest of the world to overpay the pensioner. Pension
providers and pensioners therefore have a natural incentive to
be rent-seeking. However, secondly, rents are resented by those

paying them as much as they are loved by those receiving them. It is for this reason that competition and anti-monopoly laws exist. Thus there is always the risk that your pension to some extent depends on rent collection and that those paying the rent will find a way to avoid continuing payments. Thirdly, the problem of rents applies to cross-border investment, that is, to the export of capital required to fund the pensions of an aging population such as the UK's, Europe's or China's. (China will soon be an ageing population because of its one child policy.) Just as individuals have an incentive to seek rents, so do pension funds.

Although the principle of economic rent is clear, in practice it can be hard to determine what is rent and what is a fair price for something. A prime example of this is playing out right now in patents for drugs and drug pricing across different countries. In the case of some life-saving drugs, what looks like a fair price to shareholders in advanced Western countries can look like excessive rents to those in third world countries. Even if it is agreed that the investors of the drug should be rewarded fairly, say with a pension, should that fair reward be a pension at the level of standards of living in the developed world or of the Third World? (In developed economies, shareholders are increasingly the pension funds, so this example is to the point.)

Summary

Pensions are complicated and boring, and even experts fail to understand them. However, they are also vital for you and your life. It is therefore vital that you learn about pensions. A good way to start this is to be clear in your own mind on what a pension is. It is simply saving for retirement in such a way that you can live comfortably when you can no longer earn. Formal pension schemes often give tax reliefs on savings, but then your pension payments are taxed. For various reasons, informal pension schemes, without tax reliefs, are becoming more popular. One of the big problems with formal pension schemes is that governments tend to raid them, and Gordon Brown destroyed more pension savings than anyone else in recent history. The actions of politicians like Gordon Brown create unique and significant risks to all formal pensions schemes.

A pension scheme has an accumulation (saving) and a decumulation (pay-out) phase. There are a number of risks in pensions that do not arise in ordinary savings. Besides complexity and political risk in formal schemes, both formal and informal schemes suffer from the human problem of self-discipline in the accumulation phase and from sheer uncertainty as to how long you will live in the decumulation phase.

Macroeconomics has some impact on pensions generally, and if you are serious about learning finance for better decision making, then you should turn your mind to macroeconomics, to help understand pensions and other areas of finance better. The main macroeconomic problem in pensions is that an ageing population will have declining pensions unless it can either reverse its ageing by importing labour into the country or by exporting its pensions savings into another, younger country. Neither solution is without risk.

If your pension is managed on your behalf, as most people's are, then you should review the valuation statements and perhaps ask questions of the pensions trustees or managers to satisfy yourself of their competence.

REVIEW QUESTIONS

1. If you have not already done so, answer the four key questions in the section 'Key questions to ask yourself about your pension' of this chapter (p. 000).

2. Use a calculator or spreadsheet to work out what capital sum will result if you save £250 per month for the next 15 years, assuming that you get a steady annual return of 6 percent, and ignoring inflation. What if rates are only 5·5 percent? (Hint: in Microsoft Excel, the function 'FV' may be useful, although you can also use the formula for future values to create your own equation in each cell.)

3. Taking your answers from question (1), work out how much per month would be paid if the sum accumulated in (1) is invested at 6 percent and paid out in equal instalments until nothing remained. (Hint: PMT.)

4. What is the difference between funded and unfunded pensions?

5. What is the difference between defined benefit and defined contribution pensions? What is the main advantage for the scheme member (i.e. pensioner-to-be) of defined benefit? For whom is this a disadvantage? What is the current trend in the world?

6. List five major sources of risk and complexity in pensions.

7. Find a good friend and meet them to spend an hour comparing notes on what you both understand about pensions. At the end of an hour, each list the three main things you learnt from the other person, and what difference that makes to your pension plans.

8. Some people invest in rental property as a way of providing themselves with a pension. What are the advantages and disadvantages of this compared to a defined contributions scheme run by a large employer? And compared to a defined benefits scheme?

9. For discussion: can your government afford to ensure that everyone who needs a pension has a pension that is enough to live on in old age? What are the main problems likely to be facing a government that makes such a promise? What are other governments doing that might affect what your government is doing? Which other governments are the most important ones to watch? Why?

10. Take your existing pension arrangements and find out how much they will provide you in retirement, in today's terms.

7
Financial strategy and how to make financial decisions

No decision is difficult to make if you will get all of the facts.

Patton

You will have to guess, most of your time, what is going on behind the next hill, and this is not only the whole business of war, but of life.

Wellington

Make sure that you hear what you don't want to hear.

Fergal Quinn of Superquinn (quoted in Allan Leighton,
On Leadership)

Knowin' it ain't the same as doin' it.

Old Hoosier saying

The aim of this chapter is to help you pull together everything that you have learnt in all the preceding chapters to make better decisions. To do this the chapter covers two things: it gives a framework for decision making in financial matters; and it also gives a number of practical tips and rules of thumb that successful people have followed. The decision making and strategy set out in this chapter applies equally to personal financial decision making and to business financial decision making. It is not intended to be new or surprising, and a reader who has some experience in either sphere should not find too much that is new, and, if you have read the previous chapters, nothing is that surprising. Another aim of the chapter is to give you confidence actually to apply what you now know in making decisions.

The structure of this chapter

The chapter is in four parts.

- The first part is a review of decision making in general. Financial decision making is a special case, not *sui generis*. This is important because the human mind is not well adapted to make the kinds of decisions that we face in modern times, and is especially badly adapted to make some kinds of financial decisions,[1] so it needs tools or an aide-memoire to overcome this problem.

- The second section is about the OODA loop, which is a way of reminding yourself whether you should be thinking about what to do or doing it. This is important because one of the biggest problems in personal financial decisions is rushing in and making a decision too quickly; in many businesses the opposite is the case. Using the OODA loop is the solution in both situations (and is itself decision making in the larger sense).

- The third part of the chapter is a collection of rules of thumb or heuristics that successful people have found useful. These practical tips were gathered by interviewing over 50 people in the course of writing this book. These are important because each is consistent with finance theory, is easier to remember than the theory and, moreover, has been found to work in practice – it has stood the test of time.

- The final part concerns keeping an investment diary or some other record of your financial decision making. This is because reviewing how and why you made each particular financial decision and learning from it in the light of what actually happens is one of the most powerful and effective ways you can improve your knowledge of finance and also become richer.

Decision making in general

Making financial decisions is not a different kind but a special case of making decisions. We therefore begin this chapter with a short review of decision making in general. This section is a short primer on decision making.[2]

The common mistake

The most common reaction to a problem is to think of a solution. For simple problems this is often satisfactory. For problems other than the simplest this is usually a mistake because it leads you to ignore some of the critical aspects of the problem. A structured approach to problem solving will help ensure that you consider all relevant factors and come up with a good solution.

A structured approach to decision making

Define the aim

The first step is to define exactly what has to be achieved clearly yet simply. The statement of the aim should usually be qualified by limitations of time and money. For example 'To save enough money to be able to educate our two children as doctors and retire by the age of 70.'

Factors

A factor or fact is anything which will influence the achievement of the aim. You should gather the factors and then draw deductions from each by continually asking 'so what?' until each factor is squeezed dry. The resources of information, reputation, knowledge, money, licenses and permissions, people, equipment and time are often factors. In business problems another vital factor to consider is usually the customer. An example is when deciding how to build a pension the relevant factors are your age and how much longer you wish to work, what level of pension payment do you want, for how long after retirement your life-expectancy suggests you will live, and what savings or pensions schemes are open to you, together with what risks your pension scheme faces. The 'so whats' from these factors include how much money you need to save given the length of your retirement and how much pension you want.

Courses of action open to you

Once you have thought hard about the factors and what they imply identify the various courses of action open to you and to some of the other actors involved. Suppose you want to build an extension to your house and your decision is how to pay for it. Some of the options might be: to do nothing; to use savings; to borrow the money as an ordinary loan; to increase your mortgage; to save; or to sell some investment. These are the different courses of action.

Likely responses to your actions

You should also consider the courses of action that others will take. The Hunt brothers, Nelson Bunker Hunt and William Herbert Hunt, had a great scheme to make between two and four billion dollars from the silver market in 1979. What they did was legal at the time, but involved cornering the market in silver. (Cornering a market is when you own so much of what is traded on the market that you can influence prices.) Their scheme was perfect except in one regard, which was that the US government changed the rules before the Hunts completed their scheme. Instead of making billions, the brothers were ruined. The Hunt brothers had failed to anticipate the likely government response to their cornering of the silver market. You perhaps are not in the multi-billion dollar financial decision making game as the Hunt brothers were, but a more everyday example following from the decision of how to finance an extension to your house, given above, is that if you borrow more money, will that make your bank less likely to help you for something else you need later on, for example?

Decision

Make the decision. This means selecting one of the courses of action from the steps above. This becomes the plan.

The plan and implementation

Your plan may be as simple as 'Go and buy as much silver as you can afford', or simply 'Extend the mortgage'. However, if it is more complicated you should write it down. It is always wise to have a contingency plan, which may be one of the courses of action you did not choose as the main plan. And write down why you chose that one and not the others, i.e. your rationale.

The problem of cause or effect

Very often a problem is not clearly defined and sometimes cause and effect may be confused. When you have to build a bridge the aim is obvious but what is the problem in terms of a headache, a car breaking down, paying school fees or an employee producing unsatisfactory work? With such problems it is necessary to define the basic cause and to overcome that. Aspirin for the headache is a solution but what if the cause is a brain tumour? The dirty fuel filter of a carburettor can be quickly cleared but how did it get dirty? Clearing the filter will only be a temporary solution.

The solution to these problems is only arrived at by the problem solver determining the root cause. Once you've done this you can start to define the aim and then the sequence of problem solving as already described.

Review

Problem solving can be improved by self-appraisal. If you can, write down each major financial decision you take, what you hoped to achieve and why you decided as you did – or even better all of the steps you went through as described above. Keep this in the form of an investment diary, and re-read it every few months. It can be painful reading to look back over the decisions you made if the results aren't as positive as you anticipated, but it is a good way to learn and the important thing is to avoid making the same mistakes again.

If you are serious about improving your financial literacy, use this decision making technique every day, not only for financial decisions but for all the major decisions you make.

The OODA loop and knowing where you are in decision making

The OODA loop is a four-stage cycle comprising Observe, Orient, Decide, Act. It was invented by John Boyd, a US fighter pilot and military strategist, but similar ideas can be traced all the way back to Aristotle and before him. The benefit of thinking in terms of the OODA loop or something like it is that it helps ensure you are focused on the right thing at each step of making a decision. If you rush ahead too fast in making a decision you may make an avoidable mistake or simply waste time. The point of the OODA loop is not to slow down your decision making but to speed it up as much as possible, but no more.

The four phases of the OODA loop are:

1. **Observe**: look at the context of your decisions and if necessary research the key factors.

2. **Orientate** yourself in the context of the decision. Relate your interests and strengths and weaknesses to what is going on. See the decision in context. Work out the different possible courses of action open to you. By the time you decide you should have identified all relevant factors in the decision and clarified your aim, and you should also understand how the factors affect the chances of reaching the aim by the different possible courses of action.

3. **Decide** what to do.

4. **Act**. Do it.

As an example of using the OODA loop, suppose that you have been persuaded to meet a financial adviser who wants to talk about your financial needs and which savings products might be useful for you. You could just go ahead and have the meeting, perhaps doing some preparation for it beforehand. Including time to get to the meeting, have it and deal with the adviser's follow up afterwards, this could easily be half a day of your time. Even if it is only two hours, you might want to ensure it is time well spent.

This is one way you could use the OODA loop to prepare. Note that the decision is whether you want to meet the financial adviser at all, and if you do, when, under what circumstances and why.

- **Observe**. Reflect on the financial adviser: how did they approach you, what was their manner? Polite? Deferential? Condescending? How did they find out about you? Who recommended them and do you trust their judgement and especially their financial judgement? Who owns the company for which the financial adviser works? What is the reputation of the owners?

- **Orient**. Why meet the financial adviser? What are your aims in finance right now, and how could a financial adviser help? Would it be better to put off a meeting for three months, six months or a year? What evidence is there that this financial adviser has expertise in the areas of finance where you want advice?

- **Decide** whether to meet the adviser. **Decide** what to ask – e.g. how does the adviser get paid and what percentage commission do they get on products sold.

- **Act**. Arrange the meeting or tell the adviser you do not want to meet.

This is perhaps common sense, but it can be surprising how few people do these common sense things when making decisions about their time. The most important points are to be clear about what your aim is and to ensure that before you make the decision you have understood its context, you are making the right decision, and you are ready to make the decision – that is to say *observe* and *orient*. One of the biggest problems people create for themselves when making financial decisions is to rush into things and make decisions too hastily. This is why there are laws in most countries that give people cooling off periods after making decision to take on certain kinds of financial obligations.[3]

- What is the strategic environment?
- What is your financial situation?
- How do these interact?
- How well do you understand the financial factors involved? How familiar are you with them from previous experience?
- Find out what has happened before and who the key players are now.

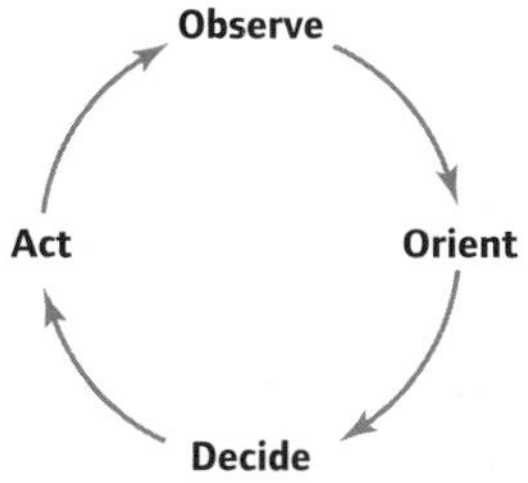

The most important phases. Fit together what you have observed into a coherent whole. Does it make sense to you? Do you really understand it? If not, do more observing and orienting.

This step includes analysis. The purpose of analysis is to enable you to make good decisions. A good test of when orientation is completed successfully is when your gut instinct coincides with the results of your analysis, and no data exists which contraindicates.

Implement and monitor the decision – which is also a test of how well you (a) gathered and (b) analysed the evidence.

Observe

Act   **Orient**

Decide

The decision is made by choosing between competing hypotheses on the basis of evidence. A decision without evidence is risky.

In this phase also, you should understand or generate different points of view, different ways of seeing the issues and especially the financial issues. Who has what interests and what incentives?

Knowledge of the strategic environment is the first priority. Then secondly, one must be able to interact with the environment and those within it appropriately. You must be able to observe and orient yourself in such a way that you can indeed survive and prosper by shaping the environment where possible to you own ends, by adapting to it where you must. Doing so requires a complex set of relationships that involve both isolation and interaction. Knowing when each is appropriate is critical to your success. In OODA loop fashion, one must continually observe, orient, decide and act in order to achieve and maintain freedom of action and maximize the chances for survival and prosperity. One does so through a combination of responsiveness, diversification, harmony, and initiative. It is these that are the core of '*Boyd's Way*'. Responsiveness is required to maintain or regain initiative. Diversification is required to manage risk, so there is no repeating pattern of the same mistakes. Harmony is the fit with the environment and others operating in it. Initiate – taking charge of your own destiny – is required if one is to master circumstances rather than be mastered by them.

FIGURE 7·1 The OODA loop

A second example of the OODA loop in use by a young couple buying their first house is as follows:

- **Observe**. What houses are available? What mortgages are available? What money of our own do we have? What insurance against unemployment is available? What are the main trends in the housing and mortgage markets right now? What are politicians, the banks and friends in the property business saying about the direction in which interest rates are going? What have our friends who have bought houses learnt from the experience – what do they advise to do differently? What websites are useful?

- **Orient**. How does what we want compare to what is available and what we can afford? What are the main factors to consider in our particular case?

- **Decide**. Whether to buy the house, and if so decide also on a budget, on what type of mortgage, and on a plan for buying and financing the house and everything that goes with it (insurance, removal fees and so on).

- **Act**. Buy the house.

What is your aim?

By the time you get to the *decide* step in the OODA loop you must be crystal clear about what your aim is. Clarifying aims and interests are real work and a valuable part of decision making, especially financial decision making.

As an example of how important it is and how hard it can be to clarify aims consider this example. Mr M is a 40-year-old man with a wife and two children aged eight and five. His financial aim, he believes, is to retire as soon as possible. Talking over his aim with a financial adviser he realizes that as he does not own a house and is working in a country in which he does not want to retire and where rental costs of housing are high, a better aim for him is to buy a house, which entails saving.

Mr M was not in a position to really consider retiring early. That was a hope, not an aim. Aims must be actionable, in that you must be able to do something to get you towards the aim; you must be able to make a plan and implement it with a good chance of achieving the aim. Picking 'retire early' was not specific enough to Mr M's circumstances to lead to any specific action. 'Buy a house in Australia' (Mr and Mrs M's home country) was specific and actionable. Without too much sacrifice they could afford to buy a property and then let it out, so that if their overseas jobs disappeared they would at least have somewhere of their own to live, and if as they hoped they reached retirement age without losing their jobs they would actually have somewhere to live, and somewhere where they wanted to live.

Some questions which may help clarify your aim are?

- What will success look like?
- Is this part of a bigger aim or is it the big, overall aim? If the latter, do I need some intermediate aims?
- How will I know when I have succeeded?
- What exactly is the decision? What is to be decided?
- Is it the right question? Does it feel right?
- What are some other ways of phrasing the question?
- How would some other person phrase the question? (Your mother, father, best friend, a political leader you admire, a businessman you admire, a boss you found inspiring.)

Top tips for financial and investment decisions

In researching this book over 50 people who are financially successful were interviewed, and their advice is given here under three headings:

- The 12 cardinal rules of investing
- Understanding your own situation
- How to use advisers, including financial advisers.

The 12 cardinal rules of investing

1 Don't invest in things you don't understand.
2 Understand what risk is.

3 Don't use financial advisers who are one-man bands or small organizations.

4 Do ensure that you understand interest rates and their effect on your investments.

5 Avoid excessive fees, don't assume that a few percent doesn't matter.

6 Do know when to cut your losses.

7 Don't stop using common sense just because it's finance. If you have money to invest you are already ahead of the game: others don't necessarily know more than you do and probably don't care as much what happens to your money as you do.

8 Don't invest in things that don't produce a revenue stream without very careful thought.

9 Don't invest in shares where shareholder rights are poor or ignored.

10 Don't try to avoid paying taxes.

11 Do work out what your long-term aim is.

12 Do ensure that you have enough mathematical skill to cope with the basic maths of the financial markets, at a minimum IRR and NPV – a little maths skill goes a long way here.[4]

1. Don't invest in things you don't understand

If there is one mistake above all others in investment decision making, it is to invest in things you don't understand.[5]

The point of investment is to make a return on one's investment, within a certain tolerance for risk that derives from one's circumstances and character. To do this requires success in one or possibly two kinds of decisions. You must be able to select the best opportunities from a range of attractive but unequal investment opportunities. And, if things go wrong, you must know when to cut your losses. Skill in both kinds of decision requires that you understand what you are investing in. This does not mean that you need to have experience of this industry in which you are investing, but you do need to understand the investment. If you are considering investing in a gold mine, you do not need to have worked in a mine or for a mining company, but you should understand what factors affect the value of gold mines in general and how these will play out in terms of the value of your specific proposed investment.

A rule of thumb for whether you can understand something is whether you can explain it in a way that your mother would understand.

2. Understand what risk is

Do understand the risk in your investments and investment ideas. What is the source of risk, where is it coming from, how can it impact your investment? Understanding what you are investing in means most of all understanding what risks inhere in that investment. Think hard about what can go wrong in any investment you are considering.

You can develop your understanding of risk by keeping an investment diary, and in it concentrating on recording what risks you understood at the time of making each of your investments.

3. Don't use financial advisers who are one-man bands or small organizations

Instead either use a financial adviser who is part of a large, well-known organization with a first-class reputation or else be your own financial advisor. Advisers have a role to play in your financial decision making, both financial advisers and others such as lawyers. One of the biggest difficulties in personal finance is that a single bad decision can wipe out a lifetime's savings. It is tempting therefore to hand over responsibility for decision making to a professional, and one of the groups claiming to be professional in this field is financial advisers, sometimes also known as independent financial advisers or IFAs. However, the problem does not go away just because it is handed over to a financial adviser.

A large number of people lose fortunes and suffer real financial distress because of mistakes made by their financial advisers. A common example of the problem is as follows. An individual is approached by their financial adviser with a scheme that promises great returns. The individual is persuaded to invest a large sum. For some time all goes well. Then for some apparently unforeseeable reason, all or most of the investment is lost. Sometimes the problem is attributed to simple bad luck, sometimes to incompetence, and not infrequently to fraud. This sorry chain of events happens very often, and even professional people such as lawyers and doctors who live their daily lives dealing with human weaknesses and ingenuity are as prone to meeting this fate of their own volition as other less skilled folk. The problem is that financial advisers who work alone or as part of a small organization operate without the safeguards and risk controls that come with a large, reputable organization.

A solution if you wish to use a financial adviser is to use one who is part of one of the largest financial institutions that has an excellent reputation. The sort of organization to look for is, in the UK, something like Clydesdale, Coutts, or HSBC; in the USA something like Bank of America, Wells Fargo, Merrill Lynch or JP Morgan; in Australasia National Australia Group, ANZ Ord Minett or Westpac; in Canada Toronto Dominion Bank, Canadian Imperial Bank of Commerce, or Royal Bank of Canada. For expatriates the same principles apply, and include names such as Zurich Insurance, Coutts, HSBC, Credit Suisse, Standard Bank, Goldman Sachs and Standard Chartered. What you will get from a financial adviser who is part of such an organization is, on the downside, a certain amount of form filling and bureaucracy, and perhaps a limited range of investment opportunities, but on the upside the processes and controls will be in place as part of its parent company's policies to ensure that your hard-won investments are not at risk of being wiped out from a single disastrous mistake.

Consider how to pay your adviser. There are reasons to believe that you can get better advice if you pay a fee rather than commission.

4. Do ensure that you understand interest rates and their effect on your investments

A classic mistake is to assume that a few percentage points don't matter in finance. A few points make the difference between a great investment and a terrible one. Investment professionals think in terms of hundredths of a percentage point, and have a special term for this, a bp, pronounced 'bip'. Retail financial products are created and sold by people who think in terms of bps. If you are thinking in terms of whole percentage points or, worse, ignoring the difference that a couple of percentage points makes over time, you are giving up your money to the finance professionals. Table 7·1 shows the effect that different interest rates have over time. We assume that a working life is on average 44 years, and so we take half this time, a period of 22 years, as a meaningful time horizon for comparing investment returns. The chart ignores the effect of inflation, so it shows very clearly what difference a few percentage points makes. Note especially the right-hand column, showing the effect of a 2 percent fee applied to a 6 percent return. This means that every year 2 percent of your asset is deducted. This kind of fee structure is very common in retail finance, especially for managed funds. Fees as large as 5 percent are not at all unusual, and have a great effect on the actual returns that you get.

What does this mean in practice? What should you do in order to understand interest rates and their effect on your investment? Simply, it means being able to work out calculations such as Table 7·1, in order to choose the best from a range of different financial products or investment opportunities. You need to be able to use either a calculator or a spreadsheet to compare the effect of the various options open to you. How to do this has already been covered in Chapter 2, on the time value of money. Key sums you must be able to work out for yourself are:

- Interest and compound interest.
- The effect of annual fees and of one-off fees.
- Adjusting for inflation if necessary, so that you are comparing either real or nominal numbers.

This last point is important but simple. Either compare numbers including inflation, or compare numbers without inflation. But never compare one set of numbers that is adjusted for inflation with another that is not.

TABLE 7.1 Effect of differences in interest rates on a £1000 investment over half a working lifetime

Initial investment £1000·00

Year	At 3%	At 4%	At 5%	At 6%	At 6% with a 2% annual fee
0	1000	1000	1000	1000	980
1	1030	1040	1050	1060	1018
2	1061	1082	1103	1124	1058
3	1093	1125	1158	1191	1099
4	1126	1170	1216	1262	1141
5	1159	1217	1276	1338	1185
6	1194	1265	1340	1419	1231
7	1230	1316	1407	1504	1279
8	1267	1369	1477	1594	1329
9	1305	1423	1551	1689	1380
10	1344	1480	1629	1791	1434
11	1384	1539	1710	1898	1490
12	1426	1601	1796	2012	1547
13	1469	1665	1886	2133	1607
14	1513	1732	1980	2261	1670
15	1558	1801	2079	2397	1735
16	1605	1873	2183	2540	1802
17	1653	1948	2292	2693	1872
18	1702	2026	2407	2854	1944
19	1754	2107	2527	3026	2020
20	1806	2191	2653	3207	2098
21	1860	2279	2786	3400	2180
22	1916	2370	2925	3604	2264

The numbers in this table have been rounded to the nearest pound. The table shows nominal growth, that is, the effects of inflation have been excluded. Note that a 6 percent annual growth rate gives over the 22-year period a return that is over 50 percent greater than a 3 percent rate. Note also how expensive a 2 percent annual fee is, in that it reduces the return of a 6 percent annual growth rate to effectively less than a 4 percent annual growth rate. The cost over the period of that 2 percent per year is almost £1000.

5. Avoid excessive fees, and don't assume that a few percent doesn't matter

Find out what fees and other charges are being applied to your investments – demand to know if necessary.

Much of the finance industry relies on retail investors not understanding just how large fees and other charges imposed by financial advisers and other intermediaries are and how little the investor gets for those fees. These fees are, in effect, optional, but most people are happy to pay them. Most managed funds that invest in developed markets do not outperform the index, so most investors in managed funds are paying for management and getting a worse return than if they bought an index tracker, which also avoids all but a tiny management fee. Many studies have shown that in developed markets most fund managers (i.e. active managers) fail to outperform the index.[6] There are two reasons for this. Active management entails knowing when to buy and when to sell, and this skill, timing, is extraordinarily difficult to exercise in investment. Secondly, the additional returns that can be gained from active management rarely exceed the additional costs associated with it. In inefficient markets such as many of the emerging markets and some kinds of commodities markets, fund managers can add value, but for investing in shares in developed markets such as the UK and USA it is best to avoid most of the actively managed funds. There are some rare exceptions to this rule. Fund managers who have a track record of regularly beating the market in developed markets include Anthony Bolton, for example, formerly the manager of Fidelity's UK Special Situations Fund.

6. Know when to cut your losses

Even the best investor makes mistakes and buys a dud investment occasionally. Generally it is a good idea to get out early rather than hanging on and hoping for the investment to come back. As traders in the financial markets say, 'The first cut is often the cheapest cut'. The psychological difficulty that many people have with doing this seems to be connected to accepting that they have incurred a loss – as if paper losses don't count. Although like paper gains paper losses do not count in one sense, the problem is that very often when it comes to realizing the loss, that is, translating it from one on paper to a real one, the loss is larger the longer it has been left. There is much evidence from research in psychology and behavioural finance showing how we are less happy to give up something we think we have than gaining something we don't know we have.[7] This is known as loss aversion. Keeping an investment diary and recording the opportunities to take your losses and when you actually did take them, and with what long-term consequence, is a good antidote to this bias in our psychological make-up.

Judgement and a sense of proportion are required when deciding how to manage investment losses. If a broad index such as the FTSE 100 or the S&P 500 falls 10 percent or 15 percent, then there is usually little reason to take any action. But if your investment in a business that you had every reason to expect would make a steady 20 percent return minimum, even in bad years, shows a 5 percent loss, then you may wish to make some thorough investigations into the causes, with a mind to cutting your losses before 5 percent becomes 10 percent or worse.

7. Don't stop using common sense just because it's finance

We've seen above the result of ignoring the difference that a few percentage points makes to the total return on one's investment; and yet many people ignore making the simple calculations that show the consequences, and thus make terrible financial decisions, in effect throwing thousands of pounds away. We also know that in the rest of life, if something seems too good to be true, then very probably it is. These kinds of mistakes are not ones that most people would make in other areas of life, and they are just as much mistakes in financial decisions. The rule is: apply common sense when making financial decisions. As one proofreader of this chapter said: 'Stop being bewildered by guys blathering about indices and using acronyms you don't understand. Ask yourself some basic questions.'

8. Don't invest in things that don't produce a revenue stream

This is not as definite a rule as the other eleven in this list. Most worthwhile investments give either a revenue stream or a mix of revenue and capital gain.

An alternative way of framing this rule is: if you invest in an asset that produces no return and your only hope is capital gain, make sure that the rationale for that gain is a good one. Art is an asset class that is an example of what some advisers suggest is an investment but which offers no revenue stream. On the contrary, as owner of a work of art you will probably want to insure it, or store it, or both, so instead of a revenue stream from art, it is an asset to which a stream of costs attach. It is possible to invest successfully in art, that is to make a living out of buying art and then selling it for more than you paid, in real terms, and after storage and insurance costs, and, further, to gain returns that are greater than you would get from putting the money on deposit in the bank. This is what professional art dealers do. It is difficult, but not impossible, for private collectors to achieve real returns from this. However, if you have an eye for art and enjoy spending time learning about art and its financial characteristics, you may have a very pleasant and remunerative opportunity.

9. Don't invest in shares where shareholder rights are poor or ignored

Not all jurisdictions ensure fair treatment of shareholders. In many, the rights of foreign or minority shareholders are not enforced by the authorities, even if they exist in law. Even within high-quality jurisdictions such as the USA and UK, the spirit with which a company treats minority shareholders can vary across companies. The problem is that if you invest in a company that ignores the rights of minority shareholders your investment will suffer.

10. Don't try to avoid paying taxes

Apart from the legal argument for paying whatever tax you owe, which is an absolute argument, and apart from the moral argument, which is less clear-cut perhaps, there is an absolute pragmatic reason for paying your taxes in full. It will probably be much more expensive if you try to avoid tax. Of course, if you have a choice between two different legitimate courses of action, one resulting in a lower tax bill than the other, you are quite entitled to select the cheaper option. But evading tax is a bad idea.

11. Do work out what your long-term aim is

As a private investor with a reasonable command of basic financial literacy you have a number of advantages over professional investors, and working out your own long-term aim is one of them. Most of the professional players in the market don't because they can't afford to do so or are incentivized by much shorter timescales. This means that you can beat most of the professionals in the long run, if you pick your market. Use your long-term aims to guide your analysis and decision making. Another advantage you have over professional investors is that you can afford to focus on small, obscure opportunities. Professional investors cannot afford to focus on the smallest opportunities because the returns do not cover their costs. This may mean for example that you can develop a better knowledge of a listed small-cap company than any professional, and thus have an advantage in the market. (A listed small capitalization company is one of the smaller companies listed on a stock exchange that you can buy shares in – a minnow rather than a whale.)

12. Do ensure that you have enough mathematical skill to cope with the basic maths of the financial markets, at a minimum IRR and NPV – a little maths skill goes a long way here

The mathematical skills meant here are the basic four functions of arithmetic, together with exponents (powers of numbers, such as squares, cubes, and so on) and percentages (which are simply repeated multiplication and division by one hundred, respectively). Maths can be terrifying to adults who are otherwise capable and successful in life. Even some accountants are frightened of maths. If you are unfortunately someone whose mind tends to freeze the moment you see a number, try to improve your basic maths skills just a little each year and don't make any financial decisions until you do. Many people find that without the pressure of exams and with a practical and relevant goal it is much easier to pick up maths.

Questions to ask an active manager before you invest

- More specifically, what is your 'base case' asset allocation policy? For example, for a US-based balanced mutual fund, it might be 60 percent equities (defined as the Wilshire 5000 Index) and 40 percent bonds (defined as the Barclays Capital Aggregate Bond Market Index).

- On an annual basis, as a percentage of my portfolio's value, how much will your services cost me? Make sure that the cost of any front-end load or commission is taken into account in this calculation.

- You claim that, in exchange for my paying you fees that are higher than what I would pay to an index fund, you will earn returns that are higher than those I could earn on those index funds. When you say this, are you comparing pre-tax or after tax returns?

- What after-tax returns have you delivered over the previous five years for investors in my tax bracket?

- What percentage of your above-benchmark returns do you expect to come from market timing, style tilts, and/or security selection?

- How do you know when to make these departures from your base case asset allocation policy? Is it because you believe you have superior information compared to other active managers, or is it because you believe you have a superior model for making sense of information that other active managers also have access to? Or is it some combination of both?

These questions are reproduced from the Index Investor website. Index Investor produces a monthly periodical aimed at educating investors about the benefits of using index trackers and updating its readers on the latest thinking about indices in investing: **http://www.indexinvestor.com**.

Apparently most investors would be happy to lose £4750

The following statement is a common way for financial advisers to feel about their clients' attitudes to investing:

In the two previous decades, the 1980s and 1990s, the stock market gained an average 18 percent compounded annual return, according to Kinniry.

> I don't think the focus was much on costs, and many investors were happy just getting a relative return of 16 percent or 17 percent . . . it didn't matter that they could have gotten 18 percent or 19 percent in an index fund.

Calculate the difference over five years of £50,000 invested at a 17 percent return and at an 18 percent return.

(http://articles.moneycentral.msn.com/Investing/MutualFunds/investors-are-flocking-to-index-funds.aspx)

For the sum of £50,000 invested over a five-year period, the difference between a 17 percent return and an 18 percent return is £4765·49. (The returns are respectively £109,622·40 and £114,387·89.) One way to interpret this claim is that many investors apparently are happy to throw away money.

Understanding your own situation

If you are not clear about your own financial situation you will not be able to make any effective financial plan, and your efforts to improve your financial situation will have to be far harder than they need be, if they succeed at all. Key questions are:

- How much debt have you?
- What is your earning capacity?
- What are your actual earnings?
- At what rate do you save, or, which is the same thing, at what rate do you pay off debt?
- What rate of interest do you pay for debt? Can you reduce this?
- How much money do you need for a rainy day? Do you have this?

- If you carry on as you are, will you end up old and in financial distress? If not, why not, what is going to save you?

- What do you need to change in your finances?

- What are the main risks to your financial security and are you protected against them?

- What would you do if you lost your income tomorrow?

- How likely is a friend or relation to run off with your life's savings? Is this possible?

- What has your financial decision making been like so far? How rich could you be compared to how rich you actually are? What are the lessons?

- Do you know enough about how to make financial decisions? What are you doing about this?

- Do you keep a diary of all your financial decisions?

- Pick two people from your class at school, one who has been more successful financially and one less successful. What have you done differently from each of these people, and do you want to change?

- Would your best friend, your muse, your confessor, your bank manager, your boss, and your teacher agree with your assessment above? What would they see differently and what does that mean for what you might want to change in how you run your financial affairs? Why not actually ask some of these people?

How to use advisers, including financial advisers

Some people do not use financial advisers but most people with money to invest do, at least from time to time. The best financial advisers may well not have the title 'Financial Adviser'. In countries such as the UK, the term 'Financial Adviser' or 'Independent Financial Adviser' is often associated with poor quality service given by individuals who are motivated by commissions. Lawyers, accountants, entrepreneurs, managers and people who have made money may be good financial advisers. The key question to ask anyone who is giving you financial advice is 'How do you get paid? And 'How do you make money out of advising me?'. Insist on being told how much commission an adviser is paid and when they are paid the commission, and do not deal with an adviser who will not answer this question.

Many people rely on friends and family as financial advisers. This is an understandable arrangement and the main attractiveness is the feeling of trust that we have in close family. However, be aware that statistics show that family members who advise or manage money for another family member are likely to be a greater risk than a third-party professional adviser. (The author would like to thank solicitor James Wilkins for this information.)

One of the most common ways that successful people, especially managers and professionals, lose money is by taking bad financial advice or by dealing with financial advisers who prove incompetent. Avoid sole practitioner firms of financial advisers and small independent firms. If you want a professional financial adviser, go to a large bank or financial institution that has a financial advice practice, or go to a firm that is affiliated to a large financial institution and has controls in place that are signed off by that institution.

> Mr Wells had bitten the dust in the hands of a crooked financial adviser.
>
> Dick Francis, *Risk*

Your secret weapon in finance – keeping an investment diary

If you are serious about improving your financial skills and making better investments, keep a financial diary. Write down for each financial decision the following:

- the date and the name of the decision
- what your aim was in making the decision
- what your decision was
- why you made the decision and the main factors you considered
- what you expected would happen, by when.

This is not the sort of diary to write every day, but do write an entry every time you make a major financial decision, e.g. to buy shares, take out an ISA, remortgage, change credit cards or lend a friend or child some money. Then go back a year or two later and write down how the decision has turned out. Read through your diary every so often. Many people find that re-reading the entries of their first couple of years is excruciatingly embarrassing – 'Did I really do that? For that reason? What a waste!' But after a couple of years your decisions will become shrewder. You may learn more from this than from any expensive courses on finance.

Summary

In this chapter we have looked at how to make financial decisions, which ties together everything we have covered so far in the book. We started with a review of decision making in general, and saw that being clear about your aim is the start to making good decisions. Clarifying your aim is real work and may take time. Simple decisions can be made without much thought, but for any complex or major decision it is worth following some decision making process to ensure that you do not overlook vital factors. This is especially true in finance, and a process for decision making was given. We then looked at the OODA loop (Observe, Orient, Decide, Act) which is a way to help avoid wasting time on decisions. Next we covered 12 rules of thumb for making good financial decisions, which came from over 50 financially successful people interviewed for this book. The main rule is not to invest in things that you don't understand. And finally, we suggested that you should keep a diary of all your major financial decisions, recording what you aimed to achieve, what decision you made and why, and then update it a year or so later with what actually happened. This is a free but effective way to learn about finance and to get richer.

REVIEW QUESTIONS

1. Pick a financial decision that is on your current to-do list. Where are you in the OODA loop on that decision?

2. You inherit £5000 which you were not expecting. The terms of the will under which you inherit this money are that you may not pay off any of your current debts but that you must invest it in something that is likely to make money, and invest in something that a reasonable person would think likely to return more than the cost of borrowing the same amount from the bank. Use the decision making tool in the first section of this chapter to decide what to do. Include 'do nothing', that is give up the inheritance, as an option.

3. You are a parent in your 50s, you have worked hard all your life, accumulated decent savings and have retired. You have some income to spare but not much capital. Your son asks to discuss with you a brilliant new investment opportunity. You know from your daughter that this opportunity is to invest in his business which he set up ten years ago. He has survived in business but has not done spectacularly well. Use the OODA loop to plot out the kinds of research, analysis and thinking that you would like to do and in what sequence to make the decision. Also write down what the decision is.

4. Your best friend has done you a massive favour recently, and is now asking you if you'd like to invest in Peruvian shrimp farming. This, your chum says, is a sure winner. The demand for shrimps is increasing all over the world, especially in restaurants and in supermarkets with middle-class clientele, and above all in China where the population is growing. Your friend is putting all their life savings into this scheme. You know nothing about shrimp farming and nothing about Peru. If you invest which classic rule of good investment decision making will you be breaking?

5. You have decided to invest £50 per month for the next five years, and you do not mind too much what you invest in, but you do want it to be a reliable and low-risk investment. Your default option is to invest in a FTSE 100 index tracker. You already have a reasonably large holding of index trackers, so you are considering an emerging markets fund that is actively managed

instead. Use the Internet to find a FTSE 100 index tracker and an emerging markets fund. For each of these find out what the annual management charges are. Using the Internet find out the expected return on each type of investment, that is, on the basis of what has happened in the past, what is the expected return on each type of investment. (The FTSE 100 gives around a 6 percent to 8 percent real return, over the long run, but see if you can find these numbers on the Internet.) Using either a calculator or a spreadsheet, work out which investment is likely to have a better pay-off for you in the long term. What is the biggest risk in the emerging markets fund, and what might you do about it?

6 Write down the 12 cardinal rules, in your own words. Consider a major financial decision you have taken in the past five years. Go through each rule and evaluate your decisions by that rule. What would you do differently if you had your time again?

7 Get in touch with two people you know well who you feel are good with money. Ask them their top three rules for investing wisely.

8 Repeat question (1), except this time the possibility of having £5000 comes not from an unexpected inheritance but from borrowing it from the bank at today's overdraft rate. Does this change your decision? If so, what does this tell you about yourself?

part

A financial product safari

Money is a strange beast. It can terrify or seduce or serve men. But a beast it is, and money can breed money or in the wrong conditions it may die.

If you go on safari in Africa, you will see all sorts of wild animals. Some are large and well known, like the lion and the elephant or the zebra, and some are less well known, at least outside Africa, like the eland and the kudu and the had-di-dah. But each one has its own unique niche in the ecosystem that is Africa.

If you had to survive alone in the wilds of Africa you would need to recognize each animal, know its characteristics and what it could be useful for. You would want to know not to leave ripe mangos out on the porch of your cave, for example, if there was a baboon in the area. Kudus are safer and easier to hunt than are lions, and so on. In this chapter we are going on a financial product safari, and on it we will see the strange financial beasts that you must understand in order to survive in that dark continent called finance.

8 Financial products

I am not struck so much by the diversity of financial products as by the many-sidedness of their marketing claims.

> With apologies to Stanley Baldwin, 1st Earl Baldwin of Bewdley, KG, PC. Prime Minister 1923–1924, 1924–1929, 1935–1937

Never invest in something that you don't understand.

> Anon.

Introduction

Each product entry has a similar format and is examined under the following headings.

What type of product is it?

We state whether the product is a wrapper or an underlying product or a composite of the two. For example, if you own what is called a stocks and shares Individual Savings Account (ISA), then the underlying product is shares (also called equity), but the ISA itself is a wrapper, specifically it is a tax wrapper.

If you go to the supermarket and buy a dozen large cans of baked beans you use a carrier bag as the wrapper to get them home. The bag is not the main point of going to the supermarket – the point is to get the cans of beans. While some carrier bags are better than others, where you decide to shop depends on the quality and cost of the beans and not the bag. So it ought to be when you choose a financial wrapper: the main factor should be the quality of the underlying product.

So we have the idea of a wrapper and of an underlying product. The function of a wrapper for financial products is to get the financial beans home, it assists us to get the benefit of the financial product where we want it. For example? Suppose that you wanted to save up over the next five years to help with the costs of sending your daughter to university in six years' time. After reviewing your financial circumstances you decide that saving into an index tracker (i.e. a wide selection of ordinary shares) is the right way to save. The financial beans are going to be an index tracker. And where is it that you want the wrapper to help you to get these financial beans? To that point in six years' time when your daughter starts university. One of the risks along the way that may reduce the amount of beans you are carrying is tax. Another is pressure to do other things with the money. Without the right wrapper the taxman will keep nibbling away at the financial beans just like a large, sharp-toothed, can-eating rat. What you need, therefore, is a rat-proof bag, otherwise known as a tax wrapper. Until recently these were very readily available, first of all as Personal Equity Plans (PEPs) and then as individual savings accounts (ISAs). These tax wrappers, as they are called, protected gains in the shares held inside them from tax, although recently the protection has been substantially reduced by Gordon Brown, when he was Chancellor of the Exchequer. While the wrapper is important, the point is the beans not the wrapper, which in our analogy means choosing the right index tracker in the first place. If you have chosen mouldy old beans then protecting them from rats will have been a waste of time.

Tax wrappers are not the only kind of wrapper for financial products. Other wrappers exist to protect against former husbands or wives seeking to acquire the assets of their former spouse or to protect against the foolhardiness of youth, for example. And just as carrier bags eventually wear out, so wrappers eventually wear out or worse, burst, spilling their goods onto the floor, where the rats are waiting for them. Guaranteed bonds are one type of wrapper, and recently some of these did the financial wrapper equivalent of splitting open above a very deep puddle.

What is the product?

Having said what type of product it is, we then describe the product. If we were dealing with the beasts of Africa, we would describe the lion as a large carnivorous cat that roams the veldt and can climb trees, that can be highly dangerous to men and other animals, and should be left well alone if you are on foot. We will take the same approach to the financial beasts. Some are honest beasts of burden, amenable to productive service like a faithful horse or honest donkey, some are admirable and magnificent, but not the sort of thing to own oneself, like a white elephant, and some have unique and useful features, like the giraffe that alone can feed on the lushest leaves high up where there is no competition.

Why was it invented? When was it invented? By whom? Who was it invented for?

Unlike the beasts of Africa which evolved over millions of years, most of the financial products which we will see on our financial safari were invented by man. Many financial animals have been well designed and made by their creators but some are financial Frankensteins, incapable of doing anything but wreaking destruction upon all close to them. To meet what needs or to mitigate what risks was the product originally designed? Do we really need to know the history of a financial product, and is it really relevant when making financial decisions in the modern world? Yes, often it is. One example, given in more detail in the life insurance entry below, is the use of endowment life insurance products to repay mortgages. Life insurance was invented for a very specific reason, and financing property deals was not part of it. Non-life insurance has a part to play in financing property purchases, but the way that life insurance was sold to repay mortgages in the UK in the 1970s and 1980s created unnecessary financial distress for millions of people and ruin for some.

How is it used well? How is it used badly?

A mule is good for carrying loads but no use at finding and following the tracks of other animals. Dogs, on the other hand, are good at tracking other animals but no good as beasts of burden. If you try to use donkeys to track your prey and dogs to carry your provisions you are in for a hard time. In the financial world thousands of people every day are trying to use financial donkeys as tracker dogs or financial greyhounds as pack-animals. At the height of the Internet boom thousands of people were taking out short-term loans to buy Internet shares. Many of those people got bitten. The people who made money tended to do exactly the opposite, they sold Internet shares and put the cash in the bank. You can have the finest carthorse in the world, but it will never win a race against greyhounds. Having learnt to recognize a financial product you should also understand how it is used well and how it is used badly.

Where to find more information?

The entries in this chapter are no more than brief introductions to the beasts that you will see on your own financial safari, and so we list further sources of information and reading for each of the financial products.

Bank accounts, i.e. savings accounts and current accounts

What type of product is it?

Fundamental product.

What is the product?

A savings account is an account with a financial institution, in which the investor deposits cash and receives interest. There are often restrictions on when you can withdraw money from a savings account, or an interest penalty for withdrawals made at no notice.

A current account is an account that has no penalties for immediate withdrawals, which are typically made by electronic transfer or cheque.

The distinction between these two basic types of bank account has become blurred now with some current accounts paying interest and some savings accounts having cheque books attached. There are also stockbroker's accounts that pay interest on cash held.

The distinguishing feature of a current account is not that it comes with a cheque book but that it is designed for current financial needs, that is everyday transactions. (The UK has announced its intention to abolish cheques by 2018[1] so in the UK at least the cheque book will not be a feature of a current account for much longer.)

The most significant risk with a savings account is that your money will not be there when you ask for it back. Despite history being liberally strewn with bank collapses the way that Africa is strewn with palm trees and bougainvillea, until 2007 few people in the UK had felt that they could lose their money in a bank collapse. Then in September 2007 Northern Rock collapsed. That was a real, undisputable bank run. Hundreds of peoples queued outside branches of Northern Rock to get their money. A bank that appeared to be being run with incompetent risk and possibly other management functions was careering towards bankruptcy. The scene of financial meltdown on our own high streets reminded us that even today banks can and do fail. Keeping one's savings safe is a task that requires skill and a certain amount of work and competence. What was surprising about Northern Rock was perhaps not that it failed, but that so many people were still banking with it after a string of other banks' and financial institution's failures, most notably with Lehman Brothers, had signalled the need to check whether one's bank was sound.

It is as if every generation must learn the same lesson, and is incapable of learning from history but must see a financial crisis and even suffer the terror of possibly losing one's life savings in it before that generation understands the need to be as careful about financial decision making as one is about whether one's food is tainted.

Northern Rock was only the most recent bank failure in the UK. How many customers of Northern Rock remembered the Bank of Commerce and Credit International which went bust in 1991 or before that the secondary banking crisis of the 1970s? The lesson is that you should not trust your money to any bank, financial institutions or anyone else without knowing about them. Are the people who manage the bank reputable, trustworthy and competent people? And if reputable and trustworthy are they competent? Or, worst of all, are they in the words of Aristotle, maimed with respect to virtue? The harsh fact is that if you lose your money, perhaps all your life's savings, it won't matter much if you lose it to crooks or lose it to the decent but incompetent. The reader might like to use Google to look at who was running BCCI and who was running the banks that had to be rescued at the time that they collapsed and to form their own views of what sort of people the chairman, chief executives and finance directors were, so as to be better able to identify and avoid this type of character in future.

There are specific steps to take when choosing a bank. Do not look first of all for an extra percentage point or so of interest. First of all find out exactly what legal entity will be taking your deposit: you want to get the full name of the bank or financial institution and the country in which is registered. We recommend that you avoid depositing significant sums of money in any country whose government has in the past 30 years performed poorly on protecting depositor's rights. One example of several countries to avoid is Iceland. On the other hand Hong Kong, Singapore, Australia, New Zealand, Switzerland and Canada are among countries that seem to be in the first division. Next, find the names of the directors of that bank or financial institution. Who are its directors and what are their reputations? Have they been involved in dodgy dealings? Have they worked for first-class organizations or not? And even if their reputations are spotless and their prior employment has been with the most respected institutions, do they understand banking and finance? Are they competent? Use an Internet search engine to find out about the institution and its directors. Imagine that you were looking for a new long-term boyfriend or girlfriend: do not put less effort into finding out about a new bank or financial institutions into which you intend to place your money than you would do in finding out about a new boyfriend or girlfriend. You might even go on a few trial dates – give a small amount of your money to a new bank and see what sort of service you get over a few months before you make the main switch of your accounts.

Why was it invented? When was it invented? By whom? Who was it invented for?

Deposit or savings accounts share their origin with current or chequing accounts. Anyone who has more money than they need immediately faces the problem of how to keep the money for use later. Before the development of the modern banking system, gold, silver or some other coin was the main form of cash in most places. When the currency was gold coin and there were no banks the problem was how to keep your gold coins safe from theft or loss. You had essentially three options: keep the gold about your person, hide it, or give it to someone else to keep. If you kept the gold on your person you might get robbed, especially if other people knew that you wandered around with pockets stuffed full of gold, and if you didn't get robbed you might just lose it anyway. Gold is heavy and it wears holes in pockets fast. If you hid it you might still get robbed, and even if the robbers didn't get it you might not remember where you hid it. Even if you remembered, you might have need of the gold when you were at some place far from the place where the gold was. The only remaining option is to give the gold to someone else to look after, but this only displaces the other two problems to someone else, and besides you would have to trust the person not to run off with the gold.

Goldsmiths realized that there was money to be made by solving this problem, and goldsmiths had several advantages over most other people in respect of being able to look after gold. First, their premises were equipped with strong rooms and other security measures that reduced the risk of robbery or losing the gold. Secondly, most goldsmiths were richer than their average client, which meant that the incentive to rob the average client was reduced. Thirdly, because the business of being a goldsmith involved dealing with gold every day a goldsmith would already have proved himself to be trustworthy in handling gold and not running off with it.

There was another advantage that goldsmiths had for looking after other people's gold and gold coins. Suppose that 100 people went each with a single gold coin to one particular goldsmith and asked him to look after their gold coins. The goldsmith would then be looking after 100 coins. Now each of the 100 customers does not need their coin immediately, but they will do at some future point. This means that the goldsmith can earn money by lending out as many gold coins as are not needed to meet the demand of people coming in to ask for their gold coin back. The goldsmith charges interest for this, and may (or may not) share that interest with the depositors. Some lenders will not repay the money, but if the goldsmith has picked *on average* the right customers and charged enough interest not just to make a profit but to cover the bad debts from people who do not return their borrowed gold then all will be well. Performing that balancing act is risk management. These are in fact the core skills and origin of banking.

As well as goldsmiths temples were another ancient predecessor of modern banking. Some temples in ancient times performed a role that went beyond pure religion and encompassed elements that today are the province of banks, fund managers, holding companies and industrial and agricultural enterprises.

How is it used well? How is it used badly?

Deposit accounts were created as places to keep spare cash and this is still the right way to use them.

If you have debt and also a large amount of cash in a deposit account, you will generally save money by using some of the cash on deposit to pay off the loans, because you will be paying more on the loans than you receive in interest on the deposits.

As a general rule it is good financial practice to keep three month's worth of outgoings (or of post-tax salary) in a savings account or in some other combination of financial products that gives the same effect as having it in a savings account, i.e. the ability to obtain cash sufficient to meet your everyday needs for three months without having to force the liquidation of any of your longer-term investments. You risk paying a high penalty for liquidating your long-term investments in a hurry.

Where to find more information?

British Bankers Association, **www.bba.org.uk/**

FSA, **www.fsa.gov.uk**

There are a great many books on individual bank scandals, such as the collapse of BCCI. The definitive overview of how banks collapse and how the US government tries to protect ordinary account holders is Irvin Sprague's.[3] Mr Sprague ended his career as Chairman of the US Federal Deposit Insurance Company (FDIC) and while at the FDIC handled 374 bank failures.

Gold and precious metals

What type of product is it?

Fundamental. (Many say that gold is *the* fundamental financial product.)

What is the product?

Gold and precious metals are available in the form of coin and bullion bars. Some are also available in the form of powder or sponge. Besides physical metal there are certificates of ownership which aim to provide you the benefits of owning the metal without the inconvenience of possession. One type of certificate of ownership is a claim on an unspecified fraction of a collective pool, another is a claim on a specified item. Gold is discussed in Chapter 1 of this book.

Gold is the lion of the financial safari. It is the king of the financial jungle. It is magnificent to look at, has an innate power second to none, and the bull lion is powerful enough to rip governments apart, ministry from ministry. It has been known to creep up silently behind self-proclaimed Keynesian economists and terrify them. This lion roars with an Austrian accent. The state of New Hampshire used to have the largest number of this beast of any state in the USA until the 1970s.

Why was it invented? When was it invented? By whom? Who was it invented for?

Some say gold was invented by God, others by Milton and Rose Friedman. A few add that His purpose was to provide citizens with a means of seeing through wicked governments who debase the currency. While there have been a few wicked governments, debasing the currency through coin clipping in times past or inflation in modern times is to some extent a necessary evil and a pragmatic choice rather than being a mark of great misfeasance on the part of governments, if inflation is moderate. Moreover, there are great practical problems to using gold as currency. While it certainly forces upon governments a necessary discipline against inflation that most governments are simply not capable of achieving themselves, the pre-monetary union government of Germany being an exception, the cure is currently thought by many to be worse than the disease, in that gold as currency prevents governments from acting to provide liquidity when it is necessary so to do.

How is it used well? How is it used badly?

Opinion today varies widely on what constitutes a good use of gold. Some hold that gold is a 'barbarous relic' from a rude and unsafe earlier period of financial history, and that prudent investors ought to have nothing to do with it. This view is based on a belief that gold is a poor investment and has no intrinsic worth, although it is never clear what 'intrinsic' means nor, if it does mean anything in the context of financial instruments, why it is a bad thing to have no intrinsic worth. Others hold that investors should do nothing without reference to gold as it is the ultimate store and measure of wealth, not least because governments will ultimately always debase their currency and defraud their populace financially. The reader must come to their own view on the matter, but take comfort that this author knows several people of each persuasion who have managed to accumulate great wealth.

A relatively uncontentious view is that gold or precious metals can be held as a small (less than 10 percent by value) part of a diversified portfolio of assets. On this approach gold should be treated as an asset and its place (and quantity) in your portfolio should be determined by comparing the risk profile of gold (or precious metals) to the other assets in your portfolio.

Be aware also that the tax and regulatory treatment of gold varies from jurisdiction to jurisdiction. For instance in the UK gold bullion can be bought and sold free of VAT by retail investors, whereas in New Zealand VAT is payable. In Switzerland many retail banks will happily buy and sell gold and regard so doing as a perfectly normal everyday banking transaction, whereas in the UK most banks treat you as little short of a raving lunatic if you ask them to sell or buy gold. In the UAE, there is even a vending machine that sells gold bullion: 'insert $1,284 and out pops a 1oz Krugerrand coin'.[4]

How governments treat gold is a barometer of their attitude to their citizens, and, some would add, their competence. Throughout history governments have oscillated between tight restrictions on ownership of gold and allowing freedom for people to own gold. For example,

> According to Feavearyear, a leading historian of the British pound, laws against the export of bullion – pieces of money in metal form, typically silver or gold – became a cornerstone of English commercial law from the 13th century onwards. In 1299, the Statute of Stepney prevented export of coins and precious metals in any form.[5]

Between 1966 and 1971 it was illegal in the UK for anyone to hold more than four gold coins, unless they had a special license to do so from the Bank of England. The USA has been no less Draconian. On 5 April 1933 the US president Franklin D. Roosevelt signed Executive Order 6102 'forbidding the Hoarding of Gold Coin, Gold Bullion, and Gold Certificates' by US citizens.[6] This made it illegal for ordinary citizens to own more than five ounces of gold. The order required those who held more than five ounces to sell the excess to the US government at $20.67 per ounce. Soon after this order the government raised the price at which it sold gold to other governments to $35 an ounce, in effect taking 41 percent of the gold of those from whom it was seized.

Those who have a view on gold tend to fall into two schools. The 'barbarous relic' school, which sees gold as an anchronism and cannot understand its continuing appeal as a financial asset, and the 'swindling government' school, which regrets the passing of the discipline on governments that gold imposed when it backed currency. The debate between these two schools of opinion matters to every investor, because it goes to the root of the problem of how to preserve wealth. One need not take sides in order to benefit from the argument. In reply it can be said to those who regret the passing of the gold standard (currency backed by gold) that the bond markets have assumed the disciplinary role on government that previously gold exercised, without loss of effectiveness but with considerable improvement. The government bond markets punish governments who appear to the consensus of financial wisdom to be making rash promises. And it can be said in response to those who see gold as nothing but a barbarous relic that their opinion, despite having been not only blessed but also created by St John of Keynes, that their assertion contradicts the very modernity it implies, which is that a large liquid market in some asset is the sole arbiter of its price and in the long run on average of its value. The reason that gold is a hedge against inflation and against government profligacy even now in these times of a well developed, mature government bond market lies not in the periodic table or the chemical properties of gold, but rather in human psychology.

Where to find more information?

Kitco, **www.kitco.com**

Prudent Bear, **www.prudentbear.com**

You might also ask your bank manager or financial adviser for their latest research note on gold. Whether they have such a thing for what is the original financial asset may itself be interesting.

Annuities

What type of product is it?

Annuities are composites of a wrapper and fundamental financial products.

What is the product?

An annuity is a type of pension, in the true sense of the word pension.

Annuities are the elephants on our financial safari. They are very large and compulsory viewing for most people. And if you are riding on a good elephant you have a sturdy, powerful and very comfortable means of conveyance, with plenty of height and leisure to ensure that you get fantastic views. You can look down from your elephant onto the toiling masses below as you progress serenely on your way.

At the time of writing, the rules governing official pensions schemes in the UK are that by the age of 75 a pensioner must use all of their pension fund to buy an annuity. There is considerable pressure from the electorate to change this, however. For example 'Nearly four in five people … would put more into pensions if they were given more flexibility over annuity purchase'.[7]

An annuity is a contract with a financial institution, typically a life insurance company, to provide a definite payment or series of payments for some defined but maybe indefinite period. The most common annuity by far is a contract between an individual and a life insurance company to provide regular payments until the individual's death. Annuities are a common mechanism by which pensions are paid. After saving a lump sum in a pension fund, an annuity provides the pension income for the rest of the life of the pensioner.

How do life insurance companies do this? They use mortality tables, which give the statistics on how long people tend to live, given certain characteristics such as age, sex, whether they smoke and so on. With this information and a sufficiently large population of people so that anomalies cancel out, an insurance company will manage the funds given to it to provide the pension payments from a combination of income and capital.

It is possible for an individual to create their own annuity. The easiest way to do this is to deposit the money in a bank and withdraw some income and some capital each month until there is nothing left. There are two practical problems to doing this. One is that it is expensive, i.e. you will need more capital for a given amount of income than getting a specialist insurance company to do it for you. The other is that you probably don't know exactly when you are going to die, which means that you risk either running out of income early or dying having benefited from less income than you could have had.

Why was it invented? When was it invented? By whom? Who was it invented for?

We do not know who invented annuities or when, but Plato has it that Socrates was aware of the idea. In modern times, the idea was developed and researched and marketed by the Equitable Life Insurance company, which was founded in 1762. The Equitable, sadly, is no longer with us in living form, but the idea of an annuity is very important for retirement planning, even if one chooses not to use an annuity product itself.

Its original purpose was to convert a lump of capital into a series of regular payments for the rest of a person's life, and it is the stream of regular payments for the rest of the person's life that is the most important part of the idea. The purpose of the invention is at least as important today as it was when originally invented.

Annuities are the main means by which private, state-approved pensions are guaranteed. The pension means a regular payment in retirement, the annuity is the most common means by which this is achieved. An annuity is to a pension as an engine is to a car.

How is it used well? How is it used badly?

Annuities are a good solution to converting a lump of capital into a series of payments over some definable (but maybe indefinite) period.

Where to find more information?

Your company's pensions department or pensions administrator.
Any of the big pensions providers. In the UK these include Royal
& Sun Alliance, Standard Life, Royal Bank of Scotland, Barclays,
Lloyds TSB and HSBC.

Association of British Insurers, http://www.abi.org.uk/

Consumers' Association, http://www.which.co.uk/

Financial Services Authority, http://www.fsa.gov.uk/

Government Actuary's Department, http://www.gad.gov.uk/

National Association of Pension Funds, http://www.napf.co.uk/

Pensions Policy Institute, http://www.pensionspolicyinstitute.org.uk/

Pension and Population Research Institute, http://home.btconnect.com/
PAPRI/

Art

What type of product is it?

Art is not primarily a financial asset but is widely used as such. As one commentator says, 'Art isn't a financial asset class with added aesthetic returns; it's an aesthetic asset class … with added financial value.'[8]

What is the product?

For the purposes of this book, art is anything that can be sold through an art dealer or at an art auction. Some financial advisers talk of art as an alternative asset class. It is never precisely clear to what this class of assets is an alternative.

Why was it invented? When was it invented? By whom? Who was it invented for?

We will not go into why art was invented. We should note that from earliest times art has been used as a financial instrument. Anything that is small and easily portable and easy to sell has exchange value. Good small works of art meet these criteria. Jewellery, carvings, paintings and rare manuscripts are examples.

Not all finance professionals believe that art is a good financial asset. On the one hand there is a view that art is generally not a good investment and that the asset price data available for art proves this. On the other hand, many people believe that the data shows the opposite, and that art makes a very good investment, particularly (like gold) as a component of a well-diversified asset portfolio. We have noticed a slight pattern while researching this book: the view that art cannot normally be a proper financial asset tend to be people who make a living out of persuading the rest of us to buy traditional financial assets; but equally, many of the more forceful proponents of art as a financial asset are art dealers or other members of the art world. However, neither group has noticeably fewer or more financially successful members than the other.

We believe that art does share many features of financial assets, both good and bad. High-quality works of art have a reasonably liquid market, not as liquid as that for good-quality shares or bonds but about as liquid as that for property. In the depths of a recession the markets for good-quality shares, bonds and property tighten, as does the art market.

Like other markets, the art market has its own peculiarities. The concepts of market manipulation, price support operations and insider dealing have reasonably clear meanings in the sphere of publicly traded equity investment, but can be meaningless or can mean quite different things in the art world. Anyone who wishes to take expertise gained in the public equity or bond markets and apply it to art may save themselves much trouble if they approach the task of learning about art as an investment *ab initio*.

At times when the stock market lacks appeal or when investors have more cash than usual the idea of art as an investment becomes more popular.[9] Hercules Brabazon Brabazon (1821–1906) is an example of what some investors in art believe is a reliable and relatively safe investment – unlikely to reach the stratosphere of prices but with a broad and deep market that may afford downside protection. While many of the Brabazons on the market now are thousands of pounds, one or two of the smaller works can be had for a few hundred.

How is it used well? How is it used badly?

For some financial assets it is straightforward to say how they are used well and badly. Art is in the other category, and much depends on where you determine art to be on the spectrum of opinion as to its merits as a financial asset, which we outline above.

As in the case of gold, there may be a place for art as a component of a well-diversified portfolio. If you are not interested in art for its own sake it would hardly be surprising if you made poor investment decisions.

Where to find more information?

Most reputable art galleries will offer advice on the investment merits of the kind of art in which they specialize. Some reputable galleries in the UK are:

Chris Beetles, **www.chrisbeetles.com**

Fine Art Society, **www.faslondon.com**

Haynes Fine Art, **www.haynesfineart.com**

The major auction houses such as Spink, Christie's and Sotheby's.

Collective investment vehicles, including unit trusts, OEICS, investment trusts, SICAVS and exchange-traded funds

What type of product is it?

Collective investment vehicles are wrappers. There is a wide variety of types, ranging from transparent to opaque.

What is the product?

The point of a collective investment vehicle is to allow the investor to gain exposure to a wider range of investments for a given quantum of investment than they could otherwise do. Suppose that you can afford to invest £50 per month. It is impracticable to invest this is shares or bonds, because it is too small a sum. It is too small because first of all, your stockbroker's commission on buying shares will eat up a high proportion of the £50; secondly, even if your stockbroker worked for free, individual shares are risky and if this is all you can afford to invest it is unwise to place it all in one share. But by banding together with a large number of others who also have £50 per month to invest, you are able to spread your risk and to reduce commission and other costs as a proportion of your investment to manageable levels.

Different jurisdictions have different kinds of collective investment vehicles. In the USA there are mutual funds, closed-end funds and exchange-traded funds (ETFs). In the UK there are investment trusts, open-ended investment companies (OEICs) and unit trusts, among others. OEICs are also known as Investment Company with Variable Capital, or ICVCs, which are similar to SICAVs. Also available in the UK and across the EU are *sociétés d'investissement à capital variable* (SICAVs) and other vehicles.

They key variables that distinguish between the individual types of collective investment vehicles are:

- The level of fees charged
- Gap between price of investment and value of underlying assets
- Closed-ended or open-ended operation
- Legal entity structure
- Ability to use derivatives.

These five factors are to some extent related. Fees are a key factor in any investment decision and are discussed below. The second and third factors on this list are closely related. There are two ways to arrange to aggregate small investments into a large fund spread over a variety of different investments, open-ended and closed-ended. A closed-ended scheme is in effect like, and often in practice is, having a company to stand between the investors and the investment. Imagine the Collective Company Ltd, with 100 shares, set up to invest in the FTSE 100. This company sells its shares for, say, £1000 each. The company then has £100,000 to invest. It buys shares in all the FTSE 100 companies with this money. Now suppose one of the original 100 shareholders wants their money back. They sell their share in Collective Company Ltd. They paid £100 for this share, how much will they get back? That depends on demand for the shares in Collective Company Ltd at the time of selling. If no one wants these shares then the seller may get back much less than the £100. Although the shares are worth £100 insofar as they are a claim on £100 worth of the assets of Collective Company Ltd, it may be that no one wants to buy those shares. Usually at some point below £100 a buyer will be found, because in effect at any price below £100 a buyer is buying free money.

Why does Collective Company Ltd not sell £100 worth of its holdings and give it back to the investor? This is precisely what a OEIC or a SICAV does, and this is the difference between closed-end and open-end investment vehicles. In an open-ended vehicle the underlying investments are sold and bought immediately upon investors buying or selling units of the vehicle. One consequence of this difference is that open-ended investment vehicles tend to track more closely the value of their underlying assets, whereas closed-ended funds trade on average at wider discounts or premia to theirs. Does this matter? First of all, remember that you are better off investing in a fund that performs well, irrespective of whether it is a closed or open ended kind. Secondly, there are sometimes opportunities to find a closed-ended fund that is trading at a steep discount to the value of its holdings, and where the value is likely to recover soon. Many private investors have made steady returns from this strategy in the past, but it does require developing some expertise in the field. And thirdly, different structures suit different kinds of underlying assets. While the ability to exit a collective vehicle at the current market valuation of the underlying assets may be an advantage to the individual investor who wants to get out, if conditions in the market are unfavourable at that time then the asset sale they force may be unfavourable to the remaining investors. Generally, closed-ended funds have some theoretical advantage where the underlying assets are less liquid, and open-ended funds where they are more liquid.

The nature of the legal entity that forms the vehicle is also a distinguishing factor. In principle collective investment vehicles can be any legal entity, including sole proprietorship, partnership, limited liability partnership, limited company, trust, foundation, or anything else according to the commercial laws of the jurisdiction in which it is set up. Some funds are structured as insurance products, either for tax reasons or to take advantage of the marketing power of an insurance company, for example. In practice investor protection laws and tax laws limit this spectrum, but in different ways in each jurisdiction. Does it matter what type of legal entity type you invest in? For the most widely held collective investment vehicles in your jurisdictions, for example an index tracker provided by a major brand name with a low fee, it probably will not matter much at all. But if you invest through collective investment vehicles we recommend that you pay attention to the legal entity type and learn about it. One example of the kind of difference that this makes is in shareholder rights. If you own £100,000 of shares spread across FTSE companies, say, you will have shareholder rights, that is to attend annual meetings and to vote, and where companies provide them to obtain other benefits to shareholders. If you own effectively the same portfolio but through a collective vehicle you are unlikely to have these rights. This will not matter to most investors, but if you are a serious investor and investing substantial sums, it is worth understanding what the legal entity structure of the investment is and its ramifications for you.

Why was it invented? When was it invented? By whom? Who was it invented for?

The first investment trust was set up in Britain in 1868 as the Foreign & Colonial Investment Trust and 'it was specifically designed to reduce investors' risk by spreading their investment between a number of stocks'.[10] The concept of sharing risk among investors however was not new, and underlay the idea of the shares in a company. The innovation in collective investment schemes is to enable smaller investors to participate.

How is it used well? How is it used badly?

The level of fees charged should be a key factor when making a decision to invest in any asset, including a collective investment vehicle. As has been said elsewhere in this book but is worth repeating, many fund managers charge fees that are excessive in relation to their actual performance. Most common in such overcharging is a fund manager who does no more than in effect track the index of a developed equity market, such as the US S&P 500 or DJIA, or the UK FTSE but charges more than the 1 percent or so that an index tracking fund charges. On the other hand, there are collective investment vehicles that actively manage investments in inefficient markets such as Brazil, Russia, China and India, and other emerging markets, who earn their fees even at 5 percent or more.

Two good ways to use collective investment vehicles are to invest in low-cost index trackers from reputatble fund managers, and secondly if you wish to invest in some particular sector or style, to find a fund that does this and which you also understand. The two criteria for good investing in collective investment vehicles are first the level of fees and secondly whether you understand exactly what the fund does and how it is managed.

An example of the breach of this second criterion was in the UK in the Split Trust scandal. Split capital investment trusts were a type of collective investment vehicle marketed by Aberdeen Fund Managers and others prior to 2002. Many investors lost significant

amounts of savings because they had not understood the risks
in these products, and indeed it is likely that those selling them
did not understand the risks either. As one financial journalist
noted at the time 'In recent weeks, share prices in many split-caps
have plunged. People who thought that they were in low-risk
investments now realize to their horror that the investments may
turn out to be worthless'.[11] In its conclusions to its investigation of
the scandal, the House of Commons reported that:[12]

- Virtually all of the holders ... were in the dark about the levels
  of borrowing...

- Even [the designers of this vehicle] appear not to have fully
  understood how they would react to falling markets; we regard
  this as a significant lapse in responsibility. They held particular
  risks in the event of a significantly falling market; and the fact
  that such market conditions were not in historical terms likely
  does not justify them being sold as low risk.

- We consider that Aberdeen's promotion material and
  statements, in particular, were recklessly misleading ...

Another example is the more recent Bernard Madoff scam. Bernard
Madoff claimed to be running an investment company but in fact
was running a Ponzi scheme. Madoff's ran the biggest investment
fraud ever perpetrated by any individual, at $50 billion in size.
He gulled investors by claiming that his funds operated a 'split-
strike conversion strategy'. Almost none of the retail investors in
Madoff's vehicle knew what this meant. Had they followed the
rule of trying to find out and then not investing when they did not
understand the answer, they would have avoided being defrauded.
In fact 'split-strike conversion strategy' is a real investment strategy
but it is complicated and no one who used it had been able to
obtain the results that Madoff was claiming.[13]

In summary, the idea of a collective investment vehicle is simple.
It collects together many investors to enable each individual
to gain exposure to investments that they could not have in
any practicable way otherwise. There are very many ways to
achieve this end, which can make this type of investment appear
complicated. However, if you the investor stick to mainstream
products from reputable vendors, and satisfy yourself on two

things, then decision making is simple: first, that the fees are not excessive given the nature of the investment; and secondly, that you understand exactly what the vehicle is investing in and what its strategy is. Most investors should invest in a collective investment vehicles, especially low-cost index trackers, as part of their investment portfolio. Collective investment vehicles that are index trackers meet these criteria and for almost all investors will be good products to buy. Avoid buying into any collective investment vehicle where you do not understand exactly what it does and how it makes its money.

Where to find more information?

Association of Investment Trust Companies, www.aitc.co.uk/ Guide-to-investment-companies/

BlackRock Investment Management, www2.blackrock.com/webcore/ litService/search/getDocument.seam?venue=PUB_IND&source=CONTENT& ServiceName=publicServiceView&ContentID=38173

Wikipedia, http://en.wikipedia.org/wiki/Collective_investment_scheme

Financial Services Authority, www.fsa.gov.uk/consumer/financial_faqs

Morningstar, www.morningstar.com/Products/Store_GuidetoMF.html

The Mutual Fund Guide, www.mutualfundguide.com/

Vanguard, personal.vanguard.com/us/whatweoffer/mutualfundinvesting

Trustnet, www.trustnet.com

Unit trusts

What type of product is it?

It is a fundamental product with some wrapping.

What is the product?

It is a type of collective investment vehicle – see previous section.

Why was it invented? When was it invented? By whom? Who was it invented for?

Unit trusts were invented in the late nineteenth century to allow ordinary investors to get the benefits of investing in a diversified portfolio of shares without suffering the prohibitive costs of buying a small number of shares in a wide range of companies. That is, they were invented to provide diversification to the smaller investor. Investment trusts and open-ended investment companies (OEICs) are developments of the idea aimed at solving some problems of unit trusts, as described in the previous section.

How is it used well? How is it used badly?

Collective investment vehicles, as these products are known, are used to enable investors to achieve great diversification for relatively small investment.

There are two dangers in collective investment vehicles, including unit trusts. One is overpaying for the product – are you getting value for the size of management fee? The starting point to avoid this is to find out what the fee is (it is usually a percentage of assets under management) and compare it to similar products. The problem here is if there are no similar products or if all are over charging. Many unit trusts and other collective investment vehicles are closet trackers, i.e. they do little more than track the index but charge much more than an ordinary index tracker. So you need to have a feel for whether you are getting value for money. A quick way to do this is to look at a graph of a comparable index, and see whether this fund outperforms it. The best way to do this is to calculate, or obtain, the beta for the fund, which is the measure of returns not attributable to the movement of the index. Remember to include any entrance and exit fees in your consideration.

The other danger is that the fund is risky. So you need to understand what the fund aims to do, and how competent the fund manager is to carry out that aim. The starting point here is to look carefully at the track record of the fund manager.

Where to find more information?

FSA, http://www.fsa.gov.uk/consumer/financial_faqs

Trustnet, www.trustnet.com

Index trackers

What type of product is it?

Index trackers are fundamental financial products.

Index trackers are the horses of our financial safari. They are widespread, versatile and the most useful animal. If in doubt about which animal to use, get a horse, because besides being useful there is a well run, 24/7 horse market.

What is the product?

An index tracker is an investment fund that tracks an index. An index is an average of several prices of individual financial instruments. If an index comprises shares in three companies and is equally-weighted, and if those company's shares are trading at $150, $110 and $40, then the index will be $100, because that is the average of the three numbers. What if the index is not equally weighted but is weighted by market capitalization? To illustrate this suppose that the first of these companies has a market capitalization three times greater than each of the other two, which are both equal. The index is then calculated as a weighted average:

$$3 \times \$150 = \$450$$

$$1 \times \$110 = \$110$$

$$1 \times \ \ \$40 = \$40$$

$$\text{Total } 5 = \$600$$

$$\text{Weighted average is } \$600 / 5 = \mathbf{120}$$

This example shows how important it is whether an index is weighted or not. Weighting is used to ensure that the index represents the value of the shares in the index, because without weighting shares in a small company would have a disproportionate effect on the index – it would not represent the value of its constituents.

Equity index trackers usually include dividend payments from the constituent companies. This is an important point because dividend payments make up a large proposition of the gains from holding equities.

Why buy an index tracker? Suppose that there are three companies, A, B and C, and suppose that over one year the share price of one of them goes up by 40 percent, another one is unchanged, and the third one falls by 25 percent. What you want, of course, is to pick the share that is going to rise 40 percent. (In order to simplify the example, let us assume that none of these three companies pays dividends.) Unfortunately, everyone else wants to do this, which means that if it is possible to do so with any certainty there will probably be no shares in that company left for most of us to buy because the world's plutocracy, high-stakes gamblers and investment banks will have got there first and locked up all the available shares. An even bigger problem is that in the real world it is just not the case that anyone can predict which company will rise 40 percent with much certainty – not plutocrats, not high-stakes gamblers, investment banks or fund managers. In fact, several experiments have proved that even chimpanzees of any age often would do better than investment banks and fund managers and that all have exactly the same chance of making the right choice of which share to buy. Picking the shares *at random* is a better strategy than trusting your money to a professional fund manager to select which shares to buy. The key problem here is the word 'select'.

Let's look at what happens if we select just one of these companies A, B or C in which to invest £100. If we get the right one, then we end up with £140. If we get the loser we lose £25 and end up with £75. If we had done nothing and left the money in the bank, let us suppose that we would have got a 3 percent return after tax, which means we would have ended up with £103.

Let's look at some of the implications of this. If we have no way of predicting which shares will do better, then we have a one-third chance of picking the winner and a two-thirds chance of not picking the winner. Even if we pick the share that doesn't change price over the year, we would have been better off not investing at all but in putting the money in the bank and getting a £3 gain. In other words, we are more likely to lose money than to gain.

What we could do instead of trying to guess which share will rise is to spread our money equally between all three shares. This will result in a 5 percent gain. This is because 5 percent is the average of a nil gain, a 40 percent gain and a 25 percent drop. This means we can replace the greater than evens probability of losing money with the certainty of gaining.

Start price	Price change (%)	End price
100	40	140
100	0	100
100	−25	75
	Average	105
	Compared to bank	*103*

But what about just leaving it in the bank? Is an extra 2 percent per year really worth it? Yes. Definitely. What separates people who have created financial security for themselves from those who have not is that they understand that small percentages matter. This is the magic of compound interest, which we have already covered, but it is so important that we will revisit what it means in a few lines here. If Jemima invests £10,000 at 3 percent and Katarina invests £10,000 at 5 percent, then after just one year Katarina will have £300 more than Jemima – not much, perhaps, but it will buy a very decent meal or even a weekend away for two. After three years there will be almost £1,000 difference between them; after ten years the difference will be £4,000; after 24 years Katarina will have twice as much money, £32,000, as Jemima; and after 48 years Katarina will have about £78,000, over four times as much money as Jemima.

Index trackers are financial products that enable you to do the equivalent of buying A, B and C. You can make you own index tracker, but usually it will be cheaper and easier to buy one ready made from a reputable fund manager. Of course, in the real world there are more than three stocks and we do not know in advance that a certain number of them will rise or fall by a certain percentage. There are also dealing costs to be paid whenever we buy or sell shares. But the principle of an index tracker is precisely as we have just described.

There are different kinds of index trackers. Some index or average across a whole stock market, for example the London Stock Exchange. Others index across several stock markets, for example worldwide index trackers will track across most of the major stock markets of the world, New York (which has two stock markets), London, Tokyo, Johannesburg, Frankfurt and others. Other index trackers follow just one industry segment. A telecoms index tracker, for example, might track AT&T, British Telecom, Cable & Wireless, Deutsche Telekom and the other big telecoms companies in the world.

Another key feature of index trackers funds is that they should normally cost less to manage than funds where a manager tries to pick stocks. This is because there is much less work to do. On the one hand, in managing an index, the manager simply divides the funds to invest by the number of shares (or apportion money in some other way) and then invests it; on the other hand, if the manager tries to pick shares, they must research each company which takes time, and usually the time of expensive people, and having invested they must keep watching to decide which companies to sell and how to reinvest in new companies. The promise of the active fund manager (as they are called) who tries to pick individual shares is that all this cost is outweighed by extra gains. There is little evidence to support that claim, and much to refute it. Typically active fund managers charge between 3 and 5 percent per year of the amount they are managing for you. This means that they have to earn 3 to 5 percent more than the index in order to make you better off, which is very hard to do. Index tracker funds often charge 1 percent or less per year. As we have seen above with Jemima and Katarina, that extra couple of percentage points is worth having. Do you want to have it or do you want to let a fund manager have it?

Why was it invented? When was it invented? By whom? Who was it invented for?

Index trackers were invented to deal with the problem of picking individual shares.

Putting money into an industry index tracker fund such as a telecoms index tracker is in effect saying 'I think this industry is going to do better than the rest of the stock market, but I don't know which companies within the industry are going to do well.' In terms of risk this is not as safe as buying into an index of the whole stock market, but it is safer than investing in just one company's shares.

How is it used well? How is it used badly?

Index funds are a good way of investing in equities.

The concept of Alpha and Beta are used in finance to distinguish two types of return. Beta is return on a share that derives from the movement of the overall market. Alpha is the return that derives from the performance unique to that share. Beta may be thought of as the rising tide that lifts all boats. As a hypothetical example, if the FTSE index rises in one year by 5 percent but shares in Outperformer PLC rise by 6 percent, then we can say that of that 6 percent, 5 percentage points was Beta and one percentage point was Alpha. Suppose a friend had recommended at the start of the year that you buy a thousand pounds of Outperformer PLC and that you did, and suppose that you agreed at the start of the year that you would pay your friend half of any profits on the investment that arose from his skill. Now, should you pay your friend half of the 5 percent or half of the 1 percent? If you are really paying him for profits arising from his skill, you should pay half of the 1 percent rise, because you would have got a 5 percent rise simply by buying the index. Alpha is a change due the factors specific to the investment; Beta is a change due to market conditional generally. In practice it is very hard to obtain positive Alpha. On the other hand, it is easy to obtain a good return on investment in the form of Beta, and there is no need to pay for it. Low-cost index trackers of efficient markets (such as the US and UK stock markets) are the cheapest way to get Beta, and Beta is a sound investment over the medium to long term.

Index funds are used well when used as a means to obtain Beta.

Where to find more information?

Indexinvestor.com

This site is an excellent reference on index investing and has both a free and a subscription-only section. Unlike many financial advice sites, the subscription is very low cost and this organization does appear to be genuinely interested in helping you to avoid getting ripped off. Its material is an excellent way to learn more about index investing.

Prudent Bear

This is a general investing site that is sympathetic to the issue of index investing.

Many fund managers offer index trackers, including Fidelity, M&G, Legal & General, Invesco, Bedlam and others.

FTSE, Standard & Poor's

The FTSE, a joint venture between the London Stock Exchange and *The Financial Times*, is a leading provider of indices, as is Standard & Poor's, the credit rating agency.

Financial Times Stock Exchange, **www.ftse.com/**

Standard & Poor's, **www.standardandpoors.com/indices/main**

Derivatives

What type of product is it?

In the introduction to this chapter we asserted that all financial products are a wrapper, or a fundamental financial product, or a composition of the two. Derivatives do not fit neatly into this categorization, but then we should never be over elegant in classifying things, especially dangerous things, at the expense of understanding them. Derivatives are not wrappers and cannot therefore be composites of wrappers and anything else. Derivatives are so called because they derive from an underlying financial product, which could in principle be any of a wrapper, or a fundamental financial product, or a composite; but usually derivatives are derivatives of financial products, or, we might say, derived financial products.

What is the product?

A derivative derives its value from an underlying asset. Derivatives include options, swaps and futures.

An option is the right to buy or sell some asset under certain conditions at a specified price. If you are buying a house and the estate agent asks for a non-refundable reservation fee, it is in effect an option to buy the house at the agreed price. A put option is the right to sell, a call option is the right to buy. Options have been covered in more detail in Chapter 6.

A swap is an agreement to swap one thing for something else, on either a temporary or a permanent basis. If you have season tickets to a football match and a friend of yours has a cottage in the Lake District, you might agree between you a swap such that you get a weekend in the cottage in return for letting him use the season tickets for a match. Note that if you had each paid the other with cash for the use of the cottage and the season ticket then there you have both earned net income, which is taxable. It is not clear that there has been any net benefit, even in kind, in the case of the swap: there has been a benefit but at the same time there has been a matching cost. Swaps are used by many large corporations and financial institutions in this kind of way to manage their tax exposure and to meet regulatory or contractual requirements efficiently. (Take professional tax advice before using this strategy, as the use of swaps for tax management is a complex area.)

A futures contract is a contract to buy or sell something in the future, and is an obligation as well as a right (which is one difference between it and an option). When you make a reservation with a travel agent for a ticket next summer, that is a kind of futures contract. You do not necessarily pay for the ticket now, but you are obliged to pay the full amount in the future. This is in contrast to the example of the reservation fee on the house, which usually does not oblige you to buy the house.

Derivatives are the snakes of the financial jungle. The rod of Asclepius, or, perhaps erroneously, the caduceus, remind us that snakes can be used for great medicinal healing. However, snakes are also fatal if not properly handled. Like real life snakes, derivatives are often seen in the company of snake charmers and snake oil salesmen.

Why was it invented? When was it invented? By whom? Who was it invented for?

Derivatives were invented for managing risk or uncertainty in the agricultural world many years ago. After cash and deposit accounts they are probably the oldest financial instruments. One example of their ancient usage, which continues to this day, is to protect farmers from the risk that prices may fall by the time the harvest is ready or the herd is ready for slaughter. The problem is this. If there is a bad harvest then prices are high, but because it's a bad harvest the farmer has little to sell; but if it's a good harvest although the farmer has plenty to sell prices are low. Because the farmer does not know what his harvest will be like nor what everyone else's will be like, and for other reasons, he does not know what the price will be or how much he will have to sell. But he can be reasonably sure that he will have at least as much to sell as in his last really bad harvest, and he can agree a price with a grain merchant for selling that quantity in advance of the crop. This means that part of his future income is certain. If the harvest is good and prices are low he will probably have got a better price than if he had waited until the crop was ready to sell; but if the harvest is poor then he would be worse off. The difference between the prices in the latter case can be thought of as the cost of buying certainty, or, which is the same thing, the cost of avoiding the risk of getting a low price in a good harvest.

How is it used well? How is it used badly?

A good way to use derivatives is to manage risk and, sticking with the example immediately above, the farmer has used the futures contract well if he has paid the right price to insure against his risk. What is the right price? There is a whole branch of mathematics, and whole legions of people who work in investment banks, that give complicated formulas for answering this question. Fortunately, however complicated and hard derivatives mathematics is, it is not the most important thing. The most important this is to understand the nature of the risks you face and then to understand how different derivatives will fit that risk, if at all. If you do this then you will probably have a very good feeling for how much to pay for insurance against the risk even without advanced mathematics.

Where to find more information?

Brealey, Richard A. and Myers, Stewart C. *Principles of Corporate Finance*, 978-0073130828, New York, NY: McGraw Hill (2005).

Liffe Options: A Guide to Trading Strategies, www.euronext.com/fic/000/010/729/107297.pdf

Ross, Stephen A., Westerfield, Randolph W. and Jaffe, Jeffrey. *Corporate Finance*, 978-0073105901, New York, NY: McGraw Hill (2008).

Forestry

What type of product is it?

Trees are a fundamental product.

Readers will of course know what forest is in the physical sense. What is not always quite so widely known is that forests often have good tax characteristics. Like art, however, forests are not a financial product but we include them here because there is a case for considering them as such.

What is the product?

From a financial point of view, there are several ways to invest in forests. You can buy a forest itself, you can buy shares in a company or trust that owns forests, or you can buy some non-forest land and plant a forest on it.

Why was it invented? When was it invented? By whom? Who was it invented for?

Investment products that are based on forests are usually designed to take advantage of the favourable tax treatment that is given to forestry in many jurisdictions, including the UK.

How is it used well? How is it used badly?

Trees take a long time to grow, and for this reason forestry, as an asset class, will usually be most appropriately used as a long-term investment. Of course, like any other investment there may be short-term opportunities to speculate successfully in forestry if there is a temporary price anomaly in the market.

If you have landholdings that are suited to forestry planting your own forest can give an investment with some of the properties of a zero coupon bond, because in n years time the forest will be ready for felling and, barring a slump in the timber market, you will get a bullet repayment of capital and interest. By matching the maturity of your forest to life events such as children going to private school or university, or your retirement age, you can use forests for long-term financial planning. However, you should do more research into forestry as an investment because like all asset classes it has its own risks which can catch out the unprepared. For one thing, you will need to insure your forest against fire and disease and possibly vandalism. You should also research the cyclicality of the timber market: it is cyclical and you should have a risk management plan against being forced to sell your forestry interest at the bottom of the cycle. In the case of retirement this need be no more than accepting that you will keep working until such time as the slump passes, but if you are planning to use the proceeds of felling the forest to pay university fees some more timeous protection will be advisable.

Where to find more information?

The New Zealand government's forestry department offers a number of publications which are useful research material for the investor contemplating forestry: **www.maf.govt.nz/forestry/**

Roger Dickie is a New Zealand corporation with a long experience of offering forestry investments designed for the individual investor: **www.rogerdickie.co.nz/**

ISAs, PEPs, TESSAs

What type of product is it?

All of these are wrappers. PEPs and TESSAs are old wrappers
and no longer available, having been replaced by ISAs: Individual
Savings Accounts.

What is the product?

ISA are wrappers into which a UK resident can place a certain
amount of money each year to be invested into equities, bonds,
savings accounts or insurance products. (At the time of writing
the limit is a maximum of £12,000.) The wrapper is a tax wrapper
and the advantage is that by investing in an ISA you will pay less
than the full normal amount of tax on income and no capital gains.
It used to be the case that all income in this kind of wrapper was
passed to you untaxed, but Gordon Brown removed much of the
income tax benefit.

Are ISAs still worth it? Not necessarily. Not only does the tax
wrapper prevent some – but not all – tax from hitting your income,
it prevents capital gains tax credits from benefiting any losses
that you have. Suppose that you had made £6,999 of taxable gains
beyond your full tax-free allowance, and you had lost £7,000 in
value from the shares in a company. (Marconi is one of many
examples where this would have been quite easy to do.) If your
loss was not held in an ISA or other tax wrapper then you could
offset your loss against your gain and you would owe no capital
gains tax. This is only fair because you would be no better off,
having a net loss of precisely £1 (i.e. £6,999 – £7,000). However,
because ISAs are a tax wrapper and the losing shares were held in
it then you would be liable for capital gains tax on the £6,999, and
with capital gains tax at 40 percent that means you have to pay the
taxman £2,799. Your situation is that not only have you made a net
loss on your investments of £1, but you have lost a further £2,799
in tax liabilities.

Why was it invented? When was it invented? By whom? Who was it invented for?

Personal equity plans (PEPs) were invented by Nigel Lawson, chancellor of the Exchequer in Mrs Thatcher's Conservative government of 1986. The PEP was invented to encourage wider share ownership, and in this it succeeded. The idea has been refined ever since, and the New Labour government that followed the Conservatives liked the idea but renamed them ISAs while retaining the essential features. However, when New Labour started to spend as much money as Old Labour had done and so needed to find ways of raising the tax take it cut back on the essential feature, the tax protection.

How is it used well? How is it used badly?

The scenario to avoid is being likely to have capital gains outside an ISA and having capital losses within it. If you invest only in index tracker ISAs and have no investments outside ISAs then they are probably worthwhile wrappers, but if your investment situation is anything else, it may be worth investigating whether the ISA wrapper is really worth having.

Where to find more information?

Any competent financial adviser and any of the large retail fund managers should be able to provide further information about ISAs. To check their competence ask (in writing) whether there is full tax relief on all financial instruments held within an ISA. You may be surprised to find many financial advisers and some very large fund managers reply with an unqualified 'yes'. This is not a right answer and you can narrow down your search by discarding such people from further consideration. You should at least keep a copy of any such written replies should you ever wish to prove their incompetence in basic financial literacy at some future point.

For example:

Fidelity Investments, **www.fidelity.co.uk**

Legal & General Retail Investments, **www.legalandgeneral.com**

M&G Financial Services, **www.mandg.co.uk**

Government bonds and corporate bonds

What type of product is it?

Government and corporate bonds are fundamental financial products, as are all similar products such as bonds issued by local governments (municipal bonds in the USA) and those issued by supranational organizations.

Bonds are the buffalo of the financial jungle. Sturdy things, plentiful and reliable, without the performance of the horse but less prone to bolting and generally less visible.

What is the product?

A government bond is a type of loan (q.v.) to the government. Loans to the UK government are also known as gilts, which is short for gilt-edged stock, the 'gilt-edged' being an allusion to the lower risk that lending to a major government carries, most of the time, compared to lending to a corporation or a private individual. Of course, lending to governments is not entirely risk free. A recent example is given by Portugal and Greece, whose governments' credit ratings were downgraded on 27 April 2010,[14] reflecting a much reduced confidence on the part of lenders that they would meet their obligations on their bonds. In 1998 the Russian government effected a default on its bonds. Both the US and UK governments had also effected defaults in the twentieth century. The US in 1933 when it required holders of gold and government issues gold certificates to take a 40 percent reduction in their value, and again on 15 August 1971 when President Nixon, in a similar move, reneged on the US's obligation to repay government debt in gold. The UK effected defaults at around the same times, and for similar reasons; it did so first by forcing a conversion of one of its main classes of gilt, 'War Loan' into a new class of gilt, entailing a massive destruction of value, and in the 1970s effected default by means of rampant inflation.

A government bond is described by three or four numbers – its:

Coupon, or interest rate
Maturity (or alternatively that it is a perpetual)
Price and
Yield.

Examples of bond prices are readily available on the Internet, for example at Bloomberg, **www.bloomberg.com/markets/rates/uk.html**.

On 30 May 2010 Bloomberg showed the following information for a 30-year UK government bond:

4·250 percent coupon, matures 7 September 2039, price £99·45.

It also showed that at this price and this coupon the yield was 4·28 percent. By convention government bonds issued by the UK government are priced for £100 worth of stock, and by the US government for $1000 worth. What these numbers mean is that in exchange for £99·45 today, plus whatever commission you pay to your broker, you get a UK government bond with a face value of £100, meaning that on 7 September 2039 you will get £100, and in the meantime, twice each year you will receive interest, at a rate of £4·25 per £100 of face value (you will get half of £4·25 in the first payment and the other half in the second). Because you are getting £100 of face value today for only £99·45, this annual £4·25 payment is not 4·25 percent as it would be on £100 but is 4·28 percent, (being 4·25 / 99·45).

Government bonds are traded on stock exchanges and can be bought either when they are first issued, direct from the issuing government, or after they have been issued though a stockbroker.

There are various types of government bond. The most ordinary kind is a simple loan in which the investor hands over a sum of money, receives interest for a number of years and then gets the sum of his original loan back.

Other types of government bond include perpetuities, inflation linked and zero coupon. Premium bonds are a type of government bond found in some countries and they are described in a separate entry in this safari.

Inflation-linked bonds pay interest according to the rate of inflation.

Perpetuities or perpetuals are bonds without a redemption date: assuming their issuer continues and remains solvent in perpetuity, the coupon is also paid in perpetuity.

Zero coupon bonds are bonds without coupon, that is, without interest. (Coupon is a synonym for interest because in their early days bonds were paper certificates, and the holder collected interest payments due by detaching from the bond coupons that were printed along its edge.) Instead of paying interest, zero coupon bonds deliver an equivalent, not always an exactly equivalent amount of value, by a higher redemption value than would otherwise be the case. An example will illustrate this. Consider an ordinary £100 bond that pays 5 percent interest annually and matures in one year. If you buy this bond today, you will pay £100 today and then receive in one year's time your £100 as principal plus a further £5 of interest, totalling £105. Now suppose you buy an equivalent zero coupon. You pay £100 now, and in a year's time you receive £105 of principal and no interest. Is there are real difference between these two cases, except some words? Yes. First of all, you will find that in the first case the bond you receive in return for your payment has a face value of £100, whereas in the second it has a face value of £105, even if it is not worth £105 for a year. The main difference, however, is that the £5 gain is income when it is interest, as in the first case, and a capital gain when it is an increase in capital value, as in the second case. If the relevant tax authorities agree to allow this difference for tax purposes, and if there is a difference between how income and how capital gains are taxed then this may be a valuable difference.

Corporate bonds are similar to government bonds but are issued by corporations rather than governments.

Why was it invented? When was it invented? By whom? Who was it invented for?

The first government borrowing is lost in the sands of time. In medieval Europe, at which time the personal wealth of a sovereign was not as clearly separated from the wealth of the state as it is today, sovereigns often borrowed to fund their projects, especially wars. Even then lending to the government wasn't always safe – Edward III of England was one king of many who defaulted.

How is it used well? How is it used badly?

Government bonds issued by G7 countries (USA, UK, Japan, Germany, France, Canada, Italy) and old Commonwealth countries (UK, Canada, South Africa, Australia, New Zealand) are low-risk investments.

Government bonds are low risk because unlike debts of private companies or private individuals, the full might and power of the state can be applied to procuring money for their payment. Theoretically, the state can send in the navy, army and air force to collect taxes in order to meet the payments due on its bonds. A corporation which is having trouble meeting its repayments does not have this option.[15] Despite the credibility of this theory, the state may be tempted instead to use its enormous powers not to obtain the money required to meet its obligations but to use high sophistry and other means to effect a default on its obligations, as we have seen in the case of the War Loan scandal, and as the UK government did in the 1970s by using inflation to destroy the value of the capital and interest income streams due to its bondholders. Gold is often a lower risk way to store capital than government bonds in inflationary times, although unlike government bonds gold produces no interest. Governments in recent times have often been incoherently hostile to the idea of their citizens holding gold, and a possible explanation is that they see it as a threat to their power to take by stealth from the investors large portions of capital and income.

Different types of government bonds meet different needs.

For any particular country, the bonds issued by corporations domiciled in that country cannot be less risky than bonds issued by the government, and on average the class of corporate bonds will be riskier, because corporations are less able to ensure repayment of their debts than are governments. If necessary a government can send in its army to collect what it is owed and if it is not owed enough to meets its obligations it can raise taxes. Corporations lack these powers.

Where to find more information?

Homer, Sydney, *A History of Interest Rates,* 978-0813522883, Rutgers University Press (1963).

UK Debt Management Office, **http://www.dmo.gov.uk**

USA and other G7 equivalents.

Premium bonds

What type of product is it?

Premium Bonds are a fundamental product of a government bond, with certain special features.

In the financial jungle, premium bonds are the geese. Small, not taken seriously by professionals, cackling in public, but plentiful, reliable and very tasty. Sometimes this bird lays golden eggs.

What is the product?

Lotteries have historically proved relatively easy ways for governments to raise money. The current success of the UK National Lottery is only a recent instance. A lesser known UK lottery is the government bond known as the Premium Bond sold to retail customers by the UK Treasury's National Savings and Investment arm. Premium Bonds are a UK government bond of a special kind, so we consider them separately on this safari from other types of government bond. With a Premium Bond the return of the principal only is guaranteed to individual bondholders. The interest is guaranteed in total, but is distributed as a lottery: all interest on all outstanding bonds is aggregated and then distributed to individual bondholders on a monthly basis by a lottery draw as prizes varying in size from £1 million to £50, with each £1 bond standing small chance of winning a prize each month (the exact chance changes with the interest rate, as it is in effect the interest rate; in May 2010 the chance was $1/_{24,000}$). The principle is thus gilt edged, but the coupon's variance is a function of the size of holding. Small holdings have highly variable returns, but large holdings fairly predictable returns approaching the interest rate paid by the government on the total holding.

Premium Bonds are an attractive product for high-rate taxpayers in the UK because prizes are free of income and capital gains taxes. Indeed, because of this the government typically sets the coupon at a percent or two below the risk-free rate. As at March 2009, £41 billion was held in premium bonds, or c. £667 per capita (ignoring the effect of holdings by non-citizen, non-residents).

There are instructive similarities and differences between the National Lottery and premium bonds. The expected return on the National Lottery is negative (between *c.* −40 to −80 percent), and the typical customer is poor and ill educated. It is because of the negative expected return that National Lottery tickets cannot be considered an investment of any sort. The expected return on Premium Bonds, on the other hand, is positive (about 1 percent nominal, tax free to UK residents), and therefore it is a proper investment. The typical holder of Premium Bonds is better educated and is more likely to be a high-rate taxpayer than the typical holder of lottery tickets. However, since the launch of the National Lottery, Premium Bond sales have increased significantly, and advertising for the National Lottery seems to spur sales of premium bonds, as if the desire to gamble in even the prudent investor, once stimulated by the right advertising, must find a home. This suggests that investor's willingness to accept below market returns derives only partly from the tax effect, but also from an innate human desire or instinct to gamble.

Premium Bonds are sold by the UK government. Similar instruments exist in other jurisdictions, although they are not always backed by the government. Bonus Bonds are the New Zealand product, Prize Bonds are the Irish product, and there is a similar product in Pakistan. There used to be a similar product in France (where winnings from UK Premium Bonds are taxable), called an '*obligation à lot*', but this is defunct.[16]

Why was it invented? When was it invented? By whom? Who was it invented for?

The idea of a premium bond is no more than a slight evolution of an ordinary bond, by adding a lottery feature. Premium Bonds per se were invented in 1957 by the UK government as a way of selling more government bonds to retail investors. These days Premium Bonds are seen as a safe, wise and uncontroversial investment, but this was not so when they were launched: they were regarded in rather the same light in which the National Lottery is today. The then Archbishop of Canterbury, Geoffrey Fisher, spoke in the House of Lords against 'debasing the spiritual coinage of the people'. He went on: 'The Government knows, as well as the rest of us, that we can regain stability and strength only by the unremitting exercise, all through the nation, of the old fashioned and essential values ... honest work honestly rewarded'.[17] (If only his grace had still been around to speak to the boards of Lehman Brothers, Lloyds TSB, Northern Rock, Wachovia and all the others of the current financial crisis.)

How is it used well? How is it used badly?

Premium bonds are a cash equivalent because they are easily and quickly convertible into cash and, being a government bond, the risk of not getting your money back when you need it is even less, by a fraction, than if one had cash in a commercial bank account.

Where to find more information?

UK National Savings, **www.nsandi.com/products/pb**

Trusts

What type of product is it?

Trusts can be used as wrappers for other financial products.

What is the product?

A trust is a legal entity of the common law countries, which means Britain and most former British territories, including Hong Kong, the USA, Canada, Australia, New Zealand. Trusts also exist in Guernsey, Jersey and the Isle of Man.

Trusts are the eland of the financial jungle. Ancient and mysterious, always in the distance.

Why was it invented? When was it invented? By whom? Who was it invented for?

Trusts in English law were invented at the time of the Crusades in the twelfth century to provide a legal entity to safeguard the possessions of knights and others who were likely to be away for some time and to safeguard the financial interests of the family and other dependents of the knight. Since then trusts have evolved in common law countries. Trusts were also developed in Muslim countries, prior to their development in English law. In Islamic law they are known as 'waqf' (وقف).

How is it used well? How is it used badly?

How trusts are used is changing rapidly because laws and especially tax laws governing their use are changing rapidly. Trusts used to offer many advantages for protecting assets from tax, especially inheritance tax. These advantages are now much diminished in the UK and other jurisdictions. Trusts are a complex and specialist area, and a good trust lawyer should be consulted by anyone who may wish to use a trust.

Where to find more information?

Duddington, John, *Equity and Trusts*, 2nd edn, 978-1405873659, Harlow: Longman (2008).

Dukeminier, Jesse, *et al.*, *Wills, Trusts, and Estates*, 8th edn, 978-0735579965, New York: Aspen Publishers (2009).

Pettit, Philip H., *Equity and the Law of Trusts*, 978-0199561025, Oxford: Oxford University Press (2009).

Shares (also known as equity)

What type of product is it?

Equity in a company, also called shares in a company, is a fundamental financial product.

Shares are the warthogs of the financial jungle. Beautiful and ugly at the same time, prone to sticking their tails up or down sharply when alarmed.

What is the product?

If you start a business you might need more money than you yourself could provide. The extra money could be got by borrowing it, in which case you would have debt financing. The other way to finance your business would be by selling equity, that is selling a share of the business, 1, 2, 5, 50 percent or whatever.

There are different legal forms of a business. The simplest is the sole proprietor form, where you, the sole proprietor, own the whole business and it is part of your property. As such you stand to gain all the benefits of ownership, which you hope will be profit, but you also stand at risk from all the potential problems of ownership. The biggest risk is that if the company owes money, whether because it makes losses or loses a legal case or for some other reason, you are personally liable for all the debts. Your friend, your mother, your father and everyone else in the world apart from you are not liable because they are not you; they are, legally and biologically, different people. It would help to reduce your risk if you could have someone else to own the company for you, but someone a bit like a slave, who you could control. This is what a company limited by shares is. Another name for a company limited by shares is a limited liability company, and in the UK these are commonly designated by the abbreviations 'Ltd' or 'plc' which are two slightly different forms of the idea. A limited company is a legal person, and in the eyes of the law has many of the same rights as you or any other biological person. As a legal person a company can own property, enter into contracts, sue and be sued in court, and it also has legal obligations, one of which is to pay tax and another is to obey the Companies Act. Unlike biological people, companies are not free agents who do as they please, they are owned by other people, and must obey all lawful commands of their owners. The mechanism of ownership is shares, so called because they are shares in ownership of the company.

There are many different kinds of shares, and the owners of a company are free to invent new kinds of shares. The most important and most common kind of share is the ordinary share.

An ordinary share in a company entitles the owner of the share to vote at meetings of the company and to receive dividends if they are payable. Dividends are payments from the company and are made only after the payments due to the company's creditors have been made and also after the operating expenses of the company have been met. (One of the main operating expenses is the salaries and other employment costs of the employees.) We say that the right of shareholders to the assets of the company are subordinated to the interest of debt holders and certain kinds of operating costs. This is to prevent companies reneging on their debts and mistreating their employees, although it does not always work. Some bondholders (i.e. holders of debt) in Barings were deprived of repayment by the shareholders, for example. On the other hand, unless the business is in a crisis, the shareholders have control over a company, which creditors do not and, at least in properly free countries such as the UK, neither do employees. (Employees can become shareholders in any publicly quoted company simply by buying shares, and many companies encourage employees to become shareholders by offering special incentive schemes to enable employees to buy shares on advantageous terms.)

What is a share worth? This is *the* question for the equity investor. On logic alone it is clear that a single share should be worth the value of the company divided by the number of shares in issue. But there never is logic alone. In valuing shares logic, if she is present at all, is always accompanied by those three confusing chaperones greed, fear and uncertainty. In principle the valuation of shares in a company is straightforward. The value of shares today is the expected future value of all dividend payments, adjusted for time. In practice the uncertainty as to what those dividend payments will be creates difficulties in valuing shares. At the beginning of this book we said that financial literacy is more important than financial innumeracy, but if you want to be able to value shares, or anything else, you must be prepare to do a certain amount of maths.

Why was it invented? When was it invented? By whom? Who was it invented for?

The first company to issue shares in modern times was the Dutch East India Company in 1606. There is some evidence that shares in joint undertakings existed in Roman times, especially in tax farming. The principle of a number of individuals coming together to jointly finance a risky project, especially a shipping expedition, and to share jointly in any resultant profits is a long established one and there is no reason why it should not have occurred to the very first merchants in history.

How is it used well? How is it used badly?

Shares are now considered to be a mainstream investment suitable for a substantial part of the portfolio of the average investor who has some time to go before retirement. This was not always the case in Britain. Before the last century shares were considered too risky for the ordinary investor. This attitude still prevails, albeit in progressively weaker form, in Germany, Switzerland and some other countries where ordinary investors hold a far higher proportion of bonds than equities in their portfolios.

Many rules of thumb for using shares as investments are discernible in the huge volume of advice that exists and continues to be generated about equity investment. Not all stand the test of time. A major problem with any system designed to outperform the index (the average of returns on all shares) is that once a system is found that works, it is soon widely copied until it becomes ineffective.

1 Shares are generally a medium- to long-term investment.

2 It is difficult to beat the market or to beat the professional fund managers by running your own investments.

3 Many fund managers are little more than what has been called closet index trackers, that is they do no better than the index, but charge in fees more than you need to pay to invest in the index yourself.

4 If you wish to invest in equities it is worth learning to read company reports and accounts.

Where to find more information?

Malkiel, Burton G., *A Random Walk Down Wall Street*, 978-0393330335, New York, NY: W. W. Norton & Company (2007).

Brealey, Richard A. and Myers, Stewart C., *Principles of Corporate Finance*, 978-0073130828, New York, NY: McGraw Hill (2005).

Holmes, Geoffrey, Sugden, Alan and Gee, Paul, *Interpreting Company Reports And Accounts*, 9th edn, 978-0273695462, Harlow: FT Press (2004).

Ross, Stephen A., Westerfield, Randolph W. and Jaffe, Jeffrey, *Corporate Finance*, 978-0073105901, New York, NY: McGraw Hill (2008).

Slater, Jim, *The Zulu Principle*, 978-1905641918, Petersfield, Hampshire: Harriman House (2008).

Smith, Terry, *Accounting for Growth: Stripping the Camouflage from Company Accounts*, 2nd revised edn, 978-0712675949, London: Random House (1996).

Also look at the research notes published by brokerage firms or ratings agencies, e.g. Charles Stanley, Credit Suisse, Morgan Stanley, JP Morgan Chase, Standard & Poor's.

Convertible bonds, preference shares and other debt/equity hybrids

What type of product is it?

Fundamental financial product.

What is the product?

The basic concept of a share in a company can be adapted and developed in various ways. There is a spectrum between an instrument that at one end is pure equity in a company and at the other end of the spectrum is pure debt. By assigning to a class of shares in a company debt-like features, it can be moved closer along the spectrum to the debt end. Preference shares are equity which has preferential rights to dividend payments and preferential rights to repayment in the event of the liquidation of the company, over and above ordinary shares. Because of these debt-like characteristics, preference shares usually do not afford their owner a vote in the running of the company in the way that ordinary shares do. At the other end of the spectrum debt can be given varying degrees of the characteristics of equity, for example in convertible bonds, which are so called because these instruments convert to become shares under certain circumstances.

Convertible bonds are the monkeys of finance. They can ape bonds or equities, move in packs and sometimes approach humans and sometimes run away from them.

Why was it invented? When was it invented? By whom? Who was it invented for?

The essential concepts in a hybrid of debt and equity are debt, equity and optionality. It is uncertain at what time these were first put together to create a hybrid product. According to Ibboston Associates, 'Financial folklore has it that in the 1880s, railroad magnate J.J. Hill issued the first convertible bond.'[18] In 1797 the French revolutionary government, facing bankuptcy, converted some outstanding government bonds into claims on land.[19]

How is it used well? How is it used badly?

It is a common fallacy to believe that hybrid securities and especially convertible bonds somehow enable a business to finance itself at a lower cost than equity or debt as appropriate. However, hybrids can be designed to help align interests and incentives of various parties participating in the financing of a venture. For example, suppose there is a brickworks with a turnover of £1 million per year, on which it makes a return of 10 percent after tax. The owner manager wants to expand into exotic tiles and offers an investor £300,000 of new shares in order to raise the £300,000 he estimates is necessary to fund the expansion into exotic tiles. The investor is interested and knows the business, but he estimates that there is only a slightly better than evens chance of the proposed new venture succeeding. If it succeeds, then his shares will be valuable because the new tile venture is expected to make a return on investment of 50 percent annually after tax, for at least ten years. If the exotic tiles venture fails, the shares will pay no dividends for three years while the business recovers from the problem. The investor thus makes a counter-offer. The investor proposes that instead of him subscribing £300,000 to new shares in the business, he provides £300,000 in convertible debt, paying 10 percent.

As debt, the claim on the earnings of the business is superior to the shareholders' claims, in other words it gets paid first. However, the £300,000 of debt converts into £300,000 of shares in the event that the new project reaches its sales targets within an agreed time. It is also agreed when the bonds (debt) will convert, as well as under what conditions. The bonds will not convert before three years after the first sale of the exotic tiles. From the owner manager's point of view this is a good deal. He is confident that the venture will succeed, and instead of paying out the 50 percent earnings on the venture to a new shareholder, he pays out only 10 percent for three years, enabling him to make enough money to buy out the bondholder before the conversion. If the new venture does not succeed, he will have to pay £30,000 of interest per year, but he should still be able to buy out the bonds from earnings before the three years is up. If things go very wrong, the owner manager will have to accept a new shareholder after three years.

Where to find more information?

Much of what is available on a search in Google or Wikipedia is unhelpful to the novice to hybrid products, and some entries are misleading, but if you keep in mind that all these products lie on a continuum between pure equity and pure debt you should be able to be usefully selective in using these resources.

Brealy and Myers or Ross, Westerfield and Jaffe, (see previous entry), and the standard textbooks for this and other subjects in corporate finance.

Pensions

What type of product is it?

Pensions are confusing. The biggest confusion is that a pension is not a financial instrument of any kind at all, but merely a description of those financial instruments intended to provide for an individual in their retirement. The purpose of a pension is to provide income in retirement.

However, for various reasons the term 'pension' has come to be used to mean a wrapper. Governments are very interested in pensions for two reasons. Unfortunately these reasons conflict, as Gordon Brown has proved so expensively. One reason is that no government wants to see the elderly population destitute and on the streets, which is what happens when people become too old to work and have no pension. But the other reason is that the government can raid pension funds to make short-term spending possible. This is why in the UK we have the farcical but tragic situation where the government tells people to put more in their pension plans (by which the government means the tax wrapper) only then to go on a raid into people's pensions.

Pensions are the whales of finance. Some types have been hunted to extinction, others are relatively plentiful, but fundamentally endangered. They are beautiful animals, and do not live on the continent of finance but swim around it, sometimes in circles. Governments are unable to decide whether to hunt pensions to extinction or to make them protected species, and have been doing both.

What is the product?

In the true sense of the word, as we have said, a pension is a periodic payment. A pension scheme is simply a set of financial instruments intended to provide you with income in your retirement. The income should be safe and secure. A pensions scheme means a scheme or plan for providing a pension. The payment has to come from somewhere, so the part of the scheme that is not the actual pension, i.e. periodic payment, is the investment required to make possible the periodic payment.

It is important to understand these basic concepts if you want to understand pensions of any kind.

The additional meaning that is usually meant when pensions are discussed in the financial pages of newspapers or sold by banks and financial advisers is the tax wrapper that goes around the pension. In the UK there are substantial tax concessions available when you put money into a government approved pension scheme; the tax concession is a deferral of the obligation to pay tax until later rather than being an outright waiver of tax.

Why was it invented? When was it invented? By whom? Who was it invented for?

The first pension scheme in England was the Royal Navy pension for officers, which began in 1738.[20] (Previously there had been ad hoc arrangements, but nothing in the form of a pension *scheme*.) Pensions had existed for many years before this, but as part of an obligation of some individual or institution in the manner of today's unfunded schemes, and were not necessarily linked to retirement as today's schemes are. Plato, for example, is supposed to have suggested that the city of Athens award him a pension as an alternative to his death sentence.

How it is used well? How is it used badly?

Investing in an approved pension scheme is a good idea provided that two factors apply. First, the value of the tax concessions now is greater than the present value of the tax payable later; and secondly, that the government does not change the rules on pensions. Unfortunately both of these factors are unknowable because they depend on how future governments will behave. If you are thinking of investing into a government-approved pension scheme now and your retirement is 40 years away how do you know what the government then will do with pensions? If the European Union has taken over the UK and there no longer exists a UK government as such, will the government of the day use UK pensions to plug the large holes that already exist in European pensions? Nobody knows for certain – and anyone who derides the question as being scaremongering either owns some powerful crystal balls or is talking them.

Many people in their 30s today are considering not trusting their pension, in the true sense, to the government-controlled pension products. Instead these people, often successful entrepreneurs and professional people, are making their own pension provisions. Buy to let property is just one example of an asset which can make a good pension. A portfolio of several buy-to-let properties, if selected to ensure a diversity of locations, types of tenant and types of property, should ensure a safe income stream from rental income. And unlike the government specified pension schemes, buy-to-let properties can be passed to your children or other people when you die. The UK government has outlawed passing any of your pension on to children or others (except in the case of a joint pension, for your spouse, but then only for them and for the rest of their life). Many people think that this is unfair.

To be extra-safe from the UK government interfering with buy-to-let pension arrangements people are putting all or part of their buy-to-let portfolio outside the UK. This also has the effect of reducing the risk of rental income varying with the UK economic cycle. One might have a portfolio of properties scattered across several countries, perhaps a house in Chile, another in Spain or the South of France, a chalet in a ski resort, an apartment in Phoenix, Arizona and a duplex in Toronto. If the tax or economic situation in the UK becomes too bad, then this would give you a range of other places where you would already have some interest and contacts. Be aware, however, that investing in property outside the UK has pitfalls and will require considerable effort to plan and execute safely. But for someone looking for a pension for 20 year's time or later, it may be worth considering. Property is only one type of asset, and any type of asset can be used to provide a pension.

Where to find more information?

Chapter 6 of this book covers pensions in detail.

Life insurance

What type of product is it?

Life insurance products are usually composite products including one or more underlying products inside an insurance wrapper. As a class of financial products they are among the most complex in the world. Within the insurance wrapper there can be any kind of fundamental product, including derivatives.

Life insurance is the hippopotamus of the financial safari. Most of the time most of the product lurks beneath the surface, invisible to the ordinary punter. Like the hippopotamus, the life insurance industry, as a rule, has its foundations firmly planted in mud, so opaque that the true nature of the product can rarely be seen. (If this sounds far-fetched, then get hold of the annual reports for the Equitable Life Insurance Company for the three years before its crisis in 2001 and see if you can work out its true assets and liabilities, as revealed by subsequent events.) Some people who work in the finance industry also feel that life insurance shares two other characteristics of the hippopotamus – it is almost totally blind and can very dangerous to human beings.

It is a great pity that the unprofessional or incompetent behaviour of parts of the life insurance industry have tainted the whole industry, because when used properly life insurance (specifically term insurance) is something that most people who have dependents should have, just as when treated properly a hippo is a pleasant and useful addition to the great African lakes. If you are unable to work out for yourself how much life cover you need, you may well be safer paying a fee to an accountant from a reputable firm to make the calculation for you instead of using a commission-based financial adviser.

We have said, above, that the insurance wrapper may wrap more than one fundamental product. There may also be, in effect, more than one wrapper on an insurance product. The fact that something is classified as insurance is itself a wrapper, as insurance products are often subject to different regulatory or tax treatment from other financial products. This means that some insurance products are, in essence, not insurance products at all, but have been designed in such a way that they will be classified as such by the authorities in order to gain preferential tax or regulatory treatment. When researching an insurance product and as part of understanding what you are looking at you should determine whether it is in essence about insurance or whether it is something else in disguise. If it is something else in disguise, make sure you know what that other thing is, why it is being disguised and whether the disguise is relevant to you. Sometimes the disguise may be purely for marketing purposes, but often the disguise is a way to navigate the complexity of various tax, inheritance and asset-protection factors to suit a particular market niche.

What is the product?

There are many kinds of life insurance and different terminology is used in different jurisdictions. The table below is an attempt to describe some of the main types or features of life insurance policy.

Endowment

An endowment policy is one which pays out a lump sum in the first of either event:

1. that the person whose life is insured dies, or
2. on the expiration of a specified period.

Endowments combine two fundamental financial products within the wrapper of an insurance policy. One fundamental product is an investment plan, the other is life cover (i.e. insurance against premature death). It is much cheaper now to make your own endowment policy by buying separately a combination of savings products (perhaps in an ISA wrapper) and insurance against death, called *term assurance* (see below).

Endowment policies were widely sold in the 1970s and 1980s as a way of repaying mortgages. It is not clear why a product originally designed for managing the risk to an individual of not being able to provide for his family should he die early would be suitable for financing a real estate transaction. Of course, an argument can be made, which need not be rehearsed here, but the way that endowments were sold for use to repay mortgages at that time is now judged to have been a disaster, and five million people were mis-sold endowment policies in this way.[21]

Non-profit

The sum assured remains fixed throughout the life of the policy, as opposed to a *with-profits* policy (see below).

Sum assured

The lump sum guaranteed by the policy, usually in the event of death, and sometimes irrespective of death.

Term insurance

Guarantees a *sum assured* if the person whose life is insured dies within the period specified. If the person survives, nothing is paid.

Unit-linked

In unit-linked policies, the policyholder can choose the apportionment of the premium between life cover and investment.

Whole-of-life assurance

Pays out a lump sum whether the person whose life is insured dies or not. Such policies can be non-profit, with-profits or unit linked.

With-profits

A supposedly irrevocable bonus is added to the sum assured from time to time during the life of the policy. The bonus originated in surplus profits of life companies, but now there is some expectation of a bonus. Bonuses are usually declared annually. We say 'supposedly irrevocable' because there are depressingly many examples in financial history where the bonuses were only too revocable when it mattered, Equitable Life being only one of the recent cases.

Why was it invented? When was it invented? By whom? Who was it invented for?

Life insurance in the form we have it today was invented by the Equitable Life Insurance Society in 1762, but had existed in some form for centuries before. Soldiers and citizens of the Roman Empire formed cooperative societies to pay for funerals,[22] and it is quite possible that the ancient Egyptians had similar arrangements.

How is it used well? How is it used badly?

In the case of genuine life insurance products rather than products disguised as insurance, the only good way to use life insurance is to protect your dependents from suffering financially in the event that you die. All other uses of genuine life insurance products are risky – see above for using them to pay off mortgages, for example.

In the case of a life insurance product that is not in essence an insurance product but rather is some other financial product masquerading as an insurance product, it should be considered as whatever product it really is to answer the question of how it is used well and how it is used badly.

Where to find more information?

Association of British Insurers, **www.abi.org.uk/**

Consumer Financial Education Body (CFEB),
www.moneymadeclear.org.uk/

Mortgage

What type of product is it?

A mortgage is a fundamental financial product, being a type of loan (q.v.).

What is the product?

A mortgage is a loan secured on a property. Most people are familiar with mortgages on residential real estate, but mortgages can be held over any asset, subject to the will of the lender. Typically this means a tangible asset, although in principle mortgages can be taken over intangible assets also. So there are mortgages over factories, ships, factory plant and equipment and mines. An example of an intangible asset on which a mortgage was given is royalties payable to the author Jerome K. Jerome.[23]

Where mortgages over residential real estate are concerned we tend to be most familiar with mortgages provided by banks or financial institutions. Note that private mortgages are also possible. In a private mortgage a private individual, usually the seller of the property, takes a mortgage over the property and loans funds to the buyer.

We stated that a mortgage is a *secured loan*. Loans can be either secured or unsecured. If a loan is secured it means that in the event of the borrower being unable to repay the loan the lender has the right to take ownership of the asset on which the loan is secured. So, if you do not keep up the repayments due on your mortgage for your house then the mortgagor can take ownership and possession of the house from you, the mortgagee.

Mortgages are the bees of finance. They pollinate life itself – but pick the wrong one and you may get stung.

Why was it invented? When was it invented? By whom? Who was it invented for?

Mortgages are probably almost as old as loans themselves.

How is it used well? How is it used badly?

The most important difference between the good and bad uses of mortgages is the ability to repay them. If you cannot afford the repayments then don't take a mortgage.

Even if you have enough cash not to need a mortgage, there may sometimes be tax advantages to getting a mortgage. There are no longer such tax advantages in the UK for mortgages on your own home, but if you get a mortgage for a buy-to-let property then the interest payments are allowable against tax (but not the repayments of capital). This does not mean that it is a good idea to borrow when you don't need to, but if you do need to borrow, or might need to at some point in the future, then it may be worth taking a mortgage on property as a means to finance the other requirement, even if that is nothing to do with property. This is because a secured loan, which for most private individuals means a mortgage on property, is generally cheaper than an unsecured loan, and the interest repayments can be offset against tax.

Where to find more information?

Every Saturday the *Financial Times* carries a league table of the best mortgages available of different kinds.

The FSA, **www.fsa.gov.uk/consumer/learn/financial_products/**

Loans or credit

What type of product is it?

A fundamental financial product.

Credits are the ants of finance. Very industrious, but too many of them and you may find the foundations have been eaten through.

What is the product?

A loan is an agreement between two parties, one being the borrower and the other being the lender. The lender agrees to provide a certain sum of money and the borrower agrees to pay it back with interest at a certain date or in instalments on certain dates.

In finance loans may also be for financial instruments other than cash. For example, bonds, shares, gold or derivatives may all be loaned, but the basic mechanism and characteristics of loans are the same whatever it is that is being loaned.

Why was it invented? When was it invented? By whom? Who was it invented for?

'Can I borrow your rock?' is probably the earliest example of a loan.[24]

Among the earliest recorded examples of loans are loans of animals and loans of crop seed such as wheat. The idea of interest payable on a loan is thought to derive from the reproduction of animals or crops. If I keep my own herd of goats it gets bigger as the goats breed. Suppose each pair of goats lives five years on average and produces on average two kids per year in the third, fourth and fifth years of their lives. At the end of five years the two original goats will no longer exist but the there will be six of their kids and two grand-kids, making a total of eight goats. So if you lent someone two goats for five years, you would not want the original goats back, because they would be dead, but you would want some or even all of the kids and grand-kids, because they are in a sense part of what was loaned in that they are the offspring of what was loaned. In addition the females of these goats will be producing milk throughout their adult lives and depending on the term of the loan you might want some part of that produce. Table 8·1 illustrates this example of goat interest. It also shows what the equivalent rate of interest is at the end of each full year. Over the full five years the annual rate of interest is 6·4 percent.

TABLE 8·1 Livestock as the original of the idea of interest

Year	1	2	3	4	5
Number of original goats	2	2	2	2	0
Kids of original goats in year 3	0	0	2	2	2
Kids of original goats in year 4					2
Kids of original goats in year 5					2
Kids of year 2's goats					2
Total number of goats	2	2	4	6	8
Equivalent compound annual rate of interest	0·0%	0·0%	26·0%	31·6%	32·0%

	Average annual rate of interest over five years		6·4%

The great historian of credit, Sydney Homer, who was also a very successful bond trader, has this to say on credit in ancient times:

> Credit is sometimes considered a modern device, or even a modern vice. It is true that new credit forms have been developed in our country, and the statistics reflecting the growth of credit during recent decades are impressive. But a glance through the pages of financial history will dispel any notion of recent novelty. Credit was in general use in ancient and in medieval times. Credit long antedated industry, banking, and even coinage; it probably antedated primitive forms of money. Loans at interest may be said to have begun when the Neolithic farmer made a loan of seed to a cousin and expected it back at harvest time. Be that as it may, we know that the recorded history of several great civilizations started with an elaborate regulation of credit.[25]

How is it used well? How is it used badly?

Borrowing more than you can afford to repay is a bad use of a loan. Borrowing on a short-term basis to meet longer-term obligations is also bad. Bad means risky. Borrowing to meet a commitment because borrowing is your cheapest option and you can afford to borrow is a good use of a loan.

Where to find more information?

The FSA, **www.fsa.gov.uk/consumer/learn/financial_products/**

Credit card

What type of product is it?

A fundamental product.

Termite.

What is the product?

Credit cards are a means of payment with a credit facility attached.

The credit facility is often but not always an interest-free period followed by the charging of interest; if the balance is paid off in full during the interest-free period, no further interest is usually payable.

In addition to charging interest, some credit card companies charge an annual fee.

In addition to the benefit of credit and convenience in spending, credit cards issued in the UK offer some protection to customers against poor-quality goods and services bought with them, when used by consumers in retail transactions within the UK. (The relevant legislation is the Consumer Credit Act and Sale of Goods Act.) In addition, card providers may offer further services as part of the card account, most often travel insurance and protection against the costs incurred if a credit card is lost or stolen.

The ten biggest providers of credit cards in the world are:[26]

1. Bank of America/MBNA
2. Chase
3. Citi
4. American Express
5. Capital One
6. HSBC
7. Discover
8. Wells Fargo
9. Barclays
10. Lloyds TSB/HBoS

Why was it invented? When was it invented? By whom? Who was it invented for?

Credit cards were invented in 1951 by Diners Club. It could be used in 27 restaurants in New York.

How is it used well? How is it used badly?

The only good way to use a credit card is to pay off the balance in full every month as it becomes due. This is because the rates of interest charged otherwise are astronomically huge, and are a very poor way of borrowing money. Credit cards are useful when travelling overseas but often if you try to rely on the travel or purchase insurance cover you will be disappointed.

Some cards refund to you a portion of what you spend each year, sometimes about 1 percent, which is worth having.

Other things being equal, the best card to have is one that charges no annual fee and gives a high rate of refund.

Credit cards are expensive if not used carefully. The CEO of Barclays Bank, Matt Barrett, told the Treasury Select Committee in 2003 that he didn't carry his own bank's credit card, called Barclaycard because he believes that borrowing on credit cards is too expensive.[27]

Some credit card providers send out blank cheques with credit card statements, for the credit card holder to use. These generally offer truly abysmal rates of interest, and should be avoided. (For a few years in the UK, Scottish Widows was an exception to this, and charged 0 percent on its credit card cheques for up to 45 days. It was possible to borrow £10,000 on these cheques and bank the funds within a Scottish Widows high interest account – a rare example of a free lunch.)

Where to find more information?

Ask Mr. Credit Card, **www.askmrcreditcard.com/**

The Consumer Association, **www.which.co.uk**

Credit Cards.com United Kingdom, **www.creditcards.com/**

UK Consumer Financial Education Body, **www.moneymodeclear.fsa.gov.uk**

Notes

Chapter 1

1 Richard Gore, Fort Lewis College; Richard Samuelson, Retired, American Accounting Association, Western Region, 43rd Annual Meeting Hotel 480, San Francisco, California, 1–3 May 2008, available at http://aaahq.org/western/2008/WAAAFullProceedings.pdf

2 Widely documented in the financial press. For example in the *Wall Street Journal*, at http://online.wsj.com/article/SB124351929640262615.html

Chapter 3

1 For example, the move from historical cost accounting to fair value accounting. In historical cost accounting an asset is valued in the balance sheet of a company at the price paid for it when it was acquired. Revaluations are possible but rare. In fair value accounting assets are revalued regularly in line with current fair value. Both methods have advantages and disadvantages. The current trend is to give up the advantage of objectivity (the price paid for the asset is a fact) in favour of the advantage of relevance (the price paid for the asset may be much less relevant than it current value), but the price paid for this shift is a loss of objectivity (what the value of the asset is worth now may be a matter of opinion, and the opinion giver may have an interest in picking a high valuation).

2 The prices quoted here take account of the bid–offer spread for gold, i.e. the buying price is the actual buying price, and the same for the selling price.

3 **Taleb, N.N.,** *Fooled by Randomness: The Hidden Role of Chance in the Markets and Life*, 2nd updated edn, 978-0812975215, Random House (2005); and also *The Black Swan: The Impact of the Highly Improbable*, 2nd updated edn, 978-0812973815, Random House (2010).

4 **Hume, David,** *An Enquiry Concerning Human Understanding*, (1748).

Chapter 4

1 **Simons, Daniel J.** and **Chabris, Christopher F.,** Gorillas in our midst: sustained inattentional blindness for dynamic events. *Perception,* 1999, 28: 1059–1074. See also **Chabris, Christopher** and **Simons, Daniel,** *The Invisible Gorilla: And Other Ways Our Intuitions Deceive Us,* 978-0307459657, Crown Publishing, (2010). The authors have a blog at **http://theinvisiblegorilla.com/blog/**

2 One example of this problem is that most people simply do not see that the interest they pay on their credit card loans is far higher than they need to pay. They would be better off borrowing the money and keeping a nil balance on the credit cards. Some of this behaviour may be to do with convenience and want of self-discipline, but research shows that the main problem is that people simply do not see the true cost of their behaviour. Once they see it, they change behaviour.

3 Dictionary, v 2.1.1. Apple Inc. 2005–09.

4 Paul Eckman is a leading researcher in this field: **www.paulekman.com/.**

Dr Eckman offers a range of training tools to help develop your skill at reading people's facial expressions. There is an iPhone app on similar principles created by Paul Dabrowski called FaceReader. A blog on the subject by an anonymous woman who claims to be able to spot liars with greater than 80 percent accuracy can be found at:

http://www.eyesforlies.blogspot.com/

Chapter 5

1 **Black, Fischer** and **Scholes, Myron,** The Pricing of Options and Corporate Liabilities, *Journal of Political Economy,* **81**(3): 637–654.

2 A large number of web pages and publications exist, some of ideal quality for those wishing to learn how to trade options, many defective in various ways. Good places to start are the chapters on options in any of the major finance textbooks, such as **Brealey** and **Myers** or **Ross, Westerfield** and **Jaffe.** To be a good amateur trader you must understand what is in one of these chapters.

Hull, John C., *Options, Futures, and Other Derivatives.* Harlow: Prentice-Hall. (2008). This is one of the classic textbooks on derivatives, although it is perfectly possible to be a very good amateur trader without touching it.

LIFFE *Options: A Guide to Trading Strategies*, London: LIFFE (2002). Available for download at: **www.euronext.com/fic/000/010/729/107297. pdf.** Anyone interested in learning more about options and about the problems of applying maths and statistics unthinkingly to finance and life should know about Nassim Nicholas Taleb. His home page is **www. fooledbyrandomness.com/**

Chapter 6

1 **House of Lords,** *Report of the Select Committee on Economic Affairs: Aspects of the Economics of an Ageing Population.* Vol. I, Session 2002–03, fourth report. Norwich: HMSO (2003).

2 This neologism, perhaps superfluous to any real semantic need, is used by such authorities at the UK's House of Lords, ibid.

3 Cost of unfunded pension schemes 'to triple in 50 years'. *Daily Telegraph*, 12 March 2010.

4 **House of Lords,** ibid.

5 **Friedberg, Leora** and **Webb, Anthony,** Retirement and the evolution of pension structure. *Journal of Human Resources*, 40(2): 281–308 (2005).

6 For a comprehensive treatment of current political factors including complexity in pensions, see **Clark, Gordon** and **Whiteside, N.** (eds) *Pension Security in the 21st Century*, 0-19-926176-8, Oxford: Oxford University Press (2003).

7 **House of Lords,** ibid.

8 The statistic of 1 in 250 is derived as follows: in 2004 there were 60,000 pensioners suffering severe financial hardship because their pensions schemes had failed (most infamous of the causes was Robert Maxwell's fraud against the pensioners of the companies he controlled). (Data from *The Economist*, Pensions: occupational hazard – why the government forked out £400m for pensioners, 20 May 2004.) Assume further that in the UK there were 15 million people with pensions other than public sector workers (whose pensions are guaranteed by the State), and dividing 60,000 by 15 million gives 0·4 per cent, and since the Maxwell pensions fraud the UK's laws on pensions have been improved to reduce the risk of fraud, resulting in a lower risk estimate. The author would welcome a better estimate of the current risk of severe financial loss from pensions malfeasance in the UK.

9 **www.zurich.ch/site/en/priv/vorsorgen/info/column_1.html**

10 Further details of various national schemes are available as follows:

Australia: http://australia.gov.au/topics/economy-money-and-tax/superannuation

Canada: www.servicecanada.gc.ca/eng/isp/cpp/cpptoc.shtml

New Zealand: www.nzsuperfund.co.nz/

UK: www.hmrc.gov.uk/

11 The questions were formulated by Robert Merton, as reported in *The Economist*. Merton gave three questions, and implied in addition the first in the list shown here. *The Economist*, Pension planning: the retiree's autopilot, a new approach to an old-age problem, 26 November 2009.

12 *The Economist*, 26 November 2009, ibid.

13 With acknowledgement to Stephen King, Chief Economist of HSBC Bank PLC, who pointed out many of the key issues examined in this section. (Any deficiency in interpretation of his points remains, of course, the author's.) Private correspondence. Mr King's analysis is set out in detail in **King, Stephen D.**, *Losing Control: The Emerging Threats to Western Prosperity*, 978-0300154320, New Haven, CT: Yale University Press (2010).

14 **Morton, John S., Rae, Jean** and **Goodman, B.**, *Advanced Placement Economics: Teacher Resource Manual, National Council on Economic Education*, 3rd Tech. edition, 1 August 2005. 978-1561835669. Quoted in Wikipedia, 28 May 2010, Economic Rent.

Chapter 7

1 Our understanding of how our psychology and its ancient evolutionary origins affect decision making including financial decision making is an area where rapid advances are being made in research. Two examples of overviews of the field are **Shermer, Michael**. *The Mind of the Market: Compassionate Apes, Competitive Humans, and Other Tales from Evolutionary Economics*. 978-0805078329, New York, NY: Times Books (2007) and **Ariely, Dan,** *Predictably Irrational: The Hidden Forces That Shape Our Decisions*, revised and expanded edn, Harper Collins, ASIN B002C949KE (2009).

2 It is drawn largely from the *RAF Manual of Decision Making*, which itself draws on leading research into decision making, as tempered by the practicalities of real life.

3 For example the Timeshare Act 1992 and the Timeshare Regulations 1997.

4 Checking that there really are only twelve items on a list titled 'The 12 cardinal rules of investing' is a very good start.

5 The psychology that explains this would be most interesting, but is beyond the scope of this book. A good overview of the literature of the psychology of financial decision making is **Nofsinger, John, R**. *Psychology of Investing*, 4th edn, New York: Prentice Hall (2010).

6 The academic literature is replete with such findings, and no real data to the contrary has been found. Typical of the academic studies are two papers by **Cuthbertson, Nitzsche, and O'Sullivan**: The market timing ability of UK equity mutual funds (2006a); and Mutual fund performance (2006b). In the former they find that 'only around 1·5 percent of funds demonstrate [statistically significant] market timing ability' in the good sense of that term, while 'ten to twenty percent of funds exhibit negative timing ability' (in the sense of a statistically significant ability to consistently get it wrong). In the latter paper:

> The authors conclude that 'the evidence suggests that there are around 2 per cent to 5 per cent of top performing U.S. and U.K. equity mutual funds which genuinely outperform their benchmarks, and 20 per cent to 40 per cent of funds that are genuinely poor ... Sensible advice for most investors would be to hold low cost index funds and avoid holding past actively managed loser funds. Only very sophisticated investors should pursue an active investment strategy of trying to pick winners – and then with much caution.'

Citations and comments are from *The Index Investor*, p. 34. February 2007, ISSN 1554-5075, **http://www.indexinvestor.com/**

Cuthbertson, Keith, Nitzsche, Dirk and **O'Sullivan, Niall,** The market timing ability of UK equity mutual funds (2006a). Available at SSRN: **http://ssrn.com/abstract=955812**

Nitzsche, Dirk, Cuthbertson, Keith and **O'Sullivan, Niall,** Mutual fund performance (2006b). Available at SSRN: **http://ssrn.com/abstract=955807**

Chapter 8

1 Notable research in the field of loss aversion and other aspects of behavioural finance has been done by Daniel Khaneman and Amod Tversky. See for example: **Tversky, A.** and **Kahneman, D,** Loss

aversion in riskless choice: a reference dependent model. *Quarterly Journal of Economics*, 106: 1039–1061, 1991. Daniel Ariely is another researcher in this field (see Chapter 7, note 1).

2 **Warwick-Ching, Lucy** and **Law, Denise,** Cheques to disappear by 2018. *Financial Times*, 16 December 2009.

3 **Sprague, Irvin S.,** *Bailout: An Insider's Account of Bank Failures and Rescues*. Washington, DC: Bear Books (1986). Before joining the FDIC Mr Sprague had been a US Army infantry officer. He was educated at The College of the Pacific and Harvard, among other universities.

4 **Mackintosh, James,** Bullion has not yet lost its shine for goldbugs *Financial Times*, 28 May 2010.

5 **Waibel, Michael,** Bit by bit – the silent liberalisation of the capital account. In **Binder, C., Kriebaum, U., Reinisch, A.** and **Wittich, S.,** (eds). *International Investment Law for the 21st Century – Essays in Honour of Christoph Schreuer*, pp. 497–518, New York: Oxford University Press (2009).

6 Wikipedia has a detailed entry on this event. See Wikipedia, Executive Order 6102.

7 The Consumer Association as reported in the *Sunday Telegraph*, 3 November 2002.

8 **Salmon, Felix,** Art as a financial asset class. In the Portfolio.com blog, 2 February 2002.

9 For example, **Stewart, C.,** A picture portfolio, *The Times*, 11 January 2003.

10 www.foreignandcolonial.com/

11 **Farrow, Paul,** Split-caps head for zero: after a year of warnings, many split-capital investment trusts are now 'walking dead', *Daily Telegraph*, 3 April 2002.

12 **House of Commons Treasury Committee,** Third Report, 5 February 2003. The full report is available at: www.publications.parliament.uk/pa/cm200203/cmselect/cmtreasy/418/41802.htm

13 **Murphy, Paul,** He Madoff with how much??? *Financial Times Alphaville*, 12 December 2008, available at: http://ftalphaville.ft.com/blog/2008/12/12/50368/he-madoff-with-how-much/

14 **Peston, Robert,** Greek credit status downgraded to 'junk', BBC News, 27 April 2010.

15 Not these days in civilized countries. The East India company did of course have such powers, but that company was to some extent the state.

16 **Connexion,** *Premium Bond wins taxable in France,* February 2010, available at: **http://www.connexionfrance.com/**

17 **Ball, G.,** How the smart money is going back into Premium Bonds, *Independent on Sunday,* 1 July 1996.

18 **Lummer, Scott L.** and **Riepe, Mark W.,** Convertible bonds as an asset class: 1957–1992. In *J. Fixed Income,* **3**(2): 47–57, September 1993.

19 **Homer, Sydney** and **Sylla, Richard,** *A History of Interest Rates,* 10-0-471-73283-4, Holboken, NJ: John Wiley and Sons (2005). Location 6482 on Kindle.

20 **Rodger, N.A.M.,** Commissioned officers' careers in the Royal Navy, 1690–1815, *Journal of Maritime Research,* June 2001.

21 The Consumer Association as reported in the *Sunday Telegraph,* 3 November 2002.

22 Dr D. Burton, Victoria University, New Zealand, personal communication.

23 Records of J.W. Arrowsmith Ltd of Bristol, 40145/L/1-10. Held in the Archives of Bristol Records Office, Bristol, England.

24 Dr D. Burton, Victoria University, New Zealand, personal communication.

25 **Homer, Sydney** and **Sylla, Richard,** ibid, Kindle location 195–202.

26 **www.creditcards.com**

27 **O'Keeffe, Alice,** The age of spend, spend, spend, *The New Statesman,* 24 November 2003.

Further reading and websites

Further reading and websites related to pure finance have been given at the end of each chapter. This list gives broader suggestions.

The 'Gorillas in our midst' experiment is worth knowing about. Derren Brown specializes in illustrating the consequences of this feature of the way our minds work. Videos of his work are available on YouTube (**www.youtube.com/**) and also at **www.channel4.com/programmes/derren-brown**

A classic and highly readable account of just how hard it can be for people to see things is given in **Jasper, Maskelyne,** *Magic: Top Secret*, London, 1949. Maskelyne was a magician who joined the British Army in the Second World War and took charge of deception operations in the Middle East theatre and elsewhere. He was able to make ships and whole army divisions disappear.

A comprehensive timeline of events leading up to and during the great financial crisis of 2007 is given at: **www.berninger.de/crisis-information-center/chronic-of-crisis-2007.html**

A number of tools and techniques of varying merit exist for determining character, your own and that of others. **Belbin** and **Myers Briggs** are two brands of psychometric test that are widely used in industry and government to categorize and grade employees. They have the advantage of giving clear answers as to how to manage people, together with an appearance of scientific rigour in so doing, but the weakness is that neither is supported by quite as much scientific rigour as the use to which they are put demands. When subjected to these tests many employees can feel that they are being pigeon-holed and told what they are thinking and feeling.

Paul Eckman's work, as detailed in the notes to Chapter 4, is scientifically sound, although in a narrower area than the whole spectrum of human character.

A classic book that sets out the idea of winner's games and loser's games in the field of investment is **Charles Ellis'** *Winning the Loser's Game: Timeless Strategies for Successful Investing*, 5th edn, 978-0071549-5, New York, NY: McGraw Hill, 2009.

For readers interested in the analogy between investment and games, **W. Timothy Gallweys'** *The Inner Game of Tennis*, 978-067977831-8, New York, NY: Random House, 1997, is also worth reading.

Many websites offer information on social trends. The UK's Office for National Statistics has detailed annual reports on trends in Britain: **www.statistics.gov.uk/socialtrends39/**

Index